AF560117

GANDHI AND ADIVASIS

Gandhi and Adivasis

Tribal Movements in Eastern India (1914-1948)

DEBASREE DE

MANOHAR
2022

First published 2022

ISBN 978-93-91928-72-8

Published by
Ajay Kumar Jain *for*
Manohar Publishers & Distributors
4753/23 Ansari Road, Daryaganj
New Delhi 110 002

Typeset by
Kohli Print
Delhi 110 051

Printed at
Replika Press Pvt. Ltd.

The book is dedicated to
my niece Shubhangi (Mishti)

Contents

Acknowledgements

The present research has been planned and documented chiefly on the basis of the perspectives of the Adivasis, the sons of the soil of our country, who once endorsed and became an inseparable part of the Gandhian movements. It is interesting to note that before the arrival of Gandhi, the Adivasi movements were mostly violent and armed, but there were instances of non-violent protests as well, because the Kherwar movement and Tana Bhagat movement began much before the inception of the Gandhian era. Congress hardly paid attention to their cause and only with the coming of Gandhi the Adivasi movements got their long awaited 'recognition' and that was also if they chose to remain non-violent, as Gandhi never endorsed violent path taken by any section of the society, be it Dalits or Adivasis. His ambivalent attitude towards Adivasis and apparent indifference sometimes cause despair on the part of the Adivasis and sometimes left his party, the Congress, with the dual policy of manipulation and championing to somehow bind the Adivasis with the 'mainstream' nationalist movement through various means, which finally led to the creation of a new state. The current study has attempted to undertake an in-depth analysis of the Adivasi predicament during the so-called Gandhian era as they had always been considered as an integral part of his 'mass' movement.

The present research has been funded by the University Grants Commission (UGC) under its Minor Research Project (MRP) programme and I am grateful to them for this. I am indebted to all the anonymous renowned reviewers for their valuable comments and suggestions. I owe my gratitude to my teacher Prof. Amit Bhattacharyya for his guidance and my colleague Prof. Arup Kumar Bhattacharyya who has always stood by me whenever I needed him. I am certain that if my father, Late Asim Kumar De were alive, he would definitely appreciate my effort and bless me. I take this opportunity to express by sense of gratitude to my mother Mrs Sonali De, sister Mrs Rajasree Dalal and brother-in-law Mr Dibyendu Dalal for always being there for me. I dedicate this work to little Shubhangi (Mishti), my niece, who has fulfilled my life with unbound love and innocence. Last but not the least my thanks are due to Mr Ramesh Jain and Manohar Publishers & Distributors for publishing the book.

DEBASREE DE

Introduction

Tribal Revolts in Chota Nagpur: Ideology, Activism and Upshots (Before the Arrival of Gandhi)

> As long as there is violence which threatens the very future of the human race, the relevance of Gandhi would continue. He would remain relevant till this danger of total annihilation of the human race is removed.
>
> J.P. NARAYAN[1]

Ulghulan and *ahimsa* or *hul* and *satyagraha*—when these come together, they make a bewildering projection of truth, though differently, yet magnificently—match the Indian case in most logical way during the British period. One can ask *how*? Because activism can be the best alternative to non-violence, if that was pursued as the ultimate means of the freedom fighters of those days. Interestingly, both have made the way together as far as the achievement of India's Independence was concerned. Sometimes in the form of revolutionary activism in Bengal, Maharashtra and the Punjab; sometimes in the form of Bose's Indian National Army, and sometimes in the form of Adivasi armed struggle, non-violence has had always remained happily or unhappily married to activism. Gandhi, the propagator of non-violence, also would have agreed to the fact that complete non-violence was something that did not work in Indian case as he himself assisted the British during the First World War by sending Indian soldiers in the battleground and the Great War even brought economic hardships for the people of the entire country. These two parallel streams—revolutionary/tribal activism and non-violence—have always worked together in bringing independence and giving mass character to all-India movements led by Gandhi.

According to Nirmal Sengupta, history has always been written with the preoccupations of the later period. Tribal movements of nineteenth century were identified as 'tribal' long after their occurrences only when the term 'tribe' came into existence. In the Santhal Rebellion or in the Birsa movement of late nineteenth and early twentieth century, some other communities too had joined hands with the tribals, write current historians. If Santhal and Munda had not been differentiated in a hundred years of sustained colonial effort the same rebellions would have been depicted as regional peasant revolts, in which some numerous communities predominated, as is true in the case of any peasant movement.[2]

The birth of tribal activism in India can be traced back from the pre-Christian era when the Aryan migration turned them into *dasas* and *dasyus* and from then on their struggle for survival began for an unending period. With the coming of the modern communications in the form of roads and railways, introduced by the British, their land was flooded with the Hindu zamindars and moneylenders that increased their hardships manifold. After years of deprival, the tribals finally rose into rebellions and hit back the zamindars, *sahukars*—the people whom they called the *dikus* or outsiders. Chota Nagpur was such a region where tribal activism had been most powerful, frequent and continuous for three long centuries, i.e. eighteenth, nineteenth and twentieth. In seventeenth and eighteenth centuries tribal movements in Chota Nagpur region were guided by radicalism or by the ideology of armed struggle, but after the arrival of Gandhi there was a remarkable shift in the mode of their struggle and it was heavily influenced by Gandhian ideology of non-violence or *ahimsa satyagraha*. According to K.S. Singh, most of the scholars have

> . . . overlooked the operation of the historical processes that led to the formation of the State [Chota Nagpur], the emergence of a complex regional system in the wake of the migration of non-tribal communities and functional castes and the penetration of cultural influences. It is evident that in the semi-exposed tribal regions the protrayal of a tribal as a Noble Savage, innocent of the operation of the historical processes, was both naive and untenable, but this led to the build-up of a myth that has bedeviled all historical writings on Chota Nagpur and inspired all tribal movements. This simplistic model also served to justify the presence of the *raj* and the role of the missionaries as the protectors of the tribals against non-tribals.[3]

The tribes were, in fact, getting integrated into a secular system of production, a market system, as it was extended to the tribal region. The Non-Cooperation movement impacted the tribal movements considerably and intensified their agrarian agitation. The impact was felt in Ranchi amongst the Tana Bhagats, in Kolhan amongst the Hos, in Santhal Parganas amongst the Santhals and in Palamau amongst the Kherwars and Cheros. It is now a well-established fact that tribal unrests of Chota Nagpur cannot be identified only in terms of a struggle between the tribals and the non-tribals, rather they were very much disturbed by the internal conflicts and national political developments of that time.[4] The tribals visualized Gandhian *swaraj* as a millennium that was going to free them from all sorts of exploitation. But before going into the detail of the tribal movements, let us first look at the geographical position of Chota Nagpur region.

CHOTA NAGPUR PLATEAU

Chota Nagpur plateau is very rich in forest and mineral resources and is also the abode of various tribal groups. The easternmost extension of the Deccan Plateau was the Chota Nagpur upland that comprised the Chota Nagpur division covering 38 per cent of the entire area of Bihar. Once a part of Bihar, Chota Nagpur was separated from it and added to the newly-formed state called Jharkhand in the year 2000. In 1765, after the Mughal rule ended, Chota Nagpur was ceded to the British. The period of eighteenth and nineteenth centuries had experienced an invasive colonial policy in Chota Nagpur in the interest of 'good governance'. The early incursions into the region had resulted in the formation of a district in about 1780 known as the Ramgarh Hill Tract, and magisterial courts were held first at Shergati to the north-west of Hazaribagh. After the Munda rebellion of 1830, the British government put the entire province of Chota Nagpur under the charge of an officer designated as 'Agent to the Governor-General'. The first legislation implemented for Chota Nagpur was the introduction of the 'Wilkinson Rules' under Regulation 13 of 1833 which made Chota Nagpur a non-regulation province of the South-West Frontier Agency after abolishing the military collectorship of Ramgarh Hill

Tract. In Singhbhum, the Munda rebellions helped the company in their 'expansionist goals' and a major portion of the territories of Porahat, Seraikela, Mayurbhanj and Kharsawan were put together under the charge of a British officer and given the name Kolhan Government Estate in 1837, and formed the south-west region of the old Singhbhum district.[5]

The agency administration was terminated by the Act 20 of 1854 and the local government was asked to appoint a commissioner who was placed under the charge of the Lieutenant Governor of Bengal.[6] Keeping their interest in mind the British implemented a dual system of administration there. A substantial portion of the region was administered directly by the British officials and the rest called as Native States, were governed by native rulers. These feudal lords were not independent and were constantly under the surveillance of the British authority. The only difference was that the acts that were in force in the British-ruled part were not applicable in this part. By the 1880s, forests in Chota Nagpur were organized under a variety of arrangements—reserved, protected, privatized and leased from the political states. As information-gathering in Chota Nagpur increased, notably by colonial officials such as S.R. Tickell (1840), Henry Ricketts (1853) and Valentine Ball (1880), new regimes of property were beginning to be put into place. On the completion of the demarcation in 1880-1, the forests of Singhbhum division comprised Saranda, Kolhan and Porahat. In 1884-5, Chota Nagpur division was constituted which embraced the whole of Singhbhum, Palamau and Kodarma. By 1925 Singhbhum was divided into Saranda, Kolhan, Porahat and Chaibasa.[7]

In 1911, the British separated Bihar from the Bengal Presidency and along with Orissa formed the province of Bihar and Orissa. In 1936, Bihar and Orissa were separated and a separate province of Bihar was created. Bihar was commonly described as comprising three parts: the land north of the Ganges was north Bihar; the plain south of the Ganges was south Bihar and the uplands in the extreme south was known as Chota Nagpur. In 1912, Bihar was constituted into four divisions—Bhagalpur, Patna, Tirhut and Chota Nagpur.

In 1854, the South Frontier Agency (formed in 1834) was abolished and Chota Nagpur was placed under a Commissioner. In 1869, the Chota Nagpur Tenure Act was passed and for the first time an effort was made to survey and demarcate the Bhuinhari tenures and the landlord tenures. The Santhal Parganas Tenancy Act was enacted in 1876. However, it failed to remove tribal grievances. The eventual break down of the traditional socio-political organization of the local tribals caused the Paharia Movement (1772-80), the Tamar Insurrection (1782-1800), the Chero Uprising (1800-1817), and the Ho Uprisings (1820-1, 1831-2, and 1837). Later due to the exploitation by the *jagirdars* and *thikadars* meted out to the tribals, the tribals again rose in arms that resulted in the outbreak of the Kol Insurrection (1831-2), the Bhumij Revolt (1832-4) and finally the Santhal *hul* (1855-7), the Sardar Movement (1859-81) and the Munda *ulghulan* (1895-1902). The Santhals again rebelled against the British in 1860 and 1871, which culminated in the Kherwar Movement under the leadership of Bhagirath Manjhi in 1874. The followers of Bhagirath Manjhi used to call themselves as *sapha hors* (pure men). In 1880 Dubia Gossian took over from Bhagirath Manjhi. The Chota Nagpur Tenancy Act was passed in 1908 to mollify the tribals and to protect some of their land rights. This led to Bihar being broadly divided into four divisions in 1912 (see Table 1.1).

TABLE 1.1: THE DIVISIONS OF BIHAR AND AREA UNDER THEM IN 1912

Divisions	Areas included
Bhagalpur Division	Districts of Bhagalpur, Monghyr, Purnea and the Santhal Parganas
Patna Division	Districts of Gaya, Patna and Shahabad
Tirhut Division	Districts of Champaran, Darbhanga, Muzaffarpur and Saran
Chota Nagpur Division	Districts of Hazaribagh, Manbhum, Singhbhum, Ranchi and Palamau

Source: Sewak Ram, *History of Bihar between Two World Wars, 1919-39*, New Delhi, 1985, p. XIV.

IDEOLOGY BEHIND THE TRIBAL MOVEMENTS OF EIGHTEENTH AND NINETEENTH CENTURIES

The tribal movements of eighteenth and nineteenth centuries are mostly marked by anti-colonial and anti-feudal radicalism. These radical movements' objective was to destroy different forms of exploitation and give birth to an independent Adivasi Raj or for autonomy of a certain kind. With the construction of the railways, the Santhals fell a prey to the hands of the *dikus* (petty traders, *banias*, zamindars, *khetwaris*, *bhuinyas* and *ghatwalls*) who, by taking advantage of their illiteracy, exploited their labour, property and womenfolks. Santhals also turned against the British interference in their traditional life. During the Santhal *hul*, their chief targets were the moneylenders, local police and the court officials. As far as the Munda *ulghulan* was concerned, it identified its principal enemies as the *dikus*, government officials and, of course, the Christian missionaries. According to Virginius Xaxa, tribal movements of the colonial period are often described more on the basis of their nature rather than on the basis of the issues on which they were based. They are commonly termed as revolts, rebellions, or insurrections. Sometimes, they have been described in terms of messianic or millenarian movements. He has further stated that since such descriptions tend to emphasize the fact that the early tribal struggles had more to do with the issue of colonial rule and administration, it would not be wrong to call them as a kind of autonomy movements. The post-colonial tribal autonomy movements were of different character from these movements and the most important difference is that, this time the struggle was far more intense as they were fought against the immediate exploiters, i.e. the non-tribals.[8]

Therefore, one of the most important components of this radical ideology is termed as millenarianism. The Santhal, Munda and Ho movements (1855-1932) believed in the supernatural intervention and reposed faith in their rebel leaders as redeemers. This belief, according to B.B. Chaudhuri, is commonly known as 'millenarianism'.

The movements illustrate two crucial elements of millenarianism: appearance of a charismatic leader as the exponent of its radical ideology, and the pervasive belief among the rebels that their cause would inevitably triumph because it had been blessed by a supernatural agency.[9]

Millenarian movements were not always spontaneous, but were quite organized, coordinated and prudent. Their conviction was firm that they would definitely be victorious. This conviction was inspired by a religious faith in a supernatural intervention, and because of the involvement of the charismatic leader, these movements are also known as the 'messianic movements'.

Another concept in connection with such movements is that of revitalization originally put forward by Anthony Wallace.[10] This idea was applied in case of India by Edward Jay. Jay talked about four principal features of revitalization movement in the Indian context. They are:

1. Expression of group solidarity and social cohesion and have acted as unifying forces for groups under conditions of social disorganization.
2. They represent attempts to establish a new moral order where the old one has been destroyed.
3. They have acted as mediators between the great and little traditions of India, or, more broadly speaking, as catalysts of acculturation.
4. They have aided in the structuring of a new social system of which both Hindu and tribal societies are a part.[11]

The cultural purification movements, like the Kherwar movement (1874-82), were mainly an important aspect of the radical political ideology of the tribals. It was through that this social reform movement would strengthen the resistance of the Santhal. But in reality it was considered as a Hinduization process, because the doctrinal foundation was very much provided by Hinduism. Monotheism, influence of *gurus*, wearing sacred thread, giving up meat and traditional liquor, cleanliness, and abandonment of witchcraft—all were the outcome of Hindu influence. According to B.B. Chaudhuri, the Kherwar movement, though influenced by Hinduism, never renounced the political path. He says,

> It is misleading to conclude that the primary aim of the programme was so-called 'rank improvement' of Santhals. Santhals did not at all abandon their political path. The only notable change was their greater caution in avoiding violence as much as possible. . . . Cultural regeneration and the political path remained inseparable. Santhals ever regarded cultural revitalization essentially as a means of promoting their political cause.[12]

If Christian influence was predominant in the Munda millenarian movement, then it was Vaishnavism that influenced the cultural or religious revitalization movements. It is generally believed that Chaitanya Dev and his followers travelled across the tribal belts of Bankura and Purulia and spread the message of Vaishnavism. This undoubtedly influenced the Adivasis. The Bhagats built up an inclination towards Vaishnavism and Shaivism as well because of which the missionaries could achieve very limited success among them.[13] The aim of these self-reliance movements was to reform or restoration of the old religious beliefs. These types of tribal movements first started with a criticism of their own religious system as well as customs and traditions and deeply influenced by Hindu religious ideology. But it does not mean that the Adivasis were inducted into the Hindufold, rather the revitalization movement emboldened their faith in their cultural uniqueness.

According to K.S. Singh, the first phase (1795-1860) of the Adivasi movements coincided with the establishment of colonial rule. Widespread spontaneous resistance was inherent in all these movements, for example, Santhal, Kol, Gond, Bhumij, Khond insurrections. The second phase (1860-1920) coincided with the all-pervasive colonialism, which witnessed a much graver intrusion of mercantile capitalism into the tribal and peasant traditional economies. The failure of the first phase of the movements had made the tribes look inward. They sought to reform the entire social system; this was the beginning of the revitalization movements. All major uprisings of the first phase were followed by the socio-cultural restructuring movements; the Santhal insurrection by the Kherwar movement (1871-80) and the Munda Oraon Sardar movement (1869-95) by Birsa Munda's and Tana Bhagats' reformative movements (1895-1921), which threw up a charismatic and 'divinely-inspired' brand of leadership. The third phase (1920-47) saw the rise of the movement of a secular and political nature, even though movements of the type mentioned above continued to occur on a smaller scale. The first involved participation of the tribes in the national and agrarian movements and second the emergence of a separatist movement in Chota Nagpur.[14]

ACTIVISM IN THE TRIBAL MOVEMENTS OF EIGHTEENTH AND NINETEENTH CENTURIES: ADIVASI MOVEMENTS BEFORE THE ARRIVAL OF GANDHI

The Chota Nagpur tribes had a tradition of militant and organized struggles going back over a hundred years. The struggles were organized around land and not forest, as elsewhere. The tribal system had survived relatively intact in this region. Tribal movements of eighteenth and nineteenth centuries showed activism in its fullest form. Be it Santhal *hul* or Munda *ulghulan*, the tribals raised their traditional arms to fight their enemies and there was no turning back until they were crushed by the over powerful British army. The tribals always exhibited their anger through armed rebellion and manifested hatred towards the native outsiders. In the later years of the nineteenth century, the influence of the Vaishnava cult made the tribals a bit non-violent and some reform movements swayed in the tribal societies before the arrival of Gandhi. According to Binay Bhushan Chaudhuri, the idea of monotheism was not new among the Adivasis, having said that, it is also important to note that itinerant Vaishnava *gurus*, mostly belonging to dissident Vaishnava sects and to very 'low Hindu castes', also preached the radical belief of monotheism.[15] Kherwar movement (later called as Sapha Hor movement) of 1874 was such a movement. To illuminate the role of activism in the Adivasi movements before Gandhi, we will discuss very briefly some of the crucial movements of nineteenth-century colonial India.

The Kol Uprising (1821-36)

There were two notable Kol movements—the Kol rebellion of 1821 and the Kol rebellion of 1831-6. The Kols and other tribes could not tolerate any outside interference in their traditional exclusive society. They called themselves as *des log*, meaning 'sons of the soil'. The non-tribals of the area were called *hatu* as they generally lived in nearby *hats* (village markets) and plainland,[16] though the word *hatu* in Mundari means 'village'. With the introduction of the British rule, the influx of a large number of outsiders, like the zamindars, merchants and moneylenders, initiated the commercialization of the tribal economy. The exploitation of the market economy eventually led them to rise in rebellion. The Porahat area is located in the north-western part of the district. It connects West Singhbhum with the Khunti subdivision of Ranchi district and with its Kompat Munda population. According to Barbara Verardo, the Porahat area is hilly, forested, and quite disconnected from the rest of the district. Porahat has a heterogeneous population of Hindu castes and 'tribal' communities like the Hos, Mundas, Santhals, and Birhors. It seems, however, legitimate to affirm that some Hos migrated to Porahat from the deeply forested southern part called Kolhan, some Hos and Mundas came from the north-eastern plains of the ex-princely states of Kharsawan and Seraikela, and that another group of Mundas migrated into the area directly from Ranchi district through the deep forests of the north.[17] In 1821 the Kols started predatory activities in Singhbhum and then in Mayurbhanj, attacked British troops, did not pay any tax, and showed indisciplined behaviour along Jackson Road. An expedition under Major E. Roughsedge was sent to subdue the tribals of Mayurbhanj at Bamanghaty to pay revenues to their overland.[18] Finally, the Kols surrendered to the British and receded into the deep forest.

After ten years the dissatisfied again revolted for a long period from 1831 to 1836 in Bamanghaty Zamindari. It was the most important revolt both against the colonial government and the 'outsiders' in which the poor Kol Adivasi peasantry participated. It was against the introduction of a complex, legalistic administrative system imposed by Lord Cornwallis. In 1831 Maharaja Kunwar Harnath Singh, a local zamindar of Govindpur, arbitrarily dispossessed the Adivasis, mainly the Kols and the Mundas, from twelve villages and gave the land to some Sikhs and Muslims. The introduction of Roughsedge's new system of dual control of administration encouraged the Sarvarakar of Bamanghaty to proclaim his independence from the control of the Maharaja of Mayurbhanj.[19] The movement from 1831 to 1836 was a continuous course of repeated disturbances. In December 1831, the four Kol *pirs* were placed under Cuttack and decided to remove the Binjhua guards.[20] Thereafter, a widespread unrest started. This rebellion was supported by the Mundas, the Hos, the Bhuinyas and the Oraons against the *dikus*. The rebels from Ranchi, Hazaribagh, Palamu and Manbhum belonged to different ethnic groups but they fought together against the outsiders under the leadership of the *mankis* (circle headman). The Adivasi peasants were often backed by the *mankis* and the Mundas in their fight against the outsiders. They attacked the Hindus, Muslims and other 'foreigners' who had settled in their villages to pursue their own agricultural and other commercial interests.[21] The notorious plunderers were arrested after military operations. The looted *daks* were recovered. The cattle stolen from neighbouring areas were restored. The rebellion was checked and later on suppressed by Captain Wilkinson, who was assisted by some of the *rajas* and the *mahajans*. All Munda and Kol *sardars* were forced to enter into direct engagements with the British.[22] The Kolhan was formed in 1837.

Bhumij Revolt (1832-3)

The revolt of the Bhumijs under the leadership of Ganga Narain was one of several uprisings which punctuated the establishment of British law and order in Chota Nagpur. The revolt of the Bhumij in the Midnapur district grew out of the ill-judged disruption of local institutions by the British during the time of Lord Cornwallis; a policy unmotivated, it seems, by anything other than a sense of bureaucratic symmetry. It was a crude form of protest against the encroachments on the tribal society.[23]

The extension of the British dominion into this hilly tract, where the tribesmen had enjoyed freedom for centuries, meant not only the political but also economic enslavement of the Bhumijs. The extension of Permanent Settlement and the Cornwallis Code to these undeveloped areas towards the end of the eighteenth century, without taking any note of tribal interests, needs and customs, did great harm to the tribesmen through ignorance and neglect of their rights and customs. The British administration, by facilitating contacts of the non-tribal people (like the subordinate officers of the courts, police and excise departments) with tribes made exploitation easy. On the other hand, the tribal chiefs, who had gradually been Hinduized, gave a foothold to Brahmins and Muslim merchants, usurers and others, who fleeced the tribal people like leeches. Moreover, the *ghatwals*, who were traditional policemen, lost their land grants because they were replaced by weak and corrupt non-tribal policemen. But the fact that in popular legend this revolt is always linked with the name of Ganga Narain serves as a reminder of the significant role of this able leader. Had there been no pre-existing general discontent among the tribal masses, Ganga Narain could not have obtained such influence. But without Ganga Narain, equally, the discontent might have continued to simmer without boiling over into violence.[24]

For twelve months Ganga Narain and his adherents carried on guerilla warfare against the British and their servants in the East India Company, killing, burning and looting, until he himself was finally killed. It is true, certainly, that the revolt helped to convince the British authorities of the necessity for the reforms that they preceded to institute, and which brought some relief. But it seems wiser to view the disturbances as the action of people, rulers and peasants alike, who took advantage of a private feud to give vent to their anger, frustration and despair, and to gain what they could from violence and plunder.[25] It was put down at the cost of thousands of tribal lives and equivalent of at least 22 years of the entire revenue of the district.

SANTHAL *HUL* (1855-7)

The Santhal rebellion of 1855-6 was not restricted to the Santhal Parganas but it reverberated as far as Birbhum, Bankura and Hazaribagh. The main leaders of this insurrection were Sidhu, Kanhu, Chand and Bhairva of village Bhagnadihi. The Santhals were exploited by the landlords, moneylenders, administrators, police, railwaymen, indigo planters and traders. According to K.K. Dutta,

> The causes of the insurrection were deeply rooted in the changing conditions of the time. It had its origin in the economic grievances of the Santhals, due to the oppressions and frauds committed to those simple minded people by the Bengali and upcountry merchants and moneylenders. The extortions of those merchants and Mahajans had become awful, and they had amassed large fortunes within an incredibly short period by recurring cash and grains from the Santhals through various obnoxious ways.[26]

The most important element in the complex of factors which forced the Santhals to revolt was their yearning for *swaraj*. According to the settlement officer H. Macpherson, the deeper cause of the insurrection, 'was the Santhal yearning for independence, a dream of the ancient days when they had no overlords, perhaps a memory of the pre-historic times when according to some speculators, they were themselves masters of the Gangetic Valley and had not yet been driven back by the Aryan invaders'.[27] The Santhals wanted to drive out the British and establish an independent Santhal Raj. Sidhu and Kanhu with their younger brothers Chand had lost their lands to the non-tribal *dikus*. In July 1885 finally rebellion broke out. The insurgents plundered the moneylenders and marched in different directions with bows, poisoned arrows, axes and swords. The insurrections extended to Godda, Pakur, Maheshpur, Murshidabad, Sangampur and Birbhum. Women also played a prominent part in the *hul* rebellion. They assisted the insurgents in plundering and carrying off goods from different villages.

Half the Santhal army was killed and the victors randomly flogged or imprisoned peasants as examples to others. In Hazaribagh, the 40th Regiment was sent for suppressing the rebellion and it was brutally suppressed. Santhal villages were raided and their property destroyed. Most of the punitive raids on villages were crowned with exemplary acts of arson, arrests and execution. According to Abha Xalxo, after the suppression of the rebellion an enquiry headed by Ashley Eden was set up to look into the grievances of the Santhals. As a consequence, a lot of administrative measures were taken by the British East India Company and one of them was the introduction of the Act XXXVII of 22 December 1855. This Act formed the territory in and around Damin-i-Koh into a separate non-regulation district called Santhal Parganas. It was placed under the direct control of the Commissioner of Bhagalpur subsequently. However, due to complaints from European indigo planters and zamindars, this act was nullified and the district was shrunk into a smaller area under the Act X of 1857. The new district created from the Santhali areas of Bhagalpur and Birbhum districts, was divided into four sub-districts—Dumka, Deoghar Godda and Rajmahal—and placed under a deputy commissioner and four assistant commissioners with civil and criminal jurisdiction.[28] Before this the boundary of Birbhum district was drawn up to Deoghar. The administrative measures also included an amendment of the existing land law and unrestricted purchase and sale of land was declared illegal in the 52 *moujas* of the newly created district.

It is often debated whether Santhal rebellion forced the British government to create a separate Damin-i-koh or it was the plan of the British to reorganize the administrative boundary. It is a well-known fact that the British rulers always wanted to make this forested land cultivable in order to increase their revenue collection. They also had the notion in their mind that if the agricultural community could be developed then it would lead to maintain law and order over there. Thus an administrative structure was formed with some parts of the then Birbhum, Murshidabad and Bhagalpur districts which was called Damin-i-koh in 1832-3. After the formation of this new structure they got the most positive response from the Santhals. They started to come to this region, settled down and make the land cultivable.[29] This helped them to have a political goal during the Santhal *hul*, that is, creation of an independent Santhal Raj which was eventually fulfilled with the formation of the Santhal Parganas.

Though the rising opened the eyes of the British officials finally to the extent of oppression which the Santhal had suffered, little was done at first to protect them against further exploitation. Therefore, soon another type of messianic movement began to grow. It was called the Kherwar Movement, since Kherwar (villager) was the original name of the Santhals. Its aim was the return of the

Santhals to their original culture and religion.[30] The nationalist histories textualized the *hul* in two ways. Santhal Parganas was either included in the nation in terms of the activities of the Bengali settlers, like Aurobindo's revolutionary terrorism, Sahajananda's Kisan Sabha movement and Gandhi's anti-liquor campaigns. Santhals were rarely mentioned except as part of the 1942 movement, when they participated in large-scale arson and destruction of telegraphic communications, acts which conformed to the Bengali image of sporadic, violent 'primitive' outbursts.[31] Or, the *hul* was included as part of the valorous events of nationalism, but 'tribes' themselves were conceptualized as tribal Hindus.[32]

Rampa Uprising (1879-80)

Rampa is an agency tribal division in Andhra Pradesh belonging now in Vizag district. Rampa was the site of a series of tribal uprisings throughout the nineteenth century. These uprisings were reactions to an increasing intrusion through the nineteenth century, and intrusion that violently and harshly affected the very social fabric of the tribal society. The pressures consequent to the attempts of the British to establish a more direct control over these rich forest tracts intensified by the 1870s, and resulted in a major confrontation by 1879. The revolt was violent and in the form of guerilla warfare. The revolt which started in March 1879 ended by October 1880 with the death or capture of more turbulent hillmen. After the revolt, the Rampa forests became the property of the state.[33]

During the non-cooperation movement, the Gudem rebellion started with an attack on the Chinta Palle Police Station in the Visakhapatnam Agency in 1922. It is also called Manyam fituri and Rampa. Increasing land alienations, exploitation of forest labour by contractors and other grievances led to the outbreak of the Girijan rebellion under the leadership of Alluri Sita Rama Raju between 1922 and 1924, which was suppressed with the killing of Raju in 1924.[34] It is important to note that there were no attacks on the outsiders as happened in the earlier rebellions and the nature of Manyam was different from the earlier tribal rebellions.

The tribals living in the Srikakulam Agency were being exploited and were in heavy debts. With the growing strength of the Girijan movement, the Girijans began fighting for better wages. These struggles for increasing wages during the time of transplantation, cutting and harvesting were fought frequently in the early years of 1960s and led to the rise of the Srikakulam movement in October 1967. Soon the movement took the character of an armed struggle and was suppressed after severe repression by the army by 1972.[35]

Khond Disturbances in Kalahandi (1882)

The Khonds of Kalahandi district of colonial Orissa lost their autonomy and self-governance with the coming of the British and this was the main reason of their rebellion. The increasing dominance and subjugation of the Hindus caused dissatisfaction among the Khonds and they got completely marginalized in the decision-making process. The Khonds were regarded as a 'notorious' and 'barbarous' race by the British, particularly so, because of their traditional practice of *meriah* or human sacrifice. In November 1835 the British army invaded Ghumsur and annexed it and thus began the infamous Ghumsur wars. The Adivasis started guerrilla warfare. The colonial records say,

> On the 14 [February] the Conds had collected in great numbers, and appeared determined to oppose their further progress. Every effort was made to avoid the necessity of resorting to extremities by explaining our object in ascending the ghauts and assuring them they had nothing to fear. For a time they appeared satisfied, but the evil counsel of Dora Bissye at length prevailed and they assailed our troops, who were in consequence compelled to fire upon them, and make good their way by force.[36]

When the first Ghumsar War ended in 1837, the British had got hold of most the king's wealth. Troops were again sent in 1846 and the Second Ghumsur War came to an end in 1848. But Dora Bissye was still free. He was captured later and was sentenced to death. These were the wars of conquest aimed at the expansion and consolidation of colonial rule.

Going beyond the palace intrigues following the death of the Rajah, the Khond disturbances of 1882, went on for over half a year. By 1882 the administration had further increased its hold over the Khonds. The 'wild' and 'excitable' Khonds had petitioned the chief commissioner regarding the enhancement of rent and forest restrictions. The colonial discourse located the problem around the policy of the late chief and his *dewan* to oust the Khond and settle the Kultas, who were considered to be more 'energetic' and 'skilful cultivators'. However, nothing was done to look into these problems. In the events that followed, the 'ferocious' and 'cruel' Khonds collectively plundered many Kulta villages 'unaccompanied by any personal violence'. The second phase saw intensive bloodshed and cruelty. Thus a great Khond rebellion took place in Kalahandi.

While nothing came out of the resistance, other than the bolstering of colonial structures within the state, the disturbance went down in the history of tribal unrest as a distinctly 'agrarian' unrest. The colonial authorities decided to intervene and persuaded the Khonds to 'return most of the stolen property'. The settlement also saw the colonial administration taking over the management of the state. However, very soon after this we are told of the British officials hanging ten Khond 'ring leaders' since they had indulged in 'large-scale massacres' of Kultas, although the records contain no formal evidence regarding the number of Kultas killed. The British official Berry's act was defended as 'retributive' and 'preventive'. Most shocking is the reference to this action being prompted by the small contingent of troops at his disposal which made it difficult for him to divert some of them with the prisoners. This act, we are told, was prompted by Berry's desire to 'keep the country in order', 'maintain communications', 'save life' (presumably of the Kultas) and 'guard his prisoners'.[37]

The Khonds had, after all, risen against the Kultas in response to the increased assessments levied upon them, their arbitrary ejection from their villages and the loss of certain ancient privileges, particularly the denigration of the office of *Umrao*. Yet seen in the larger context of the colonial process, the Khond insurrection was directed as much against the British authorities as it was against the Kultas. Such an argument gains credence from the Khonds' choice of *meriah* as a mode of protest.[38] As Nandini Sundar has argued in the context of Bastar, the Khond disturbances have to be assessed against the backdrop of indirect rule, which included the displacement of an earlier tribal functional system by the incorporation of external elements and strengthening of colonial structures in the state.[39] While these disturbances do not represent a 'customary rebellion' for reasons elucidated above, neither were they similar to the one in Bastar in 1876.[40]

The level of government control increased in the 1930s with the introduction of laws of reserving the forests, which restricted the Khonds' traditional rights to cut it periodically to make fields, to gather and hunt in it.

MUNDA ULGHULAN (1899-1900)

According to Stephen Fuchs, the Munda is an important aboriginal race in Chota Nagpur, in north-eastern central India. In course of time some Munda headmen rose to prominence and became petty kings. The Munda chiefs adopted Hinduism because they wanted to be on an equal footing with the other chiefs and nobles of Chota Nagpur. More and more Hindus invaded the Munda territory, and the Hindu and Mohammedan landlords began gradually and systematically to tighten the control of their tenants and to reduce the independence of the Munda to practical serfdom. Tenancy rents were increased, forced labour and various other forms of economic exploitation were introduced. The Mundas had seen their traditional *khuntkatti* (communal ownership) land system being eroded by *jagirdars* and *thikadars* (contractors) coming from outside. Problems of recruitment of indentured labour, *beth begari* (forced labour) and proselytization by Christian missionaries also contributed to creating a rebellious situation.[41]

The Mundas had no other choice than to fight openly for their rights or to be reduced to complete slavery which their oppressors obviously aimed at. The Munda rebelled against their oppressors seven times between 1789 and 1832, chiefly in 1811, 1819-20, and again in 1832. But the British administration was completely on the side of the Hindu and Mohammedan landlords and enforced law and order, as the colonial power understood it, with the force of its superior arms.[42]

With the coming of the First Forest Act of 1882, land measurement work began. This endangered the communal ownership rights of the forest tribes like the Mundas. Birsa Munda (1874-1901) came forward to lead the protest movement and was given the epithet of 'Birsa Bhagwan' or 'Dharti Aba'. He tried to unite the Mundas but all of a sudden was arrested by the colonial police in 23 August 1895. On 30 November 1897 Birsa was released. Birsa shifted his centre of activity from Chalkad to Dombari, a small mountainous village. In 1899 Birsa called for the complete elimination of British rule in a secret meeting. The Mundas also burnt the effigy of Queen Victoria.[43] The movement was also against the Christian missionaries.

He taught the Mundas first that he was a divinely appointed messenger come to deliver them from foreign rule, and later that he was an incarnation of God (*Bhagwan*) himself. His mission was to save the faithful from destruction in imminent flood, fire and brimstone by leading them to the top of a mountain. Beneath them, all the British, Hindus and Muslims would perish, after which a Munda kingdom would be ushered in. Birsa assembled a force of 6,000 Mundas armed with swords and bows and arrows, some of whom burned Hindu temples and Christian houses and churches, killed a constable and were finally defeated in battle by government troops.[44] The government sent a military expedition against the rebels. In the encounter in which the rebel Munda fought with great bravery though with pitifully inadequate weapons 200 persons were said to have lost their lives. Munda rebellion not only targeted the feudal structure of the society, but the British imperialism as well. Though Birsa did not have any political philosophy or ideology so to say, but there was a clear indication of class consciousness in the movement.

The Kherwar Movement (1874-82)

There is a crucial gap in the study of the tribal movements in Chota Nagpur starting from the Kol insurrection to the Tana Bhagat movement (1914-21). Due to colonial exploitation, tribals of Chota Nagpur launched a series of protests against British rule and the *dikus*, though the forms of protests were 'a curious mix of agrarian, religious and political' issues. They were followed by socio-religious or revitalization movements.[45] Though the scholars have time and again defined the Kherwar movement as a socio-religious movement, the objective to establish an independent Santhal Raj had always driven the Santhals. All the targets of the Santhal *hul* remained the same, only the strategy changed. Before the commencement of the Kherwar movement in July 1874, sporadic agitations from 1860s continued unabated and the radical ideology revived. In 1866 there came another possibility of an uprising when a famine broke out.

The movement of 1871 led by Karoo Manjhi in Santhal Parganas had hardly died down when in the fall of 1874 there was yet another serious outburst of the Kherwar movement under the leadership of Bhagirath Manjhi of the village Tardiha in Godda subdivision. He had also taken part in the rebellion of 1855. To suppress the movement, the government took strong action to check it. Ultimately, Bhagirath was arrested and sentenced to two years' imprisonment. Bhagirath died in 1879 but a new movement against the Census Operation of 1881 was launched, and it was more violent than any other movement since the Santhal Revolt of 1855.[46]

This movement was an outcry against the Census Operation which was raised by the peasants of Jamtara under the influence of Dubia Gossain. It was initiated by him and it was eagerly caught up elsewhere. The Kherwar leaders seized the opportunity quickly and headed it which advanced Kherwarism with the strength of a revival. The revival of the movement was considered by the government as dangerous, contemptible and 'not innocent'. In order to suppress the influence of Dubia Gossain, the government took punitive action and Dubia Gossain was taken prisoner and was deported to Lucknow, far away from the Santhals, as a political prisoner. The other ring leaders were also arrested during and after the Census Operation and sentenced to imprisonment or deportation.[47]

The rumours as well as the rigid stand of the Santhals against Census Operations 'reflected the community consciousness of the Santhals bound by loyalty to their leaders and to their radical ideas. . . . The new mood of solidarity created by the Kherwar movement had throughout a bitter anti-state tone. Its primary reason was the growing antipathy of Santhals towards the government'.[48] Though the Kherwar movement died down soon, but the radical faith in the creation of Santhal Raj persisted.

The Bhil Uprising (1818-31, 1900-1912)

The term 'Bhils' was often applied for all those who led a lawless life and resided in the deep jungles. When the British conquered Khandesh from the Peshwas in 1818, they found the Bhils to be a turbulent tribe. Mountstuart Elphinstone, the Governor of Bombay, suggested to Col. Briggs, the Political Agent, to drive away the Bhils into the hills. Briggs, however, preferred to make settlements with some Bhil chiefs in 1818. But the chiefs violated these agreements and continued to create a law and order problem. In 1821 a military expedition was undertaken to dislodge some refugee Bhils who did not take to the quiet life of cultivators and watchmen.[49]

The Bhil Raj started as a typical religious, Bhagat-oriented and vaguely messianic project of a reformed society rather than a fully detailed political claim to independence. Guru Govind, a Banjara by caste, preached continence, good behaviour, observance of Hindu religious norms of purity, faith in one almighty god and devoted repetition of his name. In November 1913, Guru Govind and his adherents who had assembled on the Mangarh Hill between Banswara and Sunth were attacked by a joint force and soldiers of the local princely states, destroying any resistance; the Guru, having survived the Mangarh battle, was to spend his last years between jail and exile. The vast assembly of devotees encamped at Mangarh prior to the defeat and the whole preaching of Guru Govind have been often interpreted as a claim to the restoration of a Bhil Raj in southern Rajasthan.[50]

The Bhil uprising of 1913 under Govindgiri resembled in violence and ferment the earlier Bhil uprisings of 1821, 1828, 1838 and 1881 in the southern Rajputana states, but it left a greater impact on the Bhils than those of the earlier ones.[51] Guru Govind's doctrines led to the diminution of cases of drinking and petty crimes among the Bhils of Pachmahals, Southern Rajputana states and South-West Central Agency, which showed that they were ready to listen to the voice of progress and reform.[52] Govindgiri's preachings also raised the social aspirations of the Bhils, taught them to consider them equal to the higher castes and faded the awe of the Rajput Thakurs and officials among them[53] and saved many of them from being converted to Christianity.[54]

The interaction of the Bhils of the Mewar Bhil Tract with the Bhagat Movement created political awakening among them and this made it easy for Motilal Tejawat to mobilize them to revolt against forced labour and high rate of land revenue in 1921-2.[55]

These are some of the instances of the Adivasi movements of the nineteenth-century colonial India. Santhal *hul* and Munda *ulghulan*, as subaltern movements, generated important shifts in both Adivasi consciousness and colonial policy that should be counted when considering the political and cultural aspects of more recent Adivasi activism, which Devalle called a 'culture of protest'.[56] The brutality of the terror strikes that were an integral part of the 'civilizing mission' hardly needs any elaboration. These movements were precipitated by a combination of diverse factors amongst which two most important were the erosion of the customary rights of the Adivasis and exploitation. These movements also illustrated that Adivasi radicalism was an important feature of Adivasi identity. According to B.B. Chaudhuri,

> . . . they aimed at redressing specific grievances, or reforming only some of the old institutions. Radicalism meant a complete restructuring of the old polity. The idea had its ambiguities. It basically was an aspiration for an independent Adivasi Raj in place of the British. Sometimes they meant the right to cultivate land without the obligation of paying anything for it to anybody, the State or private groups. They were even willing to pay, on the condition that the demand for payment did not transgress what they called the traditional norms. Radicalism here was the idea of a political order where there traditional position in the village land remained secure. The idea that increasingly inspired the Adivasi movements was the dream of the Raj of their own.[57]

The Adivasi movements before the arrival of Gandhi (except the Bhil and Kherwar movements) were influenced by religious superstitions. But in spite of that they had a vision of an independent state because of which they radicalized their movements. The bitter dose of radicalism was first noticed during the Santhal *hul*. According to Chaudhuri,

> It was a religiously inspired movement. At least the leader claimed the idea of the insurrection came directly from the God, who personally appeared to him, and told him to start the insurrection as the only means of getting rid of the domination of the aliens, including the British raj. His leadership of the insurrection was also God's choice, and God blessed it, assuring the rebels of victory. Particularly reassuring to them was the leader's prophecy that the divine intervention would make them invulnerable to the formidable military might of the British. The leader's claim is unverifiable. It became part of the rebel ideology because they believed what he had said.[58]

These rebellions often oscillated between both the 'external' and the 'internal' exploiters, sometimes targeting both. The form of resistance through direct confrontations was not an easy way for the Adivasis, who faced decimation under colonial rule. Besides the varying patterns of activism, there is a remarkable shift in the identification of the enemies. Gradually the confrontation with colonialism of the early nineteenth century was later transformed into direct face off with both the colonialist and its associates, such as zamindars, moneylenders and businessmen. The first half of the nineteenth century was replete with the activities of the 'insurgents' and 'rebels' who were ubiquitous up till the turbulent years of 1855-1901—to some of the major tribal rebellions like the *Santhal hul* (1855-6), the Kalahandi uprising of the Khonds (1882) and the Keonjhar *melis* (1868 and 1891-2), that ended with Munda *ulghulan* (1899-1901). Even, there was large-scale guerrilla warfare in different parts of eastern India, especially by the Gonds. British counter-offensive acts brutally quelled the movements and justified themselves as doing the right thing as a part of their 'civilizing mission'. All these revolts were, of course, eventually crushed by the British. Some rebel leaders fled into banditry or, very rarely were reinstated with less exacting revenue settlements. More commonly they were wiped out with exemplary savage.

It was believed that the primitive tribes were devoid of any consciousness and they were misled by the Hindu lower castes, as there was a huge participation of the non-tribals in the Santhal movement. It was also assumed by the colonial government that the

Santhals had no capacity to mobilize the past and to foresee the future. Therefore, they would not be able to take part in any historical act. There was a constant comparison between the Revolt of 1857 and Santhal *hul* of 1855 amongst the Bengali literary society who termed the former as politically motivated but the latter as a mere 'primitive' act. Superstition played a very crucial role in formulating such preconceived notion about the rebellion. According to Prathama Banerjee,

> Santhal rebellion did not have to happen just because Santhals were exploited by mahajans and colonial officials. Rather, the rebellion happened since the Santhals believed that it must, as much because of as in spite of their exploitation. . . . This unflinching mood of rebellion appears in colonial documents as 'primitive' superstition.[59]

THE UPSHOT

In most of the cases the British did not call the tribal movements as conquest, but insurgency or rebellion. For the British the tribal movements were not as threatening as disturbing the political equilibrium of the colonial state, but for them the more matter of concern was the acts of violence that were initiated for getting their legitimate rights back. When the Adivasis first encountered the British they discovered a completely different world before them, the Christian missionaries played a crucial role in bringing the Adivasis in direct contact with the colonial rule. The standard bearers of the so-called 'civilization' first established close contacts with the tribals with the motif of evangelization and contributed significantly in 'pacifying' these 'savage-like' Adivasis without much effort. Pacification was seen as the first stage of 'civilizing' the barbarians and that was the best way to justify *their* acts of violence. For the British,

> The violence . . . had much to do with the religious beliefs, practices, 'superstitions' and the moral attitude of the tribals. The government did not explain the relationship between the 'tribal way of life' and the articulation of their wrath against enemies through violence. It probably assumed the permissiveness of a considerable degree of violence under the tribal cultural mores.[60]

Talking about the upshot will definitely remind us the brutal suppression of all the tribal movements and creation of a separate tribal area called Santhal Parganas in 1856. It is a well-known fact that the tribals of Chota Nagpur contributed in a significant way to the nationalist movement during the Gandhian era, that is, from 1920-47, which is why it is sometimes even believed that with the Sapha Hor (in Santhal Parganas), Tana Bhagat (in Ranchi) and Haribaba movements (in Singhbhum), tribals for the first time took the plunge into the Indian national movement. Needless to say, this belief is untrue as Santhal *hul* or Munda *ulghulan* had no less contribution in raising consciousness among the tribals for a national cause. Even Birsa Munda preceded Gandhi by 43 years in asking the British to quit their country or *disum*. But the question can be raised as how did national leaders like Gandhi, Thakkar Bapa, Rajendra Prasad, and other Gandhians succeed in winning the hearts of the Adivasis of Chota Nagpur? Or, why did the tribals like the Santhals, Oraons, Hos and Gonds take part in the national movement? Or, whether Gandhi really valued the sacrifices made by the innocent tribals? Or, they were considered merely as a composition of crowd or the 'mass' in the movement led by Gandhi?

By the early twentieth century, the Sanskritization process became central to the rhetoric of nationalist mass mobilization as far as the Adivasis were concerned. They started claiming autonomy as their right and the so-called mainstream nationalist politics had no alternative except to recognize their distinctiveness within the illusion of 'unity in diversity' concept which was taken as socio-cultural-linguistic but not political. It was essentially this craft of diversification of Adivasi culture that propelled the so-called mainstream modern political *gurus* to mobilize the Adivasis on the pretext of cultural nationalism in order to include them into the realm of political nationalism. Historians such as G. Pandey, Judith Brown, more recently Pierre Birnbaum, Doron Shultziner and Sarah Goldberg and many more, have long been debating the question of how mass mobilization took place during the course of the nationalist struggle. In nationalist and imperialist historiography, there was a grave underplaying of the extent of subaltern participation in nationalist politics. The 'mass' were viewed as essentially inert.

The birth of national consciousness among the masses has been exemplified as an elite contribution. But mass participation cannot be dovetailed to elite achievement.

To the Hindu peasantry steeped in the medieval *bhakti* tradition, the Mahatma appeared like a *bhakti* preacher and to the Adivasis like a *bhagat.* He spoke in predominantly *bhakti* idioms of *ram-rajya,* of the efficacy *Ramnama,* of the service of the *daridra-narayan* (God in the shape of the poor) at his evening prayer meetings.[61] According to K.S. Singh,

> The Bhil Bhagats, the Tana Bhagats among Oraons, and the Sapha Hors among Santhals, the Haribaba movement among the Hos (1930) and the Raj Mohini movement among the Gonds, saw in the freedom movement led by Gandhi an opportunity for the recovery of the tribal raj, and the rights as agrarian communities which they had lost, as well as an opportunity to continue the social reforms such as temperance, purification and education, and for seeking social uplift and reestablishing an equation with peasant castes.[62]

It was well known to Gandhi and Congress that the Adivasis[63] would not be given back their own country (*disum*) after Independence. Nor would they be free from the exploitation of the Hindu *dikus.* Nevertheless, they made fake promises just to win their support for the 'national cause'. The Adivasis have always been looked down upon as primitive, savage, body-centric, violent, and the like in the colonial records. The middle-class educated nationalists also treated them as irrational, novice, innocent, devoid of consciousness and who can be easily allured or persuaded by the missionaries. Their resistance to the colonial modernity was always ignored in the nationalist discourse as religiously influenced or reformist or revivalist in nature as if there could not be any political motif. To quote Prathama Banerjee,

> Nationalism as political paradigm, with its inherent historicism, would then develop a relationship of desire with the Adivasi, seeking to modernize, Hinduize, and nationalize the 'tribe' on the one hand, but on the other hand, to retain the so-called 'primordiality' that allowed reckless and intractable resistance to the universalizing 'modern'.[64]

The so-called national movement failed to intermingle the currents of national and social discontent into a single anti-colonial, anti-feudal revolution—a lapse which was described by Sumit Sarkar as 'tragic'.[65] Second, it failed to ensure perfect mobilization.[66] This radical historiography pointed out that there has been a tendency of the 'elitist' historiography of Indian nationalism to concentrate on Gandhian or Congress stream of nationalism and treat popular (peasant and tribal) movements as an 'abnormal' outgrowth, peripheral to the study of the development of the Indian nation.[67] In other words, the elitist historiography labelled only the Congress-led movement as 'nationalist' and unfortunately the tribal movements still remain ostracized. This critique pointed out that, as such, it presented only a distorted picture of the reality. In fact, though the Congress-led movements and the popular upsurge in various parts of the country flowed separately, often at opportune moments the Congress leadership tried to seize control of these popular movements.[68]

Therefore, the present research attempts to analyse the contribution of Gandhi and situate Gandhian ideology in the Adivasi movements of Chota Nagpur instead of analysing the contribution of Adivasis in the Gandhian mass movement of early twentieth century. So, there will be very little discussion on the Adivasis joining 'Freedom Movement of India', or 'mainstream nationalist movement' during this time. This can be kept aside for the time being.

Studies on Gandhi continue to multiply, and in recent years a few have come out on Gandhi and Adivasi. Most of the studies on Gandhi's relation with and views on Adivasis are based on analysis of his utterances, speeches and writings on or related to Adivasis as presented to him in his time. Though Gandhi did not provide any comprehensive model for the Adivasi development, yet his principles are used during the policy making for the Adivasis even today. Gandhi's two greatest followers, Verrier Elwin and Thakkar Bapa, failed to draw a proper plan for the sustainable development of them.[69] Either forest policy or land policy, all have bombed miserably to ensure Adivasi participation as well as their well-being. Most important of all, the Adivasis are the ones who still know the secrets of sustainable living. If they disappear, they will take those secrets with them.

The present research attempts to write such a history where the

Adivasis are the main subject; where they are the sole standard-bearer of their movements; where they themselves take their own political decisions devoid of any elite interference. Though Gandhi had a profound influence on these movements, they were primarily and essentially initiated and conducted by the Adivasis themselves. There is hardly any evidence that can prove that Gandhi organized or launched any movement among the Adivasis. He could only support or disown their movements. For him Adivasis were a part of the broader nationalist struggle. His image manufactured by his associates, spates of stories about his supernatural powers and rumours planted by his party workers worked more than he himself as a person. Biswamoy Pati has rightly observed that,

> . . . the nature of the problems raised by these movements remained largely unresolved and resurfaced to strengthen and reinforce the Gandhian mass movements. Moreover, even if articulated at a different time and in a different context, the echoes of some of the issues raised by these movements are discernable even today.[70]

Finally, it should be noted that the book aims to discuss Gandhian ideology and its impact on Adivasis and Adivasi resistance movements during the colonial period and not the pre-Gandhian Adivasi movements. This is also a well-known fact that there is already a wide range of secondary literature on pre-Gandhian tribal movements. For example, *Tribal Movements in India* by K.S. Singh, *The Coming of the Devi* by David Hardiman, *Resisting Domination: Peasants, Tribals and the National Movement in Orissa 1920-50* by Biswamoy Pati, *Out of this Earth* and *Sacrificing People* by Felix Padel, *Adivasi and the Raj* by Sanjukta Das Gupta, *The Sardar and Kherwar Movements in Bihar, 1858-95* by John MacDougall, *A Land of their Own* by Paul Streumer, *Adivasis in Contemporary India* by Uday Chandra and many more. This book does not aim to reinterpret the pre-Gandhian tribal movements or try to go deep into them. Pre-Gandhian Adivasi movements have come here only as reference points in order to trace the continuity. Colonial policies did change time to time according to the course of Adivasi movements, but colonial policies are not the main theme of the present book. How the colonial administration reacted towards the Adivasi customs, whether they succeeded to mitigate Adivasi grievances—are completely different issues to be researched separately. Besides, the book has tried to delineate the impact of Gandhian ideology on the Adivasi movements of his time and later, not how the Adivasis figured in the Gandhian mass movements in the Chota Nagpur region. There are places and occasions when Gandhian perspective has been defined by Congress' policies, especially in the case of Jaipal Singh, but that certainly because of unavailability of sources about Gandhi-Jaipal Singh interactions or Gandhi's opinion regarding the Jharkhand Movement and a separate Jharkhand state. Having said that, it is also to be noted that during this time Gandhi was the sole figure who could decide Congress' policies and Congress on its part did not dare to impugn his decisions as Gandhi had an immense popularity and acceptability across the nation. Gandhi enjoyed an unquestionable authority in Congress at least up till 1944.

NOTES

1. M.P. Sinha, ed., *Contemporary Relevance of Gandhi*, Bombay: Nachiketa Publications, 1970, p. 3.
2. Nirmal Sengupta, 'Reappraising Tribal Movements II: Legitimization and Spread', *Economic and Political Weekly*, vol. 23, no. 20, 14 May 1988, pp. 1003-5.
3. K.S. Singh, 'State-formation in Tribal Society: Some Preliminary Discussions', *Journal of the Indian Anthropological Society*, vol. 6, no. 2, October 1971.
4. For more detail on the internal conflict and division, see Sanjukta Das Gupta (2011), *Adivasis and the Raj* and Sangeeta Dasgupta (1999) *Reordering a World.*
5. Vinita Damodaran, 'Colonial Construction of the "Tribe" in India: The Case of Chota Nagpur', in *Adivasis in Colonial India: Survival, Resistance and Negotiation*, ed. Biswamoy Pati, New Delhi: Council of Historical Research, Orient Black Swan, 2011, pp. 55-87.
6. M. Sahu, *The Kolhan under the British Rule*, Jamshedpur: Utkal Book Agency, 1985, p. 61.
7. Vinita Damodaran, 'Customary Rights and Resistance in the Forests of

Singhbhum', in *The Politics of Belonging in India: Becoming Adivasi*, ed. Daniel J. Rycroft and Sangeeta Dasgupta, New York: Routledge, 2011, pp. 103-18.

8. Virginius Xaxa, *State, Society and Tribes: Issues in Post-Colonial India*, New Delhi: Pearson Education India, 2008, p. 51.
9. Binay Bhushan Chaudhuri, 'Revaluation of Tradition in the Ideology of the Radical *Adivasi* Resistance in Colonial Eastern India, 1855-1932, Part-II', *Indian Historical Review*, 37 (1), 2010, pp. 39-62.
10. Anthony Wallace, 'Revitalization Movements', *American Anthropologist*, 58, 1956, pp. 264-81.
11. Edward Jay, 'Revitalization Movements in Tribal India', in *Aspects of Religion in Indian Society*, ed. L.P. Vidyarthi, Meerut: Kedar Nath Ram Nath, 1961, pp. 282-315.
12. Ibid., p. 51.
13. David Hardiman, 'Christianity and the Adivasis of Gujarat', *Labour, Marginalisation and Migration: Studies on Gujarat, India*, 2002, downloaded on 3 October 2019 from http://www.sagepub.com/textbooks Search.nav?_requestid= 73292
14. K.S. Singh, 'Colonial Transformation of Tribal Society in Middle India', *Economic and Political Weekly*, vol. 13, no. 30, 29 July 1978, pp. 1221-32.
15. For detail, see Binay Bhushan Chaudhuri, 'Revaluation of Tradition in the Ideology of the Radical Adivasi Resistance', *Indian Historical Review*, 37 (1), 2010, pp. 39-62.
16. D.M. Praharaj, *Tribal Movements and Political History in India*, New Delhi: South Asia Books, 1988, p. 104.
17. Barbara Verardo, 'Rebels and Devotees of Jharkhand: Social, Religious and Political Transformations among the Adivasis of Northern India', PhD Dissertation, Department of Anthropology, London School of Economics and Political Science, University of London, 2003, p. 12.
18. Ashok Priyadarshi, 'Tribal Rebellions in North Orissa: A Study on Kol Uprising of Mayurbhanj State, 1821-36', *Proceedings of the Indian History Congress*, vol. 71, 2010-11, pp. 696-705.
19. R.P. Chanda, *Selections from Official Letters and Records (SOLR), Roughsedge to Swaiton*, Secretary to Government of Bengal, 7 May 1821.
20. Cobden-Ramsay, *Feudatory States of Orissa (FSO)*, (Bengal Gazetiers), Howrah, 1950, p. 109.
21. P.K. Shukla, 'Adivasi Peasantry's Struggle for Land-Rights and the Quest for Identity: A Study of Colonial Chota Nagpur and Santhal Parganas

(Jharkhand)', *Proceedings of the Indian History Congress*, vol. 70, 2009-10, pp. 471-81.

22. SOLR, pp. 104-5, *Stockwell to Thomason*, 559 and 560, 8 May 1832, p. 42.
23. E.J. Hobsbawm, 'The Bhumij Revolt, 1832-3 (Ganga Narain's Hangama or Turmoil) by Jagdish Chandra Jha' (Review article), *Bulletin of the School of Oriental and African Studies*, University of London, vol. 32, no. 1, 1969, pp. 182-3.
24. J.C. Jha, 'Some Light on the Origins of the Bhumij Revolt of 1832-3', *Proceedings of the Indian History Congress*, vol. 26, part II, 1964, pp. 162-3.
25. Jagdish Chandra Jha, *The Bhumij Revolt (1832-3) (Ganga Narain's Hangama or Turmoil)*, Delhi: Munshiram Manoharlal, 1967.
26. K.K. Dutta, *Anti British Plots and Movements*, Meerut: Meenakshi Prakashan, 2006, pp. 46-7 and V.N. Dinesh, *National Movement in Jharkhand*, Rampurhat: Santhal Parganas Forum Publication, 1970, p. 3.
27. J. Troisi, *The Santhals, Reading in Tribal Life*, work in ten volumes, vol. VIII: *Social Movement and Change*, New Delhi: Indian Social Institute, 1979, p. 127 and M. Areeparampil, 'Struggle for Swaraj', *TRTC*, Chibasa, W. Singhbhum, 2002, p. 144.
28. Abha Xalxo, 'The Great Santhal Insurrection (*Hul*) of 1855-6', *Proceedings of the Indian History Congress*, vol. 69, 2008, pp. 732-55.
29. Arun Chowdhury, *Adibasi Jibon: Samaj o Sangram*, Kolkata: Gangchil, 2013, pp. 11-13.
30. Stephen Fuchs, 'Messianic Movements in Primitive India', in *Asian Folklore Studies*, vol. 24, no. 1, 1965, pp. 11-62.
31. K.K. Datta, *History of the Freedom Movement in Bihar*, vol. I, Patna: Govt. of Bihar, 1957.
32. Subodh Ghosh, *Bharater Adivasi*, Calcutta: Indian Associated Publishing Company, 1948, pp. 31, 195.
33. Prasad B. Reddy, 'Tribals in Revolt: A Study of Rampa Uprisings of 1879-80', in *Proceedings of the Indian History Congress*, vol. 48, 1987, p. 427.
34. Jaswantha P. Rao, 'Tribals' Struggle against Land Alienation', *Economic and Political Weekly*, vol. 33, no. 3, 17-23 January 1998, pp. 81-3.
35. D. Srinivas, 'From Manyam to Srikakulam Rebellion: Forests and Livelihoods in Northern Andhra 1924-52', *Proceedings of the Indian History Congress*, vol. 67, 2006-7, pp. 678-91.
36. Russell's Report of 12 August 1836, para 51, cited in *Sacrificing People:*

Invasions of a Tribal Landscape by Felix Padel, New Delhi: Orient Blackswan, 2011, p. 41.

37. Biswamoy Pati, 'The Diversities of Tribal Resistance in Colonial Orissa, 1840s-1890s: Survival, Interrogation and Contests', *Economic and Political Weekly*, vol. 48, no. 37, 14 September 2013, pp. 49-58.
38. Nongbri Natasha, 'Resistance Reconfigured: The 1882 Khond Disturbances in Kalahandi', in *Indian Anthropologist*, vol. 46, no. 1, January-June 2016, pp. 1-16.
39. Nandini Sundar, *Subalterns and Sovereigns: An Anthropological History of Bastar 1854-1996*, New Delhi: Oxford University Press, 1997, p. 103.
40. Ibid., pp. 78-103.
41. Shashank Sekhar Sinha, 'Adivasi Movements and Beyond', in *Narratives from the Margins, Aspects of Adivasi History in India*, ed. Sanjukta Das Gupta and Raj Sekhar Basu, Delhi: Primus Books, 2012, p. 218.
42. Stephen Fuchs, 'Messianic Movements in Primitive India', in *Asian Folklore Studies*, vol. 24, no. 1, 1965, pp. 11-62.
43. Arun Chowdhury, *Adibasi Jibon: Samaj o Sangram*, Kolkata: Gangchil, 2013, pp. 100-101.
44. Kathleen Gough, 'Indian Peasant Uprisings', *Economic and Political Weekly*, vol. 9, no. 32/34, Special Number, August 1974, pp. 1391-1412.
45. K.S. Singh, 'Birsa Munda and his Movement in Chota Nagpur 1874-190', in *We Fought Together for Freedom: Chapters from the Indian National Movement*, ed. Ravi Dayal, Delhi: Indian Council of Historical Research, 1995, p. 2.
46. Sumit Sarkar, *Modern India (1885-1947)*, New Delhi: Macmillan, 1983, pp. 44-5.
47. P.K. Shukla, 'Tribal Resistance in Chota Nagpur: A Case Study of the Dubia Gossain Movement (1870-80's)', *Proceedings of the Indian History Congress*, vol. 62, 2001, pp. 613-20.
48. Binay Bhusan Chaudhuri, 'Radical Adivasi Movements in Eastern India: Origins, Ideology and Organization 1856-1922', *Proceedings of Indian History Congress*, IHC, vol. 72, 2012, pp. 1-78.
49. N. Benjamin and B.B. Mohanty, 'Imperial Solution of a Colonial Problem: Bhils of Khandesh up to *c.* 1850', in *Modern Asian Studies*, vol. 41, no. 2, March 2007, pp. 343-67.
50. Marco Fattori, 'The Bhil and the Rajput Kingdoms of Southern Rajasthan', in *Narratives from the Margins, Aspects of Adivasi History in India*, ed. Sanjukta Das Gupta and Raj Sekhar Basu, Delhi: Primus Books, 2012, p. 148.
51. Vijay Kumar Vashistha, 'The Bhil Revolt of 1913 under Guru Govindgiri among the Bhils of Southern Rajasthan and its Impact', *Proceedings of the Indian History Congress*, vol. 52, 1991, pp. 522-7.

52. Proceedings, Internal-A, Nos. 18-22, F&P, NAI, March 1914.
53. Proceedings, Internal-A, Nos. 18-22, F&P, NAI, August 1914.
54. Proceedings, Internal-A, Nos. 38-47, F&P, NAI; Census of India, vol. 26, 1921; Rajputana and Ajmer-Merwara, part 1, Report, April 1916, pp. 105-9.
55. File No. 428, Political (Secret) of 1923, F&P NAI, for details about the Bhil Revolt in Kotra Bhomat under Motilal Tejawat, see, File no. 428, Political (Secret) of 1923, F&P, NAI; Morris Carstairs, 'The Bhils of Kotra Bhomat', *The Eastern Anthropologist*, VII, 3-4, March-August 1954, pp. 173-4.
56. S. Devalle, *Discourses of Ethnicity: Culture and Protest in Jharkhand*, Delhi: Sage, 1992.
57. Binay Bhusan Chaudhuri, 'Radical Adivasi Movements in Eastern India: Origins, Ideology and Organization 1856-1922', *Proceedings of Indian History Congress*, IHC, vol. 72, 2012, pp. 1-78.
58. Ibid., p. 61.
59. Prathama Banerjee, *Politics of Time: 'Primitive' and History-writing in a Colonial Society*, New Delhi: Oxford University Press, 2006, pp. 167-8.
60. B.B. Chaudhuri, 'Towards an Understanding of the Tribal World of Colonial Eastern India', in *Narratives from the Margins, Aspects of Adivasi History in India*, ed. Sanjukta Das Gupta and Raj Sekhar Basu, Delhi: Primus Books, 2012, p. 49.
61. K.S. Singh, 'Mahatma Gandhi and the Adivasis', *Man in India*, vol. 50, no. 1, January-March, 1970, pp. 1-25.
62. K.S. Singh, 'Tribal Polity: State Formation to Formation of States, Tribals in Pursuit of Sakti', in *History of Science, Philosophy and Culture in Indian Civilization*, General editor D.P. Chattopadhyay, vol. XIV, pt. II, *Social Sciences: Communication, Anthropology and Sociology*, ed. Yogendra Singh, Delhi: Pearson Education India, Centre for Studies in Civilization, 2010, p. 270.
63. Gandhi did not like the colonial terms like 'animist' or 'aboriginal' and said that, 'we were strangers to this sort of classification—'animists', 'aborigines', etc.—but we have learnt it from English rulers'. After the birth of the Jharkhand movement Gandhi started to use the term Adivasi.
64. Prathama Banerjee, 'Culture/Politics: The Curious Double-bind of the Indian Adivasi', in *Subaltern Citizens and their Histories*, ed. Gyanendra Pandey, New York: Routledge, 2010, p. 126.
65. Sumit Sarkar, *Swadeshi Movement in Bengal*, New Delhi: Peoples Publishing House, 1973, pp. 515-16.
66. Gyanendra Pandey, *The Ascendancy of the Congress in Uttar Pradesh: A Study in Imperfect Mobilization*, Oxford: Oxford University Press, 1978.

67. Ibid., p. 217.
68. Sajal Nag, 'Multiplication of Nations?: Political Economy of Sub-Nationalism in India', *Economic and Political Weekly*, vol. 28, no. 29/30, 17-24 July 1993, pp. 1521-32.
69. Sagar Preet, 'Tribal Problems: A Gandhian Perspective', *Indian Anthropologist*, vol. 24, no. 2, December 1994, pp. 29-38.
70. Biswamoy Pati, 'The Diversities of Tribal Resistance in Colonial Orissa, 1840s-1890s: Survival, Interrogation and Contests', *Economic and Political Weekly*, vol. 48, no. 37, 14 September 2013, pp. 49-58.

CHAPTER 1

Changing Perspectives on Adivasi Predicaments: Gandhi, Verrier Elwin and Amritlal Thakkar

In 1914, at the age of 44, Gandhi arrived in India. He decided to stay at Santiniketan, an educational centre founded by Rabindranath Tagore. Gandhi's first tour to Chota Nagpur took place in 1917. He first came to Patna and then to Ranchi during the indigo *satyagraha*. Famous meetings between him and Sir Edward Gait, the Lieutenant Governor of Bihar, was held on 2 June 1917. Consequently, the Sly Committee was appointed on 10 July to discuss the problem of indigo plantation. His next visit to Chota Nagpur was in September 1925. He came to Chaibasa which was the heartland of the Ho tribes. He also met the Mundas at Khunti on his way to Ranchi. He saw a silent reform movement, initiated by the Congress, among them. He was very much impressed by the innocence of the tribals and commented that:

> . . . among these tribes there is quite a colony of them called Bhaktas, literally meaning devotees. They are believers in Khaddar. Men as well as women plied Charkha regularly. They wear Khaddar woven by themselves. Many of them had walked miles with their Charkha on their shoulders. I saw nearly 400 of them all plying Charkha most assiduously at the meeting I had the privilege of addressing. They have their own Bhajans which they sing in chorus.[1]

Gandhi's third tour of Chota Nagpur started from Daltonganj in January 1927, when thousands of villagers of hill sides, such as Korwas, Pahariyas, Bhuians, Kherwars, Cheros, came from long distance.[2]

GANDHI AND VERRIER ELWIN

Verrier Elwin, who was an anthropologist, lived, loved and wrote extensively about the tribals during his lifetime. Born in 1902 in England and studied in Oxford, Elwin was later introduced to the writings of Tagore and the opinions of Gandhi by Bernard Aluwihare. He had also heard about a distinguished athlete in Oxford called Jaipal Singh who later became a famous name in Indian politics, especially during the Jharkhand Movement. Father Jack Winslow was the founder of an *ashram* settlement called the Christa Seva Sangh (CSS) which was founded to explore the possibilities of the reorientalization of the Christian religion. He worked as a missionary in western India for many years. Elwin and three of his friends got attracted by Winslow and decided to join him.

Elwin arrived in Poona on 20 November 1927 as a member of CSS. In January 1928 he was assigned by the CSS to attend a meeting of an International Fellowship of Religions, organized at Gandhi's *ashram* in Ahmedabad. That was Elwin's first meeting with Gandhi which impacted him greatly and made him an ardent supporter of Indian national movement. But Gandhi's ideas did not impress him very much. In his own words:

> He is a born leader of conduct, but not of thought. His religious position struck me as deeply unsatisfactory . . . Gandhiji's outlook . . . strikes me as neither genuinely Eastern or Hindu, nor genuinely modern in the best sense of the word. It's an amalgam of Ruskin, Tolstoy, Emerson and that gang—a type which I have never understood or liked.[3]

In June 1931, Verrier Elwin was invited by A.V. Thakkar to come on a tour of the *ashrams* he ran. Born in 1869, two months after Gandhi and in the same state of Gujarat, Thakkar had first been trained as an engineer. In 1914 he left his job in the Bombay Municipality to join the Servants of India Society, the social welfare organization founded by Gopalkrishna Gokhale. In 1921 he was sent to organize famine relief in the coastal districts of Maharashtra. This brought him face to face with the poverty of Bhil tribals: two years later he founded the Bhil Seva Mandal at Dahod, the first tribal welfare organization run and staffed by Indians. It ran schools and dispensaries for the Bhils, interceded on their behalf with moneylenders and officials, and promoted *khadi* and temperance.[4] With support from Gandhi and under the guidance of Thakkar Bapa, the Bhil Seva Mandal designed a comprehensive programme for the tribal welfare. The main features of it were:

- Improving the economic condition of the tribals through co-operative societies
- Improvement of agriculture
- Liquor prohibition
- Land conservation and educating tenants about land rights
- Providing welfare activities during droughts, famines, and floods.[5]

The positive signs of the work of Bhil Seva Mandal became evident in the 1920s itself. Gandhi believed that tribals are the most genuine people, the only thing they are required to do is to

1. Abstain from eating flesh
2. Abstain from taking intoxicating liquor or drugs
3. Use homespun clothes
4. Speak the truth
5. Live cleanly.[6]

Mahatma Gandhi was once asked why he paid so little attention to tribes. He replied: 'I have entrusted that part of our work to A.V. Thakkar'.[7] Thakkar took Elwin to the Bhil villages. This tour stimulated Elwin to work for the tribals.[8] Jamnalal Bajaj, a prosperous merchant and treasurer of the Congress in Wardha, asked Elwin once, 'Why don't you do something for a tribe, which is almost entirely neglected both by national workers and by missionaries?'[9] Gandhi's attitude towards missionaries always remained ambivalent: he did not approve high pressure evangelism. At the same time he was appreciative of their art of applying the principle of disinterested service to the disadvantaged.[10]

Verrier Elwin's disillusionment of Gandhi took place with the gradual unfolding of various incidents. Mary Gillet, a teacher trained in Roehampton, came to Poona in 1932 to join the CSS. Elwin and Mary both wanted to marry each other but Gandhi disapproved it as a defeat in leading an ascetic life. The marriage was finally abandoned and Mary left for Europe. Later when Gandhi's youngest son Devadas got married he did not object, which according to Elwin amounted to hypocrisy.

Gandhi's fast against untouchability in the palace of a rich industrialist where the lower castes were not allowed to enter, made Elwin even more surprised and disenchanted with his leadership. Later Gandhi told Elwin to go back to England and promote the cause of Congress there as he had very little interest in Elwin's *ashram*. This made him further disappointed.

In November 1934, A.V. Thakkar visited Elwin's place. Thakkar later wrote in *Harijan*:

> Father Elwin, though a Christian in the truest sense of the term, is not out for proselytization. He does not convert Gonds, but merely serves them. He has no other aim than that of pure unadulterated service from a humanitarian point of view. For this type of service, he is neither thanked by Christians nor by Hindus. The former dislike him for the departure from the orthodox way of work, and the latter distrust him as they cannot imagine any Christian tabooing conversion.[11]

In a paper written in 1944, Elwin advocated the prohibition of proselytization as in many other free countries. He said,

> Change of religion is actually harmful to the aborigines. It destroys tribal unity, strips the people of age-long moral sanctions, separates them from the mass of their fellow countrymen and in many cases leads to decadence that is as pathetic as it is deplorable, the methods employed are questionable. There is economic exploitation, exploitation of ignorance and social exploitation. Therefore, missionaries should be withdrawn from tribal areas.[12]

Responding to the question whether missionaries would be welcomed in the free (independent) India, Gandhi said,

> Every nation considers its own faith to be as good as that of any other. Certainly the great faiths held by the people of India are adequate for her people. India stands in no need of conversion from one faith to another.[13]

A simple analysis of Gandhi's statement reveals several controversial issues. Such issues include treating conversion and proselytism as synonyms, every nation owning its faith or religion, and to shut Indian citizens from the freedom to choose one's own religion or faith. All these do not conform to the secular commitment of the independent India Gandhi had fiercely fought for. It is not surprising that most intellectual writings by Hindu communal nationalists today utilize Gandhi as a basis for their anti-conversion writings. Gandhi's dislike of religious change or proselytism is unambiguous, but the meanings of his statements are often vague and sometimes they appear to be inconsistent.[14] For instance, he says he detests conversion and fails to understand its rationale, but also declares it highly desirable.[15] In one passage, Gandhi states that he regards Christianity as 'equally true' with his own religion, while he just announced that he does 'not accept the orthodox teaching that Jesus was or is God incarnate in the accepted sense that he was or is the only son of God'.[16] The implication is that the core doctrine of orthodox Christianity is false.

One of the difficulties in understanding Gandhi on conversion is his ambiguous use of the term 'conversion'. In one place he said, 'I am against conversion, whether it is known as *shuddhi* by Hindus, *Tabligh* by Mussalmans or proselytizing by Christians. Conversion is a heart-process, known only to and by God. It must be left to itself.'[17] About *shuddhi* he said,

> My Hindu instinct tells me that all religions are more or less true. All proceed from the same God, but all are imperfect because they have come down to us through imperfect human instrumentality. The real *shuddhi* movement should consist in each one trying to arrive at perfection in his or her own faith. In such a plan, character would be the only test. What is the use of crossing from one compartment to another, if it does not mean a moral rise?[18]

Lalsangkima Pachuau had shown in his research on tribal movement to Christianity in north-east India, most stories of tribal conversion in north-east India are the result of the works of early 'native' converts.[19] In many cases, missions had very little or nothing to do with the conversion of these leaders, and in other cases unlikely convert-employees of mission also served as the instruments. Cyril Firth's earlier observation concurs with this point when he said, 'It has been the converts who sought out the missionaries rather than the missionaries who sought out the converts'.[20] The initiative taken by 'native' tribal converts is an important key in understanding the nature of the movements.

There were other things on which Elwin and Gandhi differed regarding the tribal development and welfare. The book *Leaves from the Jungle* reflects Elwin's gradual denial of Gandhian principles and his rejection of Gandhian teachings in relation to the tribals. Three of Gandhi's chief principals—spinning, temperance and celibacy—were completely unacceptable for the tribals and after noticing the aboriginals and their way of life, Verrier Elwin realized this very well. Gandhi was very optimistic about the role which the Bhils would finally play. He expressed his concern for and faith in their awakening in the following words:

> The Bhils have been long neglected by the States and reformers; if they are given a helping hand, they can become the pride of India. All they need is the spinning wheel in their homes and schools in which their children can receive simple education. In the vast awakening that has taken place, no race can be left out of the calculation of the states and reformers.[21]

But Elwin said that aboriginals do not wear cotton clothes, so there was no point in encouraging spinning; rather they were more interested in rice pounding that not only fulfils their daily needs but also fits perfectly into their way of life. According to Guha,

> Why would the Gond take to spinning, he asks, when no cotton is grown anywhere in his country? And why should the aboriginal practice of temperance when his jungles are rich in *mahua*, the tree from which he distilled a most potent and liberating spirit? Asked his definition of Hell, one Gond replied: 'Miles and miles of forest without any *mahua* trees.' Another wished to be buried under the tree so that even in death he might 'suck some pleasure from its roots.' … Their view … was that 'You may eat, you may drink, but life without a wife is wasted.'… nothing worried men more than impotence: they were dismayed when Sham's dispensary had no remedies for that ailment. Premarital liaisons were frequent, adultery even more so. Verrier counted nineteen elopements in one year in their village alone.[22]

Temperance was another thing that seemed unfitting to Elwin as far as the tribal's predicaments were concerned. The traditional *mahua* liquor had always been a part and parcel of their culture, drinking was something inseparable from their day-to-day life, then how can they be able to practice temperance? But Gandhi had strongly condemned the practice of liquor consumption and its pernicious effects on the Adivasis.[23] To prove his point, Gandhi suggested that it was the drinking of alcoholic beverages that had made the British cruel and that when Indian men wasted their meagre incomes on drink, street brawls, wife-beating, and child abuse often followed.[24] Gandhian *ashrams* situated at the Adivasi areas popularized teetotalism through folk songs and picketing.

Leave Daru and toddy,
O, my people rise and awake
Be free from debts of shaukar
Increase happiness.[25]

Like prohibitionists around the world, Gandhi denied that laws forbidding the sale of alcohol violated the drinker's rights. Rather, prohibition protected the would-be drinker. Gandhi stigmatized the drinking habit as foreign to India, blaming it on British imperialism. Thus, according to Gandhi the pursuit of prohibition was a patriotic pursuit. In his book, *Key to Health*, published posthumously, Gandhi reminded his readers that he had first-hand knowledge of how drink devastated the families of poor Indians. At the same time, he did not condemn the medicinal use of toddy saying that, 'the prohibition will certainly not affect the sale of toddy for bonafide medicinal use'.[26]

There were a few spontaneous popular temperance agitations in the late nineteenth and early twentieth centuries that boosted the strength behind the call for prohibition. For example, among the Adivasis in the Devi movement in South Gujarat during the early 1920s, the worshippers of Goddess Devi helped purify themselves by their abstinence from alcohol and meat. They regarded as their principal enemy the local Parsi liquor-sellers, who were often also landowners and moneylenders.[27] After the movement got underway, Gandhian activists supported it, and in turn many Adivasis supported the nationalist cause.[28] Members of one Adivasi group, the Bhils, even took a vow not to drink 'while bowing to a portrait of Gandhi'. Likewise, a reform movement that included teetotalism transformed the culture of the Gonds, another Adivasi group, in the 1930s.[29]

Kasturba Gandhi and Vallabhbhai Patel bluntly discouraged calls for a social boycott of liquor dealers and the refusal of labourers to work for them.[30] The party sidestepped economic questions. This was partly because Gandhi's harmonizing ideology rejected class struggle, partly because of its close association with exploiting groups. Gandhi's own approach was more eclectic and pluralistic than his party men. According to the Mahatma, '. . . the strong wine of libertinism that the intoxicated West sends us under the guise of new truth and so-called human freedom.'[31] Gandhi had a horror of alcohol because it threatened to undermine self-control. Moderate in his criticism of many things he found objectionable, he was wholly immoderate in his concern to realize temperance: 'Drugs and drinks are the two arms of the devil with which he strikes his helpless slaves into stupefaction and intoxication.'[32] Gandhi clearly and repetitively dubs drinking as a 'robber of reason' so much so that he asserts that the alcoholic tends to forget 'the distinction between wife and mother, lawful and unlawful'.[33] He said, 'The drunkard forgets the distinction between wife, mother and sister and indulges in crimes of which in his sober moments he will be ashamed';[34] but this evil levels all, 'I have seen respectable Englishmen rolling in the gutter under the effect of alcohol'.[35] Having said that, it is also very true that, Gandhi never wanted to lose the support of his wealthiest backers, like the Marwari industrialists Jamnalal Bajaj and G.D. Birla. Any direct attack on Parsi liquor dealers risked straining links with his wealthy counterparts in Bombay. Gandhi lamented 'that in all India any opposition came from the Parsis'.[36]

The emphasis on prohibition of liquor rather had a negative impact on the Adivasis, because it can be doubted if alcoholism was a serious problem until liquor monopolies were enacted and traditional brewing outlawed, flooding Adivasi regions with strong drink.[37] Gandhi was interested in the success of his own experiments primarily to the extent that others might learn from them and subscribe to a regimen of self-discipline. He wanted to engage young Indians on a level that would lead to self-control rather than mandate institutional reform through policy.[38] But what he could not realize was that the suppression of the home brewed liquor, forcing the tribal to buy commercial liquor only from outlets licensed by the state, had brought him into contact with a most 'degraded type of alien', the liquor contractor. Actually, where the anthropologist defended the tribal's love of drink the reformer wished gradually but firmly to introduce prohibition.

Gandhi published his core arguments in an article titled 'Drugs, Drink and Devil', which appeared in *Young India* on 22 April 1926. Elwin believed that liquor was far more indigenous product than *khadi*. About drinking he said,

> Gandhi took a vow not to drink cow's milk. The tribesmen could not understand how, in view of this, we were doing all we could to persuade him to break his taboo on milk and give it to his children. Gandhi regarded alcohol and tobacco as bad, an estimate with which the people emphatically disagree.[39]

In the Quit India movement, the Adivasi participation was spectacular. Lakshiram Hembrom, a Santhal leader of Midnapore, led the rebels to burn down many liquor shops. In Bankura, they set aflame liquor shops as well. In Kanchanpur, Kadamghat and Belabani under Bankura Police Station, Santhal rebels were reported to have set fire to three liquor shops. According to Dhiren Baske, the Santhal insurgents targeted the liquor shops and destroyed them because these had lured thousands to liquor addiction and had caused their economic impoverishment and moral degeneration.[40] In the wake of nationalist movement, the promotion—quite successful, as we have seen—of the image of India as an abstinent culture, had allowed for the nationalist elite's assertion of moral superiority against the intemperate colonizers. Moreover, the prohibition of alcoholic drinks, a forceful demand of nationalists and temperance activists since the 1900s, was a means to severely diminish the colonial state's resources. Boycotting liquor, imported spirits, and toddy was a prominent strategy within the *swadeshi* campaign of 1905, which sought to further economic self-sufficiency and national identity.[41] In India, the standard of abstaining from alcoholic beverages was closely linked to various efforts to appreciate or impose upper caste norms, which became part of modern middle-class *bhadralok* culture.

A decade later when Congress acquired partial control of most provinces, Congress ministries adopted legislation that restricted alcohol sales. The result was a rush of law breaking, sometimes with the connivance of local officials. In a memorandum about the ministry in Bihar province, Vallabhbhai Patel complained: 'prohibition has been a fiasco, an utter fiasco if some reports are to be believed'.[42] Gandhi himself sadly acknowledged, 'Prohibition in the Congress provinces is not going on in the spirit in which it was conceived.'[43]

With the growing interaction with the Gonds, Elwin found that they practice not only premarital sex, but also a very simple process of separation from marriage ties. For them, marriage is a must. He wrote,

> . . . one of the drawbacks of semi-tribal India is domestic infidelity. Divorce is universal, elopement common, adultery an everyday affair. The ghotul villages have a much higher standard in this respect. The incidence of divorce in Bastar was under 3 per cent. An examination of 50 marriages in Patangarh showed 23 divorces or 46 per cent.
>
> We may also consider how the ghotul boys and girls were almost completely free from those furtive and unpleasant vices that so mar our modern civilization. There was hardly any masturbation; where it was practiced, it was due to the mistaken efforts of reformers to improve the ghotul. Prostitution was unknown, unthinkable. No motiari would ever give her body for money.[44]

Elwin himself had referred to this issue in his autobiography,

> In July 1939, he [Gandhi] wrote to me about spinning, whose utility for the Gonds I had questioned. He replied that he did not want us to spin unless we had a living faith in it. The cause of spinning, he said, 'is passing through' a severe trial. To me it is on the same level with the war against untouchability. Even if Indian humanity did not rise to them, I should be spinning and warring against untouchability. Without them non-violence cannot be established nor truth vindicated.[45]

* * *

> During the forties my links with Gandhi weakened. . . . For Gandhi my affection never wavered, but I allowed the difference between us to keep me away from him. I suffered a great disillusion when I discovered that the khadi programme was not suitable for our tribes. I have always been a strong supporter of handloom weaving, but spinning, for very poor people and in places where cotton did not grow, seemed to me artificial and uneconomic.[46]

Elwin was even against the reform movements launched among the tribals on the Gandhian line. He was dismissive of such reformist activities, which he believed, only resulted in emasculating tribal life. He thus argued,

> The real danger of these movements is that they give the aboriginal a parody of Hinduism instead of the lofty and ennobling teaching of that religion in its true form; they deprive him of an essential part of his diet and provide no substitute; they lower the dignity and freedom of his womenfolk; they rob him of his natural and innocent recreations; they stimulate the spirit of communalism, arrogance and caste exclusiveness; and in the long run they destroy tribal religion, art and organization.[47]

This may be contrasted with the ideas of nationalist anthropologists like D.N. Majumdar. Majumdar has clearly indicated that Adivasi culture (Ho culture) was inferior to that of the Hindus. He has expressed his concern regarding the reformist programme of prohibiting Adivasi dances:

> . . . the stoppage of dances in the village, within a couple of years, will be an accomplished fact. We have got to wait to find out the effects of this prohibition but in the meantime, it is not idle to speculate the prospects of this taboo. The majority of the Hos take dance as a regular exercise after their evening meal. When they are free from other engagements, the dances take up their time and afford opportunities for the young people to spend their energy in some way. Now if they are not given sufficient useful work, as a compensation, this time they will remain unoccupied and idle, and want of taste and culture may lead them to things which may not be conducive [to] or compatible with their newly awakened consciousness. If they had sufficient education, they would themselves realise that the dances were opprobrious to their conduct. They would also realise the evils associated with these dances and could find out means to end these scandals. But where ninety per cent of the people possess no knowledge of alphabets, it is idle to expect any such thing.[48]

On the other hand, Elwin stressed on the gaiety of aboriginal life that comes through most vibrantly in their love for dance. Elwin wrote that without dance,

> . . . tribal life sinks into utter monotony. . . . The tribesmen like their recreation to have a kick in it, and they find small consolation in missionary tea-parties

or Congress meetings to discuss agricultural reforms. Without the dance, the tribesman is overwhelmed with boredom; he is swallowed by his work and his anxieties: there is no tower into which he can escape.[49]

The Gandhians attacked Adivasi culture time and again, but more grave concerns were always bypassed, like exploitation by the zamindars, moneylenders and shopkeepers. They were never given any honourable positions or respectable tasks in Gandhi's *ashram*, which were very often given to the caste Hindus. Many upper caste Hindu Congressmen even objected the claim of the Adivasis being followers of Gandhi. During the Gudem Rampa uprising that took place in 1922-4 by the Gond tribals under the leadership of Alluri Sita Rama Raju across Andhra-Orissa border, Raju used the 'constructive' programme of Gandhi as an effective camouflage to educate and prepare the masses for a showdown with the British and his camouflage was so effective that he caught both the Congress leadership and the British rulers by surprise in August 1922 by openly looting the three police stations and declaring a liberation war. The revolt had been brewing from January 1922, a period of intensive no-tax campaigns in the plains. It was in this period that the Gandhian promise of *swaraj* in one year had also caught the imagination of tribal masses in the hills.

Raju was moved by the Gandhian ideology of temperance and promoted *khadi* among the Gonds. It was observed by M. Annapurniah,

In the whole programme of Gandhiji, boycott of courts and liquor appealed to him. He started in the Agency tracts of Godavari and Vizagapatnam Districts a campaign of prohibition. His piety and devotion attracted huge crowds around him. His word was law for the Agency folk. They were guileless and his eloquent appeals touched their hearts. 'Don't dance attendance at the courts and don't drink' was his message to the villagers. His message spread like wildfire. But not one in the Agency responded to his bugle call. A new consciousness dawned on the innocent folk. People gave up drink in large numbers. Courts were deserted. A number of panchayat courts sprang up in the villages and justice was administered locally. Raju is reported to have been a regular Khadi wearer. From the confessions in the *fituri* trials, it is clear that Raju supplied only Khadi uniforms to his troops. Rallapalli Kasannla, a non-cooperator and Khadi producer of Tuni, was put on trial for having supplied khaki Khadi uniforms to Shri Rama Raju.[50]

But he encouraged the Adivasis to arm themselves with guns and adopt guerrilla method of fighting the enemy. During the national movement, Raju was seen actively working among the tribals for the spread of *khaddar*, in the anti-liquor campaign, and for the establishment of *panchayat* courts, all parts of the Congress programme.[51] It is not at all surprising to see such a militant man raising slogans like 'Gandhi-ki-jai' after looting the Chintapalli Police Station, and on another occasion he 'spoke highly of Gandhi'.[52] This means that Raju was in 'close communication with the plains',[53] and the main currents of the nationalist movement led by the Congress. In the course of his discussion with the Deputy Tehsildar, Malkanagiri, he is reported to have said after praising Gandhi, that violence is necessary. He will continue his campaign till *swaraj* is established.[54]

The Congress leaders did not show him an iota of sympathy on the pretext of using violence. But the actual reason of their hostility against the poor Gonds was, as David Arnold has rightly identified, that they themselves shared the same class interest of the zamindars and moneylenders against whom the Gonds were revolting.[55] To Raju's utter disappointment, while the reaction from the Congress in the plains was hostile, the response from other political elements was either passive or negative. A prominent nationalist paper, *Andhra Patrika*, for instance, no doubt demanded an immediate enquiry into the grievances of the hill tribes, but was the first to denounce the suggestion that Raju had any links with non-cooperation under the leadership of Gandhi in the plains.[56] After Raju's death the same paper observed in its editorial that 'the *fituri* conducted by Raju is another illustration to show that violence is quite a useless weapon. Hence all will do well to adopt the excellent non-violent non-cooperation preached by Mr. Gandhi. . .'[57] At the ideological level, Raju failed to perceive the class interests operating in the nationalist movements under Gandhian leadership in the plains.[58]

In 1929, in the course of an Andhra tour, a portrait of Raju was presented to Gandhi. Reacting to it at a later date, he wrote:

> Though I have no sympathy with and cannot admire armed rebellion, I cannot withhold my homage from a youth so brave, so sacrificing, so simple and

so noble in character as young Shri Rama Raju . . . Raju was (if he is really dead) not a *fituri* but a great hero. Would that the youth of the country cultivated Shri Rama Raju's daring, courage, devotion and resourcefulness and dedicated them for the attainment of *swaraj* through strictly non-violent means. To me it is daily growing clearer that if the teeming millions whom we the articulate middle classes have hitherto suppressed for our selfish purpose are to be raised and roused, there is no other way save through non-violence and truth. A nation numbering millions needs no other means.[59]

Therefore, imposing anything from above would be rejected by the tribals, which would not only affect their life but also generate a sense of subordination by the dominant culture. Gandhi always reminded Elwin that spinning is a form of *tapasya*, or ascetic discipline, but Elwin replied that these principles were not for the tribals. He started believing that celibacy is hypocritical and a hopeless attempt to suppress human desires.[60] He knew that the Gonds would never appreciate celibacy, but rather see it as a perversion. He used to believe that it was impossible to reconcile with Gandhian philosophy of love because according to Gandhi lust must not enter into marital ties.

Elwin was very disappointed and disheartened to see the indifference of the so-called intelligentsia, leaders of the national movement and especially members of the Congress party. He believed that tribal people were no less important than the Dalits (the untouchables), but still ignored by the society at large. He wrote in a journal,

. . . that one has become a problem of all-India importance: the other remains buried in oblivion. Indian national workers and reformers—with the exception of the heroic little band associated with the Bhil Seva Mandal—have neglected the tribes shamefully. The Congress has neglected them. The Liberals have neglected them. The Khadi workers have neglected them.[61]

Though Adivasis whole-heartedly supported Gandhian movements, Gandhi paid very little attention to the Adivasi situation in India. For him Adivasi issues always remained at the bottom of the priority list. He convinced Amritlal Thakkar to devote his time and energy more on Harijan issues and made him the secretary of the Harijan Sevak Sangh. Thakkar Bapa was preoccupied with the tribal problems and was persuaded by Gandhi to accept the secretaryship of the Harijan Sevak Sangh. Gandhi said,

There is no limit to your greed. By all means satisfy it to the top of your bent. Your secretaryship surely is no hindrance. . . . You can give as much of your time as you like to the Adivasis while discharging your duty as Secretary of the Sangh. You do not want to tell me that you want to resign even after that latitude. . . . But the eradication of the sin of untouchability calls for the moral force of the pure in heart. Do not forget that the irreligion of untouchability is today being sanctioned as religion. That is not so in the case of Adivasis. I do not mind therefore your dedicating yourself to the service of the Adivasis, but it must not be at the cost of the Harijans.[62]

Gayatri Chakravorty Spivak while evaluating Mahasveta Devi's pathbreaking work *Draupadi*, has stated that, in giving the name Harijan (God's people) to the untouchables, Mahatma Gandhi had tried to concoct the sort of pride and sense of unity that the tribes seem to possess. But Mahasveta Devi had followed the Bengali practice of calling each so-called untouchable caste by the name of its menial and unclean task within the rigid structural functionalism of institutionalized Hinduism.[63] Thakkar Bapa was more inclined to do the social work for the Adivasis, mainly the Bhils. Bapa had to shift from the Adivasi area to shoulder the responsibility of Harijan work at Delhi, leaving the work of the Bhil Seva Mandal at Dahod and Jhalod in the hands of his co-workers—Lakshmi Shrikant and Dayabhai. Later he mounted pressure on Gandhi to relieve him from the growing burden of Harijan Sevak Sangh so that he could devote the rest of his life to the upliftment of the Adivasis. In his reminiscences about Thakkar Bapa, S.G. Vaze stated that 'he (Gandhi) in no way depreciates the service of the Adivasis, he thought that service of Harijans must have the first claim of all Hindus.'[64] But Gandhi replied to Bapa:

Our ancestors have sinned grievously by putting Harijans virtually out of the pale of Hindu society. It is our sacred duty to give them once again an honoured place amongst ourselves. The work is nothing less than that of reforming the current Hindu religion. No, Thakkar, while you and I live, that must be our primary duty. Everything else must come after, however, important it may be in itself. All you can do is to leave a large part of the actual work to your colleagues and, confining yourself to general supervision, give as much time to the *Adivasis* as you can spare, but the responsibility for the Harijan Sevak Sangh will lie on you. Neither of us can divorce ourselves from that work.[65]

Gandhi never took much interest in Elwin's work for the Gonds. Gandhi's ignorance of the tribal plight is quite evident from the letters that he wrote to Elwin between 1932 and 1933. During Elwin's illness he even advised him to give up his work and returned to England.[66] But Elwin continued his work in Mandla. During the 1930s a movement was sweeping through the Gond community in which the Adivasis abandoned liquor, meat, dancing and singing. The Gandhians heavily influenced such movements, but Elwin's grudge was that the Adivasis were manipulated by the Congressmen because according to him, Adivasis who changed their way of life in this way went 'flat, like stale beer: there was no more kick in them'. Elwin's work among the Gonds was soon jeopardized by the wave of the reformist movements under the auspices of the Gandhian ideology and in 1938 he shifted his headquarter to a place where the influence was less pervasive.[67] In 1938, Elwin changed the name of his organization to Bhumijan Seva Mandal. 'Bhumijan' means 'sons of the soil' and he chose the term instead of the Gandhian term Adivasi, which defined the tribals in terms of their place of residence rather than in terms of their attachment to this earth. According to Elwin, Bhumijan were the original inhabitants.

In the Constitution of 1935, many Adivasi areas were enumerated as 'excluded' or 'partially excluded', which meant that the Adivasis were regarded as politically unfit for any electoral representation. This was definitely a very important matter on which Gandhi could negotiate with the British government. But both he and his party kept mum on the issue. Lakshmidas Shrikant, a renowned Gandhian and a member of Thakkar Bapa's Bhil Seva Mandal, wrote an article in *The Times of India* in 1938 supporting the British move for excluded and partially excluded areas for the Adivasis. He argued that the Bhils had no social cohesion or any sense of social responsibility, and were not suited for democratic forms of local government.[68] Later in 1946 when Gandhi realized that in order to have freedom from exploitation of the caste Hindus the Adivasis were gearing up for demanding separate statehood, he made a comment on this issue. In an address to the Congress workers of Midnapore district in Bengal, which was mostly an Adivasi inhabited region, he said:

> The 1935 Act had separated them [the Adivasis] from the rest of the inhabitants of India and had placed the 'excluded areas' under the Governor's direct administration.[69]

Differences between Elwin and Gandhi became so wide that he finally broke away with Gandhi and Congress. In his own words,

> It has been evident that sooner or later I should find myself in opposition to the Indian nationalists, and in the last three years there has been a steadily increasing difference between me and the Congress Party, for which at one time I had considerable sympathy.
>
> For example, it seems to be the aim of the Congress politicians to bring the aboriginals within the Hindu fold and then to treat them as though they had no special claims; they resent the establishment of Excluded and Partially Excluded Areas [established by the British government to protect the aboriginals]; they dread the claims of Anthropology to guide these areas. This company of vegetarians and teetotalers would like to force their own bourgeois and Puritan doctrines on the free wild people of the forests.
>
> On the other hand I myself consider the aboriginals to be pre-Hindu and that the adoption of Hinduism will be a major disaster for them; I welcome the Excluded Areas, and only wish that there were very many more of them; I consider that scientific anthropology should guide and regulate the administration of all primitive peoples and that they should not be handed over to elected politicians who have no knowledge of their special problems; and I think that the social and moral outlook of the Congress would cut the tap-root of vitality of aboriginal India. . . .
>
> I want therefore to make it clear that although I have still a few personal friends within its ranks, I am no longer a supporter of the Indian National Congress, and I want rather to carry on my work for the aboriginals in the closest co-operation with the local officers of the British Government. . . .[70]

Elwin always wanted the tribals to develop keeping their old and traditional practices intact and only to repudiate their malpractices like witch-hunting and black magic. With the victory of Congress in the elections of 1937, the Raj Gond movement swept the Gond world. In August he visited Gandhi at Wardha to talk to him about the condition of the tribals, but found that he was so busy with Home Rule that he did not even pay heed to the tribals' cause. Elwin understood that the Congress,

> . . . wished on the one hand to use the tribals as cannon-fodder in their political campaigns and on the other to convert them all to vegetarianism, abstinence and settled cultivation—the plough was everywhere the symbol of the Congress-Hindu culture that is sweeping tribal areas.[71]

Guha wrote that Thakkar Bapa had once told Gandhi that while Elwin's learning was very great, his commitment to 'truth' was uncertain. By 1946 the breach between Gandhi and Elwin was more or less complete.[72] Elwin had not spoken to Gandhi after 1940 or 1941, and there is no record of his reactions to the events of the last years of the Mahatma's life—the Quit India Movement, the fasts and walks for communal harmony, the Partition of India.[73] Thakkar complained that he was an isolationist who wished to keep the aboriginals away from the national movement and all it offered. Bapa rejected isolation and hoped for a 'healthy comradeship' would develop between tribals and non-tribals. He wrote that by the policy of isolation,

> The aborigines should form part of the civilized communities of our country not for the purpose of swelling the figures of the followers of this religion or that, but to share with the advanced communities the privileges and duties on equal terms in the general social and political life of the country. Separatism and isolation seem to be dangerous theories and they strike at the root of national solidarity. We have already enough communal troubles, and should we add to them instead of seeing that we are all one and indivisible? Safety lies in union not in isolation.[74]

Having said that, Bapa had also reiterated that,

> But how can the aborigines realize their present backwardness and work for their own economic, social and political progress if there is no contact with people more advanced than ourselves? When contact is advocated, I do not for a moment suggest that large populations of the plains should be transplanted to aboriginal regions and made to live amidst and dominate the Adivasis. Also, I do not discountenance the need for protection of aboriginal

interests against any possible exploitation by some sections of the advanced people of the plains. What I mean to say is that a healthy comradeship should develop between the aborigines and the non-aborigines and each should profit culturally from the other and in course of time work hand in hand for the welfare of India as a whole. I am one of those who strongly advocate reservation of seats, but in a general electorate, for the Adivasis in the legislatures and Local Boards for some time to come. All the same, I feel that there is no cause for getting alarmed over imaginary evils resulting out of the contact with non-aborigines and their civilization sharply reacting to creation of self-governing tribal areas.[75]

Elwin replied that he was a protectionist who wished to protect the aboriginals from aggressive and insensitive outsiders.[76] The difference between Elwin and Thakkar Bapa can be understood from this passage of Ramchandra Guha where he says,

Where Elwin gloried in their joyful attitude to sex, Thakkar upbraided the aboriginals for their 'crude marital relations and promiscuity in sexual matters' (he had been horrified by what he read in *The Baiga*). Where the anthropologist defended the tribal's love of drink, the reformer wished gradually but firmly to introduce prohibition. And where Elwin wished for protection to be given to shifting cultivation, Thakkar prescribed that the plough everywhere replace swidden, which he condemned as a 'wasteful' form of cultivation which only encouraged the tribal's 'proverbial' laziness.[77]

G.S. Ghurye published *The Aborigines: So Called and their Future* (1943) and attacked Elwin as a 'no-changer' and 'revivalist', as one who wished to see 'the aborigines reinstated in their old tribal ways, irrespective of any other consideration'.[78] In his memoirs Elwin was to write of what made him move away from Gandhi:

Gandhi's emphatic views on prohibition (which I considered damaging to the tribes), his philosophy of sex relations, especially as exaggerated by some of his followers (which I considered damaging to everybody), and what seemed to me a certain distortion of values—the excessive emphasis on diet, for example, further separated me from him. Today I feel very sorry about this, for it was in his last years that Gandhi reached his highest stature and I deprived myself of the warmth of his affection and the strength he would have given me during a difficult period. But it was a feeling about Truth that kept me from going to see him and from this point of view my instinct was right.[79]

Ramchandra Guha has admitted that Elwin later became disenchanted with Gandhism, whose credo of puritanical reform (asceticism, vegetarianism and prohibition) he found too restrictive for communities who liked their liquor, their sex and their hunting. These shifts in loyalties are captured in *Leaves from the Jungle* (1936), Elwin's diary of his early years in Mandla. The book provides revelations, through flashes of irony and wit, of his growing rejection of Gandhi and Christ: as in a description of a *khadi* mosquito net which 'though utterly patriotic and highly mosquito proof, appears to admit no air whatsoever', or a confession that he spent a day of rest reading Agatha Christie 'though aware it would be more suitable for me to employ my leisure reciting the Penitential Psalms'.[80] In a novel written in the early 1950s, Elwin noted how homespun *khadi*, once 'the symbol of insurgence against British rule', had now become 'an almost official uniform, the sign of authority and power'. The rebel had become the governor; even so, the association of *khadi* with decency and honesty stayed a while.[81]

Elwin had more admiration for Nehru than Gandhi. He believed that Nehru combined a scientific intelligence with a broad humanity.[82] Nehru also admired Elwin's work. Later in January 1954 he became the tribal adviser of North Eastern Frontier Agency on the recommendation of Nehru. A final printed comment of sorts was called for when Elwin was asked in May 1954 to write a book introducing Gandhi to the north-east. For the Adivasis, Elwin wrote, Gandhi's

> life and teaching has vitally important lessons. There is first the lesson of peace. Disputes between villages and individuals can never be really solved by violence. . . . Love is the only way of progress, forgiveness is the true discipline and bond of social life.
>
> Then there is the lesson of self-reliance. We are to be ourselves, not imitations of other people. We are not to be ashamed of our own culture, our own religion, our art, our dress; however simple it may be, it is ours and we may be proud of it. That is the meaning of *swadeshi*. . . .
>
> And then there is lesson of tolerance, which is also the lesson of unity. Bapu loved India as a whole. He saw it, in all its diversity of hills and plains, as a single unity. He saw its people, with their different languages, their varied dress, their

distinct religions, blended into one great nation, a family united in the love of Truth and Peace, moving forward to a time when all men could live together in friendliness and equality.[83]

Later he changed his position in regard to the north-eastern tribals. In his book *A Philosophy for NEFA*, he proposed for integration instead of isolation, which was his former position and assimilation, position of his critiques. Policy of integration was rather a middle way to foster loyalty for the state of India. He wanted to introduce modern education, medical facilities, and agriculture in the interior tribal regions without hampering their own way of life. Nehru was of the opinion that this policy of integration should be applied outside NEFA as well.

It is important to note that, Nehru's involvement in tribal affairs was very marginal. In contrast, Gandhi, Thakkar Bapa and Rajendra Prasad were more aware of tribal problems. Gandhi called the Adivasis the last but not the least of India's sons, and A.V. Thakkar and Rajendra Prasad formulated the first set of measures for their welfare and development along the lines of the Gandhian reconstruction programme. At various stages of constitutional debates, the leaders who influenced the formulation of the tribal policy were Thakkar Bapa, Vallabhbhai Patel, G.B. Pandit, B.R. Ambedkar and the tribal leaders like Nichols Roy and Jaipal Singh. Nehru did not effectively intervene in debates.[84]

Ambedkar felt that the aboriginal tribes 'have not yet developed any political sense to make the best use of their political opportunities and they may easily become mere instruments in the hands of either a majority or a minority and thereby disturb the balance without doing any good to themselves'.[85] He recommended that a statutory commission administer the Agency areas in which the aboriginal tribes lived, compelling the governments of the parent provinces to contribute to their upkeep. In a newspaper response to Ambedkar's speech, Amritlal Thakkar responded characteristically with feigned surprise 'this doughty champion of the oppressed, depressed and exploited should have so completely ignored the aboriginal tribes who are worse off than the harijans'.[86] Thakkar argued that if Ambedkar's principles of weightage based on social and educational status were applied, the aboriginal tribes might even qualify for an absolute majority. In the bitter exchange that followed, Thakkar argued that Ambedkar's proposal was nothing short of a refusal of the right to vote to the aboriginal tribes, and that his excessive favoritism for the Harijan resulted in a complete denial of justice to the aborigines. This ambiguity which arises between Thakkar and Ambedkar is a symptom of a rapidly changing historical process within which the tribal was being reconfigured as the hapless being at the margins of the caste hierarchy.[87] Rejecting Thakkar's charge of 'partiality and small mindedness' on himself, Ambedkar explained his position thus,

> The reason why I did not include the Aboriginal Tribes in the scheme of distribution of seats in the Legislature is not the result of my antipathy to them, but is entirely due to my belief that these Aboriginal Tribes do not as yet possess the political capacity which is necessary to exercise political power for one's own good.[88]

In Ambedkar's partisan perspective, the tribal was politically uneducated and educationally backward, but his social status was better than that of the untouchable. Thakkar on the other hand championed the aboriginal's marginal status and had little time for the subtleties of poll politics; the right to vote was supreme, and the need to provide the aboriginals the right to vote was symbolically primary. The similarity of the positions between Ambedkar and the Gandhian initiative in so far as the tribal is concerned, shows that both their thought processes are bound by the emerging governmental modes of modern Indian politics. This archaeological similarity underlies the profound differences in their political projects.

Elwin's *A Philosophy of Love* can be taken as the last of his encounter with Gandhian philosophy. He said,

> Gandhi once said that Ahimsa makes exploitation impossible and perhaps the greatest danger to the tribes is not cultural destruction but economic exploitation. They have lost and still are losing vast areas of their land; millions of them are in bondage to the moneylender. Many have been reduced almost to the condition of serfs. The great industrial projects inevitably lead to the dispossession of their traditional lands and the task of rehabilitation has not always been implemented properly.[89]

Elwin, in his autobiography, categorically explained why he did not support some of the principles of Gandhi. He believed that India is not a Puritan country. Puritanism invaded India from the West which influenced Gandhi to a great extent. Self-conscious and self-righteous Puritanism can be proved ruinous for the simple and gullible tribal folk by destroying their traditional customs and values. He himself had reminded us that he accepted Gandhi's teachings which appealed to him, but also rejected his philosophy which he found unfit for the tribals. He said, 'There are a lot of things I have never been able to accept in Gandhism, particularly its Puritan aspect, but there were at the same time many other things of great inspiration.'[90]

Archana Prasad in her book *Against Ecological Romanticism: Verrier Elwin and the Making of an Anti-Modern Tribal Identity* has attempted to question the assumptions of Elwin's ecological romanticism and challenged the unrealistic interpretation of tribal history on which they are based. Prasad argues that the tribal people of Central India depend on shifting cultivation, hunting and gathering only as a result of their marginalization into the forested tracts by the settlement of caste Hindu cultivators in the Maratha period. In the third essay 'Paying the Way for Hindutva: The Tragic Tale of the Transformation of Elwin's Romanticism', Prasad has categorically stated that Elwin's change of heart may lie in the inability of his ideas to deal with the modernist challenge. According to her, being a failure Elwin was forced to reconcile with the Gandhian movement and formed a Hindu nationalist front against the Christian missionaries. That is why, she has ended by saying that the source of the transformation of Elwin's stand lay in the inability of ecological romanticism to cope with the problems of tribal life in mid-twentieth century. Prasad has vividly argued that Verrier Elwin's model of tribal development was anti-modern, unrealistic, romantic and fruitless, detrimental to the cause of sustainable development of this community. She has grievously charged that Elwin was used by the Hindu nationalist leaders. She said,

> The polarity that is created between Christianity and Islam on the one hand and Hinduism on the other is strikingly close to Elwin's position at the advent

of independence. By siding with Hinduism as a more inclusive religion than others, the ideas of contemporary environmentalists are likely to be misused by the same right wing Hindu forces who used Elwin's position to make their inroads into the tribal areas to ban Christian Missionaries in Tribal Areas and thereby paving the way for Hindutva.[91]

In her third essay 'The Baiga and Its Eco-Logic: Reinterpreting Verrier Elwin's Cultural Ecology in Central India', she indicates that the 'cultural ecology' on which the Baigas relied was based more on anthropological particularism. According to her, Elwin framed an anti-modern tribal identity in his prolonged narrative. But in a recent research, Koutuk Dutta has justly pointed out that Elwin spent over a hundred nights in different *ghotuls.* His field research was enormously helped by the presence of his wife Kosi, who, as a member of the greater Gond family could claim kinship with the Murias. He believd that 'reverence for all life' is the prime essence of all forms of ecological romance. His description, receding and representation of aboriginal people and their surroundings strictly followed this revelation. The tribals of India worship nature as their mother and their cultural ecology was spiritedly romantic. So the theory of anthropological particularity of Prasad, which is used to interpret Elwin's discourse about the tribals of central India, fails to understand his views on tribal India. Not only that, in defending the *ghotul* from the obvious criticisms of the so-called civilized world, Elwin pointed out that there were virtually no cases of venereal disease among the Murias. Prostitution, rape and child marriage, so visibly present in more advanced societies, were all too absent in Muria community. Muria art and handicrafts as presented and recorded by Elwin is a clear mark of modernity as there is an extraordinary presence of newness. In his seminal book *The Baiga*, Elwin vividly represented that all the tribal societies were socially superior to modern ones because women enjoyed more freedom in the tribal community. This discussion categorically states that Elwin's representation of Indian tribal world is in no way anti-modern. The proposition of Prasad, that is, against ecological romanticism and making of an anti-modern tribal identity is sharply contradictory.[92]

GANDHI AND AMRITLAL THAKKAR

Amritlal Thakkar, popularly known as Thakkar Bapa, was born in 1869 in Saurashtra in a middle-class family. After completing his schooling he went to Poona to do a three-year course in engineering. His father had married him off when he was still in school. He lost first his only son and then his wife at the age of thirty-nine. He married again, but within two years his second wife died. Then he gave up family life and devoted himself to social service. After coming into contact with Gopal Krishna Gokhale and D.K. Karve, he resigned from the post of chief engineer under Bombay Municipality in 1914 and joined Servants of India Society. Thakkar Bapa started his social service work with famine relief. In 1932 he took up the secretaryship of the Harijan Sevak Sangh which came into being after Gandhi's historic fast in the Yeravada prison in 1932. He also established Adim Jati Seva Sangh for the cause of the tribals which was headed by the first President of Independent India, Dr Rajendra Prasad. Gandhi had always appreciated Bapa's dedication towards the Adivasis:

> If we are to regard the tribesmen and the aborigines as our fellow beings, this can only be done by observing Thakkar Bapa's mode of life. It has always been his inordinate ambition to mingle with the needy and the distressed and the moment he is away from them he feels distressed.[93]

According to Thakkar Bapa, the main handicaps the tribes suffer from are poverty, ill health, inaccessibility of the regions inhabited by them, defects of the administration and lack of leadership and literacy. While defining poverty among tribes he wrote, '. . . the aboriginal does not differ from the non-aboriginal so far as fundamental human equalities are concerned. Only due to his ignorance, his problems assume a slightly different garb from those of the non-aboriginal'.[94] He said,

> Lack of leadership in the tribal communities is a great handicap. Amongst the Christianized aborigines, e.g. of Chota Nagpur, there are a few educated people, but they generally seem to be interested chiefly in Christian aborigines than in their non-Christian brethren. Amongst the latter, leaders are fewer still. This is one of the reasons why aboriginal interests fail to receive proper attention from the authorities and from the general public.[95]

Thakkar Bapa had his first contact with the Bhils during his famine relief work in the Dahod and Jhalod talukas of Panch Mahals (Gujarat) in 1919 and 1922. He, in association with Indulal Yagnik, Gandhi's prominent lieutenant, raised funds from capitalists in Bombay to buy food that was then distributed among the Bhils.[96] Yagnik established a National Bhil Hostel and was joined by Thakkar Bapa in early 1922. Another hostel was opened, called the 'Bhil Ashram'. Thakkar Bapa decided to set up a permanent organization for the service of the Bhils. In 1922 he finally established the Bhil Seva Mandal, which was in overall control of work amongst the Bhils. This organization laid the foundation for his life's work amongst the Adivasis of India.[97] During 1919-20, Sukhdev Vishwanath Trivedi with the help of Purushottam Das took the first step on behalf of the government for drought relief and rehabilitation work among the Bhil Adivasis. Purushottam Das was the Secretary of the drought relief committee of the Indian National Congress. When Gandhi was informed about the plight of the Adivasis he sent Thakkar Bapa immediately and Bapa started the Bhil Seva Mandal in 1923. One of the greatest achievements of Bhil Seva Mandal was the education of Bhil girls. Two girls of Bhil-Patelia community were admitted in *ashramshalas* of Jesawada and Mirakhedi in 1930-1. Later, four more girls joined the Jesawada Kanya Ashramshala.[98]

On instructions from the Servants of India Society and Gandhi, Bapa went to Puri in 1920 to organize flood relief. Gandhi was very much impressed by the relief operations organized by Bapa in Orissa. On his request, Gandhi himself went to Puri to see the situation over there. Thakkar Bapa and Devadas Gandhi with the help of hundred leading persons of the country formed an organization for the service of women in India. It was named after Kasturba Gandhi and called Kasturba Trust. Thakkar Bapa was appointed as the secretary of this memorial fund. Though Bapa cannot be called a Gandhite, his personal attachment and loyalty to Gandhi amounted to hero-worship. Gandhi looked to Bapa as the father of the Trust. He very often used to say that if in any case his opinion was at variance with that of Thakkar Bapa, Bapa's opinion should prevail.[99] An admirer wrote in 1928 that Thakkar Bapa,

. . . was a friend of the poor, the untouchable and the aborigine. The cry of torment, anguish and torture attracts him from one remote corner to the other. Whether it be a famine calamity or a flood devastation, official persecution or temperance work, khaddar organization or opening wells and tanks for untouchables, you cannot miss the mark and the guiding and unerring hand of Amritlal. The theatre of his activities is among the depressed and the oppressed in out-of-the-way places or among forest tribes in the hills.[100]

Gandhi's disapproval of the missionary, his appropriation of the pastoral effort for Hinduism, the nature of the social work, and the character of the cultural assault on the Bhils of western India, all come through in one of his notes on the subject:

Shri Amritlal proposes once again to hold a fair for the Bhils on the forthcoming Ramanavami day. On that occasion a temple to Ramachandra is to be declared open, that is, there will be 'prana-pratishta' (Invocation of life) into the idol of Rama. Why may we not call it prana-pratishta into the Bhils? Shri Amritlal has shown us our duty towards them. We hardly ever accept them as human beings. The government has also classified them as a scheduled tribe. Thus neither society nor the government takes interest in them. These so-called uncivilized communities are bound to attract the attention of the missionaries, for it is the latter's duty to get recruits for the Christian army. I do not regard such proselytization as a real service to dharma. But how can we blame the missionaries, if the Hindus take no interest in the Bhils? For to them any one who is brought into the Christian fold, no matter how, has become a Christian, has entered a new life and become civilized. If as a result of such conversion, the converts rise spiritually and morally, I personally would have nothing to say against their conversion. But I do not think that this is what happens. I, therefore, say that the prana-pratishta into the idol in this temple will in fact be prana-pratishta into the Bhils themselves, for I suppose that they will from that time onwards understand the holy power of the name Rama, will feel god's presence and resolve to give up eating meat and drinking and be filled with new life. The building of the temple, however, is but the beginning of our service to them, not its end. There are many things we can do to serve them; but workers are few, and that is our misfortune.[101]

Gandhi was sensitive about religious conversion. He believed that religion was a personal matter between an individual and his God. He said,

It is a conviction daily growing upon me that the great and rich Christian Missionaries will render true service to India if they confine their activities to humanitarian service without the ulterior motive of converting India, or at least her unsophisticated villagers, to Christianity, and destroying their social superstructure, which notwithstanding many defects has stood now from time immemorial the onslaught upon it from within and from without. . . . Every living faith must have within itself the power of rejuvenation, if it is to live.[102]

On the other hand, C.F. Andrews justified proselytization as a means of conferring freedom from primitive terrors and savageries on tribes. He wrote to Elwin,

I cannot at all agree with Bapu that most forms of 'religion' which are really evil in their essence, are not to be conditioned. I believe in South India the devil worship is absolutely hideous in some of its forms and utterly unworthy of man made in the image of God. . . . Have you not gone too far in following Bapu about 'conversion'? I fully accept that these hill tribes must be freed from the suspicion and fear that you must have some ulterior motive. But the joy which we have in our own hearts owing to the love of Christ must find its expression, because it is the one motive power in our own lives. Bapu would seem to suggest that even to wish in one's own heart to give to another that joy, which has been the strength and stay of one's own life, is itself wrong.[103]

As early as 1909, Gandhi observed in the *Hind Swaraj* that for the attainment of *swaraj* even 'the Bhil, Pindari and Thag who are our brethren' be won over. He advised the people not to be 'scared of your brother' in bringing them in the mainstream of national life.[104] In his presidential speeches in the public meetings of the Bhils of Panch Mahals and the Kaliparaj (later known as Raniparaj) of Surat district between 1925 and 1927, Gandhi adopted a religious approach in the extension of his constructive programme among the Adivasis of Gujarat. In the public meeting of the Bhils under the auspices of Bhil Seva Sadan at Dahod on 2 January 1925, Gandhi in his presidential address impressed upon the Bhils to cherish Thakkar Bapa, as their religious preceptor and follow his Thirteen Commandments,[105] directing the Bhils to abjure liquor, bride-price and stealing, observe cleanliness and worship Babadev. Along with this, he impressed upon them to spin *khadi*—'the elixir of life'—for self-sufficiency and use *swadesi* as *swaraj* could not be achieved without boycotting foreign clothes. He emphasized for the education of Bhil children and exhorted their teachers to teach them the *Ramayana* and the *Mahabharata.* He exclaimed that as Hindus the Bhils should chant *dwadasha mantra* (*om namo bhagavate vasudevaya*) instead of slander and filthy words.[106] Thakkar Bapa as the president of the Bhil Seva Mandals in the Panch Mahals and the constructive workers, toured the Princely States of Pratapgarh and Banswara between 1923 and 1928 for initiating social reforms among the Bhils. However, the princes of these states resented the entries of these 'Gandhian and Congress agitators', and 'protagonists of Home Rule' in their dominions. Specially, the fame of A.V. Thakkar was afloat in southern Rajputana States that like Govindgiri he would galvanize the Bhils to revolt, and therefore, the Diwan of Devgarh-Baria in 1923 had ordered him to quit the state. Such fears of armed revolt were not without foundation as the communion of the Bhils with the Bhil *ashrams* went to the extent that they had politicized them and participated in non-violent movements in the Panch Mahals.[107]

This religious approach to constructive programme revealed that Gandhi and Thakkar Bapa aimed at discouraging conversion among the Adivasis of the Panch Mahals where the Christian missionaries had started philanthropic activities much earlier than the Gandhian workers. Gandhi acknowledged Bapa's efforts for popularizing the Tulsi version of *Ramayana* in Bhili dialect among the Bhils and in their schools and the singing of *bhajans* based on *Ramayana* by Dattoobhai Barlokar among them.[108] He also appreciated Bapa's contribution in opening a temple of Rama on Ramanavami (26 April 1926) for the Bhils at Jesawada, and called it 'the beginning of our service to them, and not its end'.[109] Gandhi even objected to the conversion of the Adivasis 'in the areas like Khond Hills where aboriginal races were animists'. He had emphatically clarified it to Dr Chesterman, a Medical Secretary of the English Baptist Mission that:

> . . . in spite of being described as animists these tribes have from time immemorial been absorbed in Hinduism. They are, like the indigenous medicine, of the soil, and their roots lie deep there. But you can only endorse this if you feel that Hinduism is as true as Christianity.[110]

Gandhi's stream-of-consciousness Sanskritization proposed for the Bhils, and his rock-like faith in his own interpretation of the relative values of Bhil and Hindu cultures, lays bare the force relations between the caste-Hindu centre and the tribal periphery. This is in stark opposition to Verrier Elwin's valorization of tribal life in *The Baiga* opens a genuine possibility of thinking critically about modernity and its discontents.[111] It is also quite in contradiction to the colonial administration's trepidation in handling insurgent tribals. His cultural confidence presumes that the tribal is incapable of resisting the actions taken on his behalf, and marks the colonial superiority in the service provided to the tribal.[112]

Thakkar Bapa devoted his entire life in the work of the upliftment of the aboriginal tribals. He has even talked about the grievances of the tribals against the system of bonded labour called *Kamiauti* in Chota Nagpur district. He said, 'Kamias are bound servants of their masters; in return for a loan received they bind themselves to perform whatever menial services are required of them in lieu of the interest due on the loan. In practice the system leads to absolute degradation of Kamias.'[113] Bapa once expressed his concern about the indifference of the political leaders towards the tribals. He said,

> . . . our national conscience towards these tribes has still not awakened—not even to the extent that it has towards the untouchable classes. There is a greater and stronger barrier between these aboriginal tribes and ourselves than between the untouchable classes and ourselves. We do take service from the untouchables; we do let them live, though in locations, in our villages: but there are hardly any points of contact between the forest tribes and ourselves except money-lending and purchasing their forest and other produce at very cheap rates.[114]

He has expressed his opinion in several articles published in *Servants of India* in different times. He said,

- A devoted worker living among the tribals should inculcate in them the habit of cleanliness and abstinence from drink. They should teach the tribal children the habit of reading and writing and the adults the habits of industry and hard work.
- To give them protection from *sahukars*, police, forest and land

revenue subordinates and to start cooperative credit society and stores societies.

- To read to them stories from the *Ramayana* and other religious books and give them information from the newspapers. Erect a temple of Rama.
- To reform their customs in respect of marriage, birth, death and guide their caste meetings.[115]

Bapa was also aware of the plight of the other tribal people of the country. He devoted the first four months of 1926 to a tour of Raipur and Mandal in the Central Provinces, the Santhal Parganas of Bihar and Bengal and the hill districts of Assam. On his return, he wrote two articles in the *Navajivan*, drawing attention to the neglect of aborigines in these regions. Commenting on these articles, Gandhi wrote:

> Brother Amritlal Thakkar does not don the yellow robes of a sanyasi (who renounces the worldly pleasures and pursuits) but he has enriched and adorned the institution of sanyasis. He does not describe himself as a sanyasi but all his work pertains to that institution. He is old but he does not rest, nor does he let those around him rest. And who can relax when misery like a wild fire engulfs the people? . . . Brother Amritlal is already a Guru of Harijans and now he is striving to be a guru of the hill tribes as well.[116]

In 1939, on the occasion of Thakkar Bapa's 70th birthday celebrations, Gandhi wrote in the *Harijan Bandhu*, 'Thakkar Bapa is a rare servant of the people. Conceit and ostentation are unknown to him. He does not need praise from anybody. His only contentment and only recreation are his work. Even in old age his zeal for work has not flagged. He is himself an institution.' Gandhi later sent a handwritten message for him where he said, 'Bapa was born only to serve the downtrodden, whether they be untouchables or Bhils, Santhals or Khasis. Even the appreciation of his service means some little service to these downtrodden people. His services have carried India considerably forward towards the goal.' In response Bapa replied, 'it is a happy augury that Harijans sit with us in the legislative assemblies as our equals. But the Adivasis have no representation there. The Government has done so little for them. The Hindu society has not even tried to go to them. Their uplift is, therefore, urgent and important.'[117]

About the habit of the liquor consumption Bapa was of the opinion that,

> the Adivasi prepares and consumes liquor by himself. . . . People must be made to understand the benefits they would derive if prohibition is introduced. Temperance propaganda must be carried on for some time before attempting to introduce prohibition. I am in favour of gradual introduction of prohibition even amongst the aborigines, as I fully believe that prohibition of liquor and intoxicating drugs confirms a great and everlasting benefit on the people. . .[118]

Thakkar Bapa believed that the tribal children should be taught through the medium of the provincial language besides their various tribal dialects and the teachers must be conversant with the tribal dialects.

Gandhi always emphasized on cleanliness, i.e. *atmashuddhi*, or self-purification, according to which the Adivasi world has to be cleaned to make worthy citizens of the Indian nation. Though Bapa and Narhari Parikh often had to fight the local elites who profited by exploiting the Adivasis, their superior attitude towards the Adivasis was quite evident as they believed that the 'primitive' people should be 'civilized'.[119] Bapa once said that the Bhils were 'hardly conscious of being human'. He saw his task as being that of winning the Adivasis 'back to the country and to humanity'.[120] The glimpses of Gandhian approach about primitiveness can be had from the following quotation,

> The primitives (Adivasis) should be approached on the basis of non-violence, accepting the principles of a democratic society and the fundamental equality and unity of man, in a spirit of love, service and humanity. It must not be a process of social domination and political imposition, but a process of common effort and understanding. The so-called primitives should retain the naturalness, health and physical beauty of primitive life and environment and they should take to civilization without its neurosis . . . to seek prosperity and success of a few, through the exploitation of the many.[121]

Thakkar Bapa used to consider shifting cultivation as an evil practice and one of the greatest difficulties in the administration of the tribal areas. He said,

> The tribals, most probably due to traditional habit, have almost a passion for this method of cultivation, and illiterate as they are, they do not easily realize

the harmfulness of the practice. . . . The aboriginals must be taught the use of the plough, plots must be allotted on the lower slopes of the hills and in the valleys for cultivation, and aboriginal children must be instructed in the art of good cultivation in special vocational schools as well as in ordinary schools. In the meantime, 'shifting cultivation' must be limited by law to two years, and not more, on each plot of land, to enable the regrowth of forest wherever possible.[122]

But Verrier Elwin was firmly against prohibiting shifting cultivation. While speaking about the Baiga tribe, Elwin gave a detailed analysis of *bewar* or shifting cultivation and the effects of its prohibition on the Baiga life. It also deals with the conflict between the requirements of soil and forest conservation with native custom in many parts of the world. The Baiga evidence should be considered before thoughtlessly condemning 'wasteful' native methods of cultivation without realizing how these are bound up with the lives of the people who practice them. Shifting cultivation involves the destruction of the forest by fire, in order to grow grain in the ashes. To the Baiga, the earth is so sacred to be profaned by the use of the plough. Hence, the almost entire prohibition of shifting cultivation in the interest of forest preservation had heavily affected the prosperity of the Baiga and similarly situated tribes in India. Elwin made a well-phrased plea for relaxation of these restrictions in his book *The Baiga.* In a letter written to Bapa, he said,

I have been striving to get the Imperialist Government to allow a few human rights to the aboriginals. First and foremost among those rights is that of shifting cultivation. Just as a certain impression has been created, the fruit of hour after hour of patient and often weary work, you come and cut the ground underneath my feet. . . . And in whose interests would you stop *bewar*? The forests belong to the aboriginal. I should have thought that anyone who was a nationalist would at least advocate *swaraj* for the aboriginal! It is a sad and grievous thing for someone like yourself arguing . . . in favour of taking away from the poor yet another of their treasured rights. I am absolutely convinced that the policy you have set in the Orissa Report will lead to nothing but the degradation, the decay, the demoralization of these poor people, and children yet unborn will curse your honoured name.[123]

In response to this concern Thakkar Bapa said that,

Mr. Verrier Elwin has discussed the subject of 'shifting cultivation' at great length in his book on the Baigas. But his views seem to incline towards the policy of allowing this kind of cultivation with certain alterations and restrictions. I cannot agree with the opinion that *bewar* or *podu* is almost a religious necessity to some of the tribes. The argument of the Baigas that they do not plough the land because they consider it a sin to 'lacerate the womb of Dharti Mata' (Mother Earth) does not justify the practice, though surely that sentiment of the Baigas may be borne in mind when we have to deal with the problem, in order to avoid hasty action, which will estrange the feelings of the aborigines, who generally are easily irritable.[124]

It is pertinent to note that Elwin was quite concerned about the adverse effect of shifting cultivation. It is evident in his following words:

Shifting cultivation is a bad thing: unfortunately it is often the only possible thing. . . . Obviously, even where a tribe had a religious passion for this type of cultivation, it could not be permitted on a large scale and forever. But where only a few tribesmen practised it—and the Baigas were a very small tribe— and where a regular rotation of at least twenty years was observed, the harm it did to the forest was greatly exaggerated. The Baigas have practised this form of cultivation for centuries in Mandla and Balaghat, yet nowhere is there better forest today.[125]

Having said that Elwin also expressed his dissatisfaction about the introduction of plough cultivation forcefully that resulted in poverty, as they hated the tabooed implement and thus suffered from mental disturbance deep in their soul. They were reduced to the position of impoverished and inferior cultivators. 'Robbed of their bows and arrows, they are no longer lords of the forest.'[126]

Thakkar Bapa clearly stated that, among those interested in the welfare of the tribals, there are two schools advocating two different policies, which are generally called 'Isolationism' and 'Assimilation'. Isolationists believe that the tribals should be kept in their areas untouched by the civilization of the plains. They fear that contact with the non-tribals, especially Hindus, will break the solidarity of the tribal society and bring many social evils into tribal areas, such as untouchability, child marriage and *purdah*, hitherto unknown to them. Bapa was not convinced with this argument. Bapa was of the opinion that the indigenous social workers should not be intervening in the internal affairs of the Adivasis rather they should be called as the advocates of the policy of assimilation. According to him, it is not right to consider that the contact will bring only bad customs into tribal life. Safeguards may be instituted to protect them from exploitation by the non-tribals. But to keep these people confined to and isolated in their inaccessible hills and jungles is something like keeping them in glass cases of a museum for the curiosity of purely academic persons. He said:

> They live on the hills and in the jungles, and are even more backward than the Scheduled Castes. They are far less organized. . . . The Scheduled Castes have had a lead over them the Scheduled Tribes for as long a period as the Scheduled Castes will enjoy it, viz. for 25 years.[127]

The differences between Elwin and Bapa first surfaced in September 1940, when Elwin received a letter from Bapa proposing the creation of a non-political, all-India association to be called the 'Indian Aborigines Friends Society' (in Hindi, 'Bharatiya Adimjati Sevak Sangh', the Sevak connoting 'social worker' or 'helper' rather than friend). The provisional aims of the Society were:

1. To study the living conditions of the members of the Hill and Forest Tribes who live an isolated life, to bring them nearer to their own tribals living in the plains and to be familiar with their customs and manners.
2. To organize, coordinate and assist welfare work conducted for their benefit, such as schools, dispensaries, sanitation and hygiene, which, it is always understood, is conducted on humanitarian lines only [that is, without a view to religious conversion].
3. To represent to the provincial governments concerned their disabilities and to suggest schemes for their moral, cultural, economic and political uplift with a view to bring them on a par with the advanced classes in the community.[128]

Elwin welcomed the idea of a countrywide association for aboriginal welfare, yet worried that it might come to be dominated by 'Congress-minded Hindus'. Elwin went on to suggest an alternate set of six aims for the new association. Three clauses from them are versions of those drafted by Thakkar—the need to study tribal life, undertake welfare work, and intercede on their behalf with government—but taking care to remove all phrases smacking of 'uplift'. A fourth called for the devising of means of economic progress with minimum of dislocation and distress. A fifth asked for special protection for the aboriginals from their traditional exploiters—'oppressive landlords, grasping moneylenders [and] corrupt officials'—as well as from 'ignorant politicians [and] proselytizing missionaries of any religion. . . .'[129] His own preferences were expressed most clearly in the last clause, which asked the association,

> . . . to do everything possible to revive and encourage all that is good and that has survival-value in the traditional tribal culture. This will include the revival of aboriginal village industries, restoration of hunting rights, stimulation of dancing and singing and the worship of ancient gods.[130]

Bapa might be evincing to Elwin as he was an anthropologist holding the notion of isolationism. It is important to remember that Elwin does not want an 'anthropological zoo' or 'museum' for that matter. What he said was the first necessity is the establishment of a sort of National Park, in which not only the Baigas, but the thousands of simple tribals in their neighbourhood might take refuge. He envisages a more positive constructive policy to follow upon the protection of the innocent tribals from official repression and the depredations and fanaticism of other non-tribal Hindus. Mere segregation seems an inadequate policy for a people who are among the poorest in the world. It would be preferable to the present deleterious policy, the cruelty of which is fully demonstrated by him.

The debate between Elwin and Thakkar Bapa became public during the 1940s. Elwin said that the Congress would be making a 'profound mistake' if it were to disregard the warnings of anthropology and follow a 'reactionary policy of oppression and interference' in tribal areas. If it did, there might even be rebellion and bloodshed. Elwin claimed that the Khond of Orissa, bearing the burden of Thakkar's report, which he had submitted to the Orissa government on tribal policy, had 'threatened to offer a human sacrifice to the "New God Gandhi" so that they will not be deprived of any more of their elementary human rights'.[131] The struggle with the missionaries later brought an opportunity for Elwin to reconcile with Bapa. Elwin asked for support from the industrialist Purshottamdas Thakurdas, the veteran Congress leader Bhulabhai Desai and A.V. Thakkar. After visiting Mandla in March 1944, Thakkar deputed his associate P.G. Vannikar to organize a Gond Sevak Mandal in cooperation with Shamrao Hivale and Verrier Elwin. They were soon joined by a Hindu service organization, the Arya Dharma Seva Sangh. In a short while, the three groups were able to close down 25 mission schools and the advance of Dutch missionaries was successfully halted.[132]

Bapa believed that nobody except the missionaries took care of the Adivasis and it was their love and affection that attracted him. He said:

> True, we Hindus rarely show that love and sympathy to the distressed and semi-wild people of our country, which we human beings should show to one another. On the other hand, we shun them and even hate them as if they were not creatures of God with the same feelings and passions as ourselves. Whose fault is it if such people find consideration, love and happiness amongst people of another religion, and so embrace it?[133]

In October 1940, Bapa became a member of the Aboriginal Welfare Board which was set up in Bihar. When the Interim Government took over, he prepared a Five-year Adivasi Welfare Plan for Bihar and Central Province. He was appointed as a member of the Advisory Sub-committee of the Constituent Assembly formed to enquire into and report on the political, economic and social set-up to be accorded to the hill-people of Assam. After Gandhi's death, in a public meeting held during 23 September 1949, Thakkar Bapa recollected Gandhi's memory and said,

> Our Gandhi Bapu has left us. My days too are numbered. But the work being done here is Bapu's; this is not to be forgotten. We have attained independence, but its defence is our responsibility. There are many communities like the Bhils in this country—Santhals, Gonds, Jawangs, Hoes, Mundas

and others. You should take up the type of work being done in Panch Mahals in other tribal communities. It is everybody's duty today to be selfless. . . . The country has 25 million Adivasis and 50 million Harijans. These 75 million people cannot be neglected if India wants to defend its independence, honour and glory. . . .[134]

Many more Gandhians educated and trained at 'Gujarat-Vidyapith', Ahmedabad, gradually turned for the cause of *sarvodaya*[135] and started working among the tribes in several parts of India. A few notable examples of them are: Jugatram Dave, who began his activities with the Chodhara tribes of south Gujarat from Vedichi in Surat (1923), Narsing Bhavsar, who began work with Bhils of Sabarkantha from his *ashrama* Shamalaji (1927), Chhotubhai Naik, who worked with Kukna Bhils of Dangs since 1948. Some Gandhians also began their work independently in pursuance of village upliftment. Harivallabh Parikh started working among the tribals at Rangpur near Chhota Udepur from his Anand Niketan Ashram, 1949.[136] Therefore, it can be said that it was mostly the Gandhian workers, and not Gandhi himself, who built upon the socio-religious reform movement among different Adivasi communities, like Oraon, Bhil, Gond, Santhal, Ho, Vedichi[137] and so on, which were originally started by the Adivasis themselves and aimed to embrace temperance and vegetarianism, later enjoined by the Gandhians. The next chapter will shed light on this issue.

Other than Bhil Seva Mandal (1922), there were other welfare organizations not directly established by Gandhi, but modelled on Gandhi's rural reconstruction programme. In the 1930s, Shakti Ashram in Assam (1931) and Barama Ashram (1936) were founded. In the 1940s, a number of organizations were formed on the model of the Bhil Seva Mandal: Andhra Sramik Dharma Rajya Sabha (1942); Vanavasi Seva Mandal, Mandla (1944); Adivasi Seva Mandal, Tohana; Adimjati Seva Mandal (1944), Santhals and Paharia Seva Mandal (1942), etc. The apex organization, Bharatiya Adimjati Seva Sangh, was established by Thakkar Bapa in 1948 to promote:

(a) social, economic and educational advancement of the tribal communities, including nomadic and de-notified tribes to enable them to take their legitimate place in the national life of the country as equal citizens; and

(b) coordinate the activities of bodies engaged in similar activities. The body is non-political, and it does not engage itself in any proselytizing activities.[138]

These organizations have proliferated since Independence and have a multi-pronged programme for the welfare of the tribes.

1. Education through Ashram schools assisted by the grant of stipends
2. Medical relief through Ayurvedic dispensaries
3. Village and cottage industries
4. Promotion of *khadi* and spinning
5. Debt-relief and
6. Forest co-operative societies.

These centres projected powerfully the image of Gandhi as Disum Aba (Father of the Nation) and brought a sizeable section of the tribals, apart from the bhagat, into the mainstream of the national movement. These organizations became the channels for communication of ideas of nationalism and freedom to the tribal people. A nationalist perspective on tribal problems emerged in contradistinction to the isolationist standpoint of the missionaries and the officials. In the course of time, the approach of these organizations came to be identified too closely with the stance of a political party, and this together with other constraints handicapped their secular development to some extent.[139]

NOTES

1. S.P. Sinha, 'Gandhi's Impact on the Tribals of Chota Nagpur 1920-30', in *Gandhi and Social Sciences*, ed., L.P. Vidyarthi et al., New Delhi: Bookhive, 1970, pp. 157-8.
2. S.P. Sinha, *Conflict and Tension in Tribal Society*, New Delhi: Concept Publishing Company, 1993, pp. 267-8.
3. Ramchandra Guha, *Savaging the Civilized: Verrier Elwin, His Tribals, and India*, Haryana: Penguin Books, 2014, p. 37.
4. Ibid., p. 53.
5. Dahyabbai Naik, *Bhil Sewa Mandal—Dahod: Progress Report*, Ahmedabad: Navjivan Press, 1967, p. 2.

6. Charles F. Andrews, 'An Aboriginal Tribe, Khaddar and Drink', *Young India*, 30 April 1925, p. 155.
7. Quoted by Elwin in a note of 17 November 1961, File 69, *Elwin Papers*, Nehru Memorial Museum and Library (NMML).
8. Guha, *Savaging the Civilized*, 2014, p. 54.
9. Verrier Elwin, *The Tribal World of Verrier Elwin: An Autobiography*, Oxford: Oxford University Press, 1964, p. 58f.
10. Anthony Parel (ed.), *Gandhi: Hind Swaraj and Other Writings*, Cambridge: Cambridge University Press, 2009, p. xlvi.
11. A.V. Thakkar, 'My Tour Diary', *Harijan*, 28 November 1934.
12. Verrier Elwin, *The Foreign Missionary Danger*, published by H.C. Vidyarthi, Ranchi: All India Divine Light Mission, 1944.
13. M.K. Gandhi, Foreign Missionaries, *Young India*, 23 April 1931, p. 83. See also 'Mr. Gandhi's Revised Statement', *National Christian Council Review* 51(6), June 1931, pp. 301-2.
14. Lalsangkima Pachuau, 'A Clash of "Mass Movements"? Christian Missions and the Gandhian Nationalist Movement in India', *Transformation*, vol. 31, no. 3, Special issue: Christian Missions in Asia, July 2014, pp. 157-74.
15. Sarah Claerhout, 'Gandhi, Conversion, and the Equality of Religions: More Experiments with Truth', *Numen*, vol. 61, no. 1, 2014, pp. 53-82.
16. M.K. Gandhi, *The Collected Works of Mahatma Gandhi*, vol. 23, Delhi: Ministry of Information and Broadcasting, 1964-94, pp. 85-6.
17. M.K. Gandhi (n.d.), *The Message of Jesus Christ*, ed. A.T. Hingorani, Bombay: Bharatiya Vidya Bhavan, p. 33, originally published in *Young India*, 6 January 1927.
18. M.K. Gandhi, *The Collected Works of Mahatma Gandhi*, vol. 24, Delhi: Ministry of Information and Broadcasting, 1964-94, pp. 148-9.
19. See Pachuau Lalsangkima, 'Church-Mission Dynamics in Northeast India', *International Bulletin of Missionary Research* 27(4), 1964-94, pp. 154-61.
20. C.B. Firth, *An Introduction to Indian Church History*, Madras: Christian Literature Society, 1976, p. 203.
21. M.K. Gandhi, *Collected Works of Mahatma Gandhi*, vol. 22, 1921-2, p. 497.
22. Verrier Elwin, *Leaves from the Jungle: A Diary of Life in a Gond Village*, New Delhi: Oxford India Paperbacks, pp. 6, 11, 12-13, 38, 41, 62, 65, 83, 114, cited in Guha, op. cit., 1936; rpt. 1990, p. 89.
23. N.R. Malkani, 'Among the Backward Classes', *Young India*, 24 June 1925, vol. IV, C.F. Andrews, 'An Aboriginal Tribe: Khaddar and Drink', *Young India*, 30 April 1926, no. 16.

24. 'Non-Cooperation Means Self-Purification', *Navajivan*, 27 January 1921, *Collected Works* 19: 285. See Shekhar Saxena, 'Country Profile on Alcohol in India', in *Alcohol and Public Health in 8 Developing Countries*, Leanne Riley and Mac Marshall, ed., Geneva: Substance Abuse Department, Social Change and Mental Health, World Health Organization, 1999, pp. 37-60.
25. Shirin Mehta, 'Social Consciousness of Tribals of South Gujarat', in *Gleaning of Indian Archaeology, History and Culture*, K.D. Bajpai, Rasesh Jamindar and P.K. Trivedi, eds., New Delhi/Jaipur: Publication Scheme, 2000, p. 318.
26. M.K. Gandhi, 'The Use and Abuse of Toddy', *Harijan*, 9 October 1937, vol. V, no. 35.
27. David M. Fahey and Padma Manian, 'Poverty and Purification: The Politics of Gandhi's Campaign for Prohibition', *The Historian*, vol. 67, no. 3 (FALL 2005), pp. 489-506.
28. David Hardiman, *The Coming of the Devi: Adivasi Assertion in Western India*, New York: Oxford University Press, 1987, Chapter 7, 'Drink and the Parsis', pp. 99-128.
29. David Hardiman, *Gandhi in his Time and Ours: The Global Legacy of his Ideas*, New York: Columbia University Press, 2003, pp. 138, 148.
30. David Hardiman, *The Coming of the Devi*, Chapter 10.
31. M.K. Gandhi, *Self-restraint vs. Self-indulgence*, Ahmedabad: Navajivan Publishing House, 1927, 1958, p. 39.
32. M.K. Gandhi, Reprinted from *Harijan*, 10 May 1942, in *Gandhi, Drink, Drugs and Gambling*, Ahmedabad: Navajivan Publishing House, 1952, p. 130
33. M.K. Gandhi, *Prohibition at any Cost* (compiled by R.K. Prabhu), Ahmedabad: Navajivan Publishing House, 1960, p. 3.
34. Ibid., p. 5.
35. Ibid., p. 6.
36. 'Meaning of Prohibition', *Harijan*, 17 June 1939, *Collected Works*, 69: 337. See also 'To Parsi Friends', *Harijan*, 3 June 1939, Collected Works, 69: 309-11.
37. Shashank Kela, A *Rogue and Peasant Slave: Adivasi Resistance 1800-2000*, New Delhi: Navayana Publishing, 2012, pp. 285-89.
38. For more information on Gandhi's attitude towards alcoholism, see D.M. Fahey and P. Manian, 'Poverty and Purification: The Politics of Gandhi's Campaign for Prohibition', *The Historian*, 67, 3, 2005, pp. 489-506.
39. Verrier Elwin, *The Tribal World of Verrier Elwin: An Autobiography*, Oxford: Oxford University Press, 1964, p. 240.

40. Dhiren Baske, *Gana Andolene Saontal Samaj*, Calcutta: Maitreyi Prakasani, 1996, p. 24.
41. Harald Fischer-Tine and Jana Tschurenev, eds., A *History of Alcohol and Drugs in Modern South Asia,* New York: Routledge, 2014, p. 5
42. Enclosure (Report on the working of the Bihar Ministry) (confidential), sent with Vallabhbhai Patel to Rajendra Prasad, 17 July 1939, *Dr. Rajendra Prasad: Correspondence and Select Documents*, New Delhi: Allied Publishers, 1984, 3: 178.
43. 'Prohibition', *Harijan*, 24 December 1938, *Collected Works*, 68: 221.
44. Verrier Elwin, *The Tribal World of Verrier Elwin*, 1964, p. 168.
45. Ibid., p. 84.
46. Ibid., p. 85.
47. Verrier Elwin, *The Loss of Nerve: A Comparative Study of the Contact of Peoples in the Aboriginal Areas of the Bastar State and the Central Provinces of India*, 1941, Bombay: Wagle Press, cited in *Adivasis and the Raj* by Sanjukta Das Gupta, New Delhi: Orient Blackswan, 2011, pp. 285-6.
48. D.N. Majumdar, 'The Cry of Social Reform among the Aborigines', *Modern Review*, March 1925, p. 287.
49. Prithish Nandi, ed., 'The Dance in Tribal India, Part 1', *The Illustrated Weekly of India*, Bomaby, vol. 76, 22 May 1955 cited in Ramachandra Guha, 'Savaging the Civilised: Verrier Elwin and the Tribal Question in Late Colonial India', *Economic and Political Weekly*, vol. 31, no. 35/37, Special Number (September 1996), pp. 2375-89.
50. Report by M. Annapurniah, Congress (Telugu) editor, sent to Gandhi, *Young India*, 18 July 1929, p. 234; *Letter from F.W. Stewart*, ICS, Agency Commissioner, to the Chief Secretary to Government, dated Camp, Narsapatam, 11 September 1922, p. 4.
51. M. Venkatarangaiya, *The Freedom Struggle in Andhra Pradesh (Andhra)*, Hyderabad, vol. III, p. 366; Demi-official from F.S.S. George, dated Narsa patam, 28 August 1922 (up to 5 October), Pub Dept (Confid), p. 23; Letter from F.W. Stewert, op. cit., dated, Narsapatam, 11 September 1922, p. 4; Govt. of Madras, Pub Dept., dated 21 November 1922, no. 974 (Mis); 20 December 1924, no. 894 (Mis); 2 February 1925, no. 108 (Mis); Madras Legislative Council Proceedings, 13 November 1922, vol. IX, no. 1-5, 1965, p. 538.
52. Letter from Stewart, op. cit., dated 11 September 1922, p. 4; Weekly Report from Huggins, dated 23 June 1923, enclosed report from Deputy Tehsildar, Malkanagiri, to the Agency Commissioner, dated 13 June 1923, Pub Dept. (Confid), p. 270.
53. *Madras Legislative Council Proceedings*, 13 November 1922, vol. IX, no. 1-5, p. 535.

54. Murali Atlury, 'Alluri Sitarama Raju and the Manyam Rebellion of 1922-4', *Social Scientist*, vol. 12, no. 4, April 1984, pp. 3-33.
55. David Arnold, 'Rebellious Hillmen: The Guden-Rampa Risings 1839-1924', in *Subaltern Studies I*, Ranajit Guha, ed., New Delhi: Oxford University Press, 1982, pp. 134-40.
56. *Andhra Patrika*, 28 August and 5 December 1922; 15 June 1923; 8, 9, 10, 11 May and 17, 1924. Also see, RNNPM, Reel no. 27, 1923, pp. 1098-9 for the translation of one report from *Andhra Patrika*, which demanded an enquiry.
57. *Andhra Patrika*, 17 May 1924. This English Para is taken from RJVJNPM, Rccl no. 28, 1924, p. 701.
58. For a theoretical critic of Gandhian ideology and specified forms of struggles, see E.M.S. Namboodiripad, 'Non-Violent Non-cooperation—The Technique of the Indian Bourgeoisie', *New Age*, 8 August 1954, pp. 34-18; 'Gandhism in Evolution-Retreat and Regrouping', *New Age*, 9 September 1954, pp. 51-60.
59. *Young India*, vol. XI, no. 29, 18 July 1929, p. 234.
60. Guha, *Savaging the Civilized*, 2014, p. 90.
61. Verrier Elwin, 'Gonds', *Modern Review*, November 1933, pp. 547-8.
62. Pyarelal, 'Bapa of Bapu', in *Thakkar Bapa: Eightieth Birthday Commemoration Volume*, ed. T.N. Jagadisan and Shyamlal, Madras: Diocesan Press, 1949, pp. 81-2.
63. Gayatri Chakravorty Spivak, 'Draupadi' by Mahasveta Devi', *Critical Inquiry*, vol. 8, no. 2, *Writing and Sexual Difference*, 1981, pp. 381-402.
64. S.G. Vaze, 'Thakkar Bapa—A Tribute', *The Hindustan Times*, 18 December 1948, *Thakkar Bapa: Eightieth Birthday Commemoration Volume*, 1949, pp. 86-7.
65. K.S. Singh, *Tribal Society in India*, New Delhi: Manohar, 1985, p. 175.
66. Letter to Verrier Elwin, *CWMG*, vol. 59, 14 January 1933, p. 13.
67. Guha, *Savaging the Civilized*, pp. 107-9.
68. *The Times of India*, 24 January 1938.
69. Discussion with Midnapore Political Workers, *CWMG*, vol. 89, 2 January 1946, p. 157.
70. Guha, *Savaging the Civilized*, pp. 104-5.
71. Ibid., p. 108.
72. Ibid., p. 144.
73. Ibid., p. 187.
74. A.V. Thakkar, *The Problem of Aborigines in India*, R.R. Kale Memorial Lecture, Poona: 1941, pp. 23-6.
75. Thakkar Bapa, 'The Problem of Aborigines in India', Gokhale Institute of Politics and Economics, R.R. Kale Memorial Lecture, 1941, T.N. Jagadisan

and Shyamlal, eds., *Thakkar Bapa: Eightieth Birthday Commemoration Volume*, Madras: Diocesan Press, 1949, p. 372.

76. Kodanda P. Rao, 'Aboriginalisthan: Anthropologist's Imperium', *Social Science Quarterly*, vol. 30, no. 2, October 1943.
77. Ramachandra Guha, 'Savaging the Civilised: Verrier Elwin and the Tribal Question in Late Colonial India', *Economic and Political Weekly*, vol. 31, no. 35/37, Special Number, September 1996, p. 2385.
78. Guha, *Savaging the Civilized*, p. 157.
79. Verrier Elwin, *Tribal World of Verrier Elwin*, p. 85.
80. Ramchandra Guha, 'Between Anthropology and Literature: The Ethnographies of Verrier Elwin', *The Journal of the Royal Anthropological Institute*, vol. 4, no. 2, June 1998, pp. 325-43.
81. Ramachandra Guha, 'A Nation Consumed by the State', in *Outlook*, 31 January 2011, pp. 30-44.
82. Verrier Elwin, 'Ancient and Modern Man', in *Nehru Abhinandan Granth: A Birthday Book*, New Delhi: Nehru Abhinandan Granth Committee, 1949.
83. Verrier Elwin, *Gandhiji: Bapu of His People*, Shillong: North East Frontier Agency, 1956, pp. 44-5.
84. K.S. Singh, ed., *Jawaharlal Nehru, Tribes and Tribal Policy*, Calcutta: Anthropological Survey of India, 1989, pp. 1-2.
85. Ambedkar cited in A.V. Thakkar, 'Education among Tribal People Very Backward: State's Responsibility for their Advancement', published in *Leader* dated 11-7-1945, reproduced in *Aboriginals' Cry in the Wilderness: Controversy between Dr. Ambedkar and A. V. Thakkar with Facts and Figures Regarding Aborigines and Hill Tribes, their Education and Representation in Legislature*, Published by A.V. Thakkar, Servants of India Society, Bombay, n.d., p. 11; Also see Gyanendra Pandey, *A History of Prejudice: Race, Caste and Difference in India and the United States*, Cambridge: Cambridge University Press, 2013, p. 32.
86. Letter to the Editor, *The Times of India* dated Poona 12 May 1945; from A.V. Thakkar, *The Times of India*, 17 May 1945, p. 6.
87. Ibid.
88. Ibid.
89. Verrier Elwin, *A Philosophy of Love*, Delhi: Publications Division. Ministry of Information and Broadcasting, 1962, p. 97.
90. Verrier Elwin, *Tribal World of Verrier Elwin*, p. 340.
91. Archana Prasad, *Against Ecological Romanticism: Verrier Elwin and Making of an Anti-Modern Tribal Identity*, 2nd edn., Three Essays, 2011, p. 10.
92. Koutuk Dutta, 'Problematizing Verrier Elwin's View of the Tribal World',

Journal of the Department of English, Vidyasagar University, vol. 12, 2014-15, pp. 46-55.

93. K.J. Chitalia, 'Bapa the Servant of India', in *Thakkar Bapa: Eightieth Birthday Commemoration Volume*, ed. T.N. Jagadisan and Shyamlal, Madras: Diocesan Press, 1949, pp. 18-25.
94. B.H. Mehta, 'The Problem of Aborigines in India', in *Thakkar Bapa: Eightieth Birthday Commemoration Volume*, op. cit., pp. 360-7.
95. Thakkar Bapa, 'The Problem of Aborigines in India', Gokhale Institute of Politics and Economics, R.R. Kale Memorial Lecture, 1941, in *Thakkar Bapa: Eightieth Birthday Commemoration Volume*, op. cit., pp. 354-77.
96. Indulal Yagnik, *Atmakatha*, vol. II, Ahmedabad: Gujarat Grantharatan Karyalay, 1970, pp. 158-61.
97. Indulal Yagnik, *Atmakatha*, vol. III, Ahmedabad: Grantharatan Karyalay, 1970, pp. 58-76.
98. C.F. Andrews, 'An Aboriginal Tribe, Khaddar and Drink', *Young India*, 30 April 1925. For more detail see Kakali Chakrabarty, 'Tribe and Tribal Welfare in Gandhian Thoughts', *Journal of the Anthropological Survey of India*, 68(2), 2019, pp. 225-33.
99. Shyamlal, 'Thakkar Bapa and the Kasturba Trust' in *Thakkar Bapa: Eightieth Birthday Commemoration Volume*, op. cit., pp. 245-52.
100. H.P. Desai, 'A.V. Thakkar: The Man and his Work', *The Modern Review*, January 1928.
101. See *The Collected Works of Mahatma Gandhi, Compact Disc* (*CWMGCD*), Delhi: National Book Trust, vol. 30, 2000, pp. 311 ff.
102. M.K. Gandhi, *Christian Missions and their Place in India*, Ahmedabad: Navajivan Press, 1941, p. 78.
103. Verrier Elwin, *The Tribal World of Verrier Elwin: An Autobiography*, Oxford: Oxford University Press, 1964, p. 97.
104. M.K. Gandhi, *Hind Swaraj*, Ahmedabad: Navajivan Publishing House, 1951, pp. 41-2.
105. Thirteen Commandments, *Navajivan* (Gujarat), *CWMG*, vol. 25, 7 December 1924, pp. 406-7.
106. Mahadev H. Desai, *Day to Day with Gandhi: Secretary's Diary*, vol. V, Varanasi: Sarva Seva Sangh Prakashan, 1970, p. 115.
107. Vijay Kumar Vashishtha, *Role of Gandhi's Ideas in Mobilization of Adivasis of Southern Rajputana Princely States (1921-48)*, Shimla: Indian Institute of Advanced Studies, 2014, pp. 194-5.
108. Viyogi Hari, *Thakkar Bapa*, New Delhi: Publication Division, Government of India, 1977, pp. 50-1.
109. *Navajivan* (Gujarat), *CWMG*, 18 April 1926, p. 312.

110. *Harijan*, *CWMG*, vol. 68, 25 February 1939, p. 422.
111. R. Srivatsan, 'Native Noses and Nationalist Zoos: Debates in Colonial and Early Nationalist Anthropologies of Castes and Tribes', *Economic and Political Weekly*, vol. 40, no. 19, 7-13 May 2005, pp. 1986-98.
112. R. Srivatsan, 'Concept of "Seva" and the "Sevak" ', *EPW*, op. cit., 2006, pp. 427-38.
113. B.H. Mehta, 'The Problem of Aborigines in India', in *Thakkar Bapa: Eightieth Birthday Commemoration Volume*, op. cit., pp. 354-77.
114. A.V. Thakkar, 'The Servants of India', in *Thakkar Bapa: Eightieth Birthday Commemoration Volume*, 6 December 1923, op. cit., p. 299.
115. Ibid., 22 June 1922, p. 298.
116. Viyogi Hari, *Thakkar Bapa* (translated from Hindi by Krishna Kumar Misra), New Delhi: Publications Division, Ministry of Information and Broadcasting, Government of India, 1977, p. 50.
117. Ibid., pp. 81-9.
118. A.V. Thakkar, 'The Problem of Aborigines in India', in *Thakkar Bapa: Eightieth Birthday Commemoration Volume*, pp. 354-77.
119. David Hardiman, *Gandhi in his Time and Ours*, New Delhi: Permanent Black, 2016, p. 144.
120. *The Servant of India*, vol. 6, no. 26, 26 July 1926, p. 311.
121. Kishorelal Mashruwala, *Gandhi-vichar Dohan*, New Delhi: Sasta Sahitya Mandal, 1991, pp. 76-86.
122. A.V. Thakkar, op. cit., pp. 354-77.
123. Elwin to Thakkar, 7 July 1941, P. Kodanda Rao Papers, New Delhi: Nehru Memorial Museum and Library, (NMML).
124. Ibid.
125. Verrier Elwin, *Tribal World of Verrier Elwin*, op. cit., p. 148.
126. Ibid.
127. Thakkar Bapa, 'Protection of Minorities', *The Hitavada*, 4 December 1948, cited in *Thakkar Bapa: Eightieth Birthday Commemoration Volume*, 1949, pp. 349.
128. Circular letter from A.V. Thakkar of 12 September 1940, in Box VIII, File D, Hyde Papers, Cambridge: Centre for South Asian Studies.
129. Ramachandra Guha, 'Savaging the Civilised', op. cit., pp. 2375-89.
130. Elwin to Thakkar, in Box VIII, Hyde Papers, 5 October 1940.
131. *The Times of India*, 22 November 1941, 30 January 1942, and 6 March 1942.
132. Ramachandra Guha, 'Savaging the Civilised', September 1996.
133. Thakkar Bapa, 'Aborigines of Orissa', *Modern Review*, September 1938, p. 78.

134. Viyogi Hari, *Thakkar Bapa*, 1977, pp. 53-4.
135. *Sarvodaya* means literally 'the rise of all'. The welfare of the depressed communities like dalits and Adivasis remains a priority under this theme. Thus the term is often referred as *Antyodaya*, i.e. welfare 'unto the last'. Jhaverbhai Patel and Allubhai Shah, *An Experiment in Antyodaya*, Surat: Sarvodaya Ayojan Kendra, p. 17 cited in Sengar, Bina Kumari, 'Gandhian Approach to Tribals', *Proceedings of the Indian History Congress*, vol. 62, 2001, pp. 627-36.
136. Jayant Pandya and Amrut Modi, ed., *Sarvodaya: Gandhi Sevaso Smithi Granth*, Bhavnagar: Bhartiya Sarvodaya Sammelan, November 1994, pp. 60-5.
137. The social reconstruction programme of the Vedichi's of Surat, which led to the outbreak of the Vedichi Movement (1922-47) shows that the reform had already been initiated among the Adivasis long before the Gandhians took over the leadership.
138. K.S. Singh, 'Mahatma Gandhi and the Adivasis', *Man in India*, vol. 50, no. 1, January-March 1970, pp. 1-25.
139. Ibid.

CHAPTER 2

Impact of Gandhian Ideology on the Tribal Movements of Chota Nagpur in Twentieth Century

With the unprecedented expansion of the railways, roads and other modern communication system, the non-tribal element started flooding the tribal areas. In Chota Nagpur alone, for instance, between 1871 and 1931, the incidence of immigration rose from 96,000 to 3,07,000. The most striking feature of this period was the breakdown of the communal mode of production and the emergence of private right in land.[1] A further stage in the development of the peasant system was the penetration of tribal economy by market. With the market came the middle men, merchants and moneylenders. Large-scale incidence of alienation of land from tribals to non-tribals took place. The tribal handicrafts declined. Out-migration from Chota Nagpur alone was 3,30,000 in 1891, 7,07,000 in 1911 and 9,47,000 in 1921.[2] The result was that the tribals began to emulate the way of life and values of the non-tribals. This process has been referred to as 'Sanskritization' in social anthropological literature. The origin of these movements can be traced back to the beginning of the twentieth century; they gained momentum in the 1920s and 1930s.

The colonial government enacted the Chota Nagpur Tenancy Act in 1908 and with this act restrictions were imposed on the landlords' rights. Another act that reflects the colonial tribal policy of segregation was the Scheduled Districts Act (1874). Behind the Government of India Act of 1919 the belief was that the tribals need special law as they are a separate ethnic community than the caste. Thus the concept of the backward areas was shaped during the colonial era. Later the tribal and non-tribal areas were both partly and fully 'excluded' in the Government of India Act of 1935.

Gandhi did not support the policy of segregation implemented by the colonial government, especially for the tribals. He, in fact, criticized the policy of 'isolation and *status quo*' as defined in the Act of 1935 and was of the opinion that this would detach the tribals from the so-called mainstream society. The 'Excluded Areas' were kept under direct colonial administration. The Adivasis were put into watertight compartments and classified as tribal people by the government. Gandhi said, '. . . it was a shame that they had allowed them to be treated like that. It was up to them to make the Adivasis feel one with them'. In strategically situated Assam, in 1946, he reminded the people that 'it was their shame that the Adivasis should be isolated from the rest of the nation of which they were an inalienable part'.[3] While including Adivasis Welfare as the fourteenth item Gandhi said:

> Adivasis have become the fourteenth item in the constructive programme. But they are not the least in point of importance. Our country is so vast and the races are so varied that the best of us, in spite of every effort, cannot know all there is to know of men and their condition. As one comes upon layer after layer of things one ought to know as a national servant, one realizes how difficult it is to make good our claim to be one nation whose every unit has a living consciousness of being one with one another.[4]

Gandhi directed that a constructive worker should engage himself in the constructive work among the Adivasis of north-east and resort to individual civil disobedience to overcome 'Government's opposition' to his work. Tendulkar has remarked that,

> If the Government prevented him (Gandhi) from going among them he would simply disobey the order. The Government might put him in prison; he would welcome it. It would be a most auspicious beginning for his work. The very fact that he had gone to prison in order to serve the Adivasis would enshrine him in their hearts.[5]

From 1910 to 1935 the tribal inhabited Chota Nagpur was quite calm as peace prevails for the time being. During this time the religious reform movements were renewed with great zeal and social purification movements influenced the tribals of Chota Nagpur to a large extent. Hazaribagh was a crucial centre of Brahmoism from where Brahmoism spread to many towns of Chota Nagpur and more significantly to Ranchi and Giridih. Arya Samaj established its branch at Ranchi in 1894.[6] Both Brahmo Samaj and Arya Samaj started disseminating the message of nationalism among the tribes of Chota Nagpur. The Ramakrishna Mission opened its branch at Ranchi in 1917.[7] Another branch was opened in Santhal Parganas in 1922, later shifted to Deoghar in 1923.[8] They also carried on many educational activities among the Adivasis of the region. Vaishnavism and Kabir Pathis also converted Mundas and Oraons of Chota Nagpur.[9] All these spiritual and cultural movements impacted the tribals of Chota Nagpur and in 1914-15, around the time when Gandhi emerged on the political scene of the country; the revivalist movement called Tana Bhagat swiped the Oraons of Chota Nagpur under the leadership of Jatra Oraon. There were other tribal movements as well that actively supported the freedom struggle of India and became the torch bearers of Gandhi's ideals in Chota Nagpur.[10]

Adivasi movements of pre-Gandhi era did want to generate an alternative structure of political power, establishment of Adivasi Raj and expulsion of *dikus.* But after the arrival of Gandhi, the Adivasi movements in Chota Nagpur aimed to enter the existing power structure and did not visualize any alternative structure of power. Their association with Gandhi and Congress by and large was devoid of any reservation.[11] These movements essentially pertain to the cultural domain, and have been enumerated by K.S. Singh as 'Sanskritization' and 'cultural' based on their nature, but Surajit Sinha has employed the term 'reform' for 'Sanskritization' and 'ethnicity' for 'cultural' to describe them. The origin of the Sanskritization or social mobility movements can be traced back from the inception of twentieth century and they gained momentum in the 1920s and 1930s. So, they all have been taken place during Gandhian era and are also known as the Bhagat movements. N.K. Bose also believed that Munda and Oraon of Chota Nagpur were interested in adopting Hindu caste norms. He said,

> In other words, in surrendering themselves to the productive arrangements of the brahmanical society, they tacitly accepted the caste system and the *varna* creed. . . . Instead of taking the path of Christianity, they began to make

greater efforts to have themselves incorporated into the social arrangements based on the *varnashrama* system and on caste distinctions, or, to raise themselves to a higher station or level in that system.[12]

But there are other points of view regarding the Sanskritization theory. It has been found that among the Oraons of Chota Nagpur, it was only the educated who were Sanskritized and only a section of the Tana Bhagats adopted some of the practices of Hindu upper caste society or if they have adopted then is this a clear sign of their aspiration for inclusion in the Hindu caste fold? Certainly not as S.C. Roy has categorically mentioned that it was only certain well-to-do families, ambitious of rising in the social ladder, who had embraced the services of the Brahman priests. Tana Bhagats were not really interested in obtaining the service of Brahman priests and refused to succumb to any sort of hierarchy.[13]

According to Xaxa, these movements are imbued not so much by the desire for social mobility as by the desire to gain respectability in the eyes of the larger society. From that perspective, they are more of a political than a cultural movement. They were also directed at reforming the inner world of their own societies including religion. These movements either aimed at replacing their indigenous gods and goddesses with the Hindu gods and goddesses or going back to the original form of indigenous tribal religion in order to withstand the forces of change.[14] When the Indian national movement gained momentum, these tribal movements became a part of the Non-Cooperation and Civil Disobedience, movement launched by Gandhi. Now, we will separately discuss them in order to get a clear idea about their ideology and dynamism in relation to the Gandhian paradigm. They are,

- Tana Bhagat movement of the Oraons
- Sapha Hor movement of the Santhals
- Haribaba movement of the Hos
- Raj Gond movements of the Gonds

TANA BHAGAT MOVEMENT OF THE ORAON TRIBES

Tana Bhagat movement (1914-22) among the Oraons of Chota Nagpur was a cultural revitalization movement in nature and was caused by the rise of political radicalism in the wake of Gandhian Non-Cooperation movement. It established a new sect, the Tana sect, which was markedly different from the Oraon community. Though started much earlier the Tana Bhagat movement was heavily influenced by the Gandhian ideology and later participated in the non-violent Non-Cooperation movement called upon by Gandhi. The movement was an obvious reaction to the repressive tax system brought forward by the erroneous survey and settlement in Chota Nagpur region in 1902-8. The immediate targets were the landlords, moneylenders, British administrators, police and the *dikus.* The Oraons blamed their age-old gods and goddesses for all their hardships and started worshipping a new religious cult preached by the Vaishnava *gurus* called Bhagat in lieu of that. As Binay Bhushan Chaudhuri has rightly observed, the millenarian beliefs of Tana Bhagat leaders did not perhaps owe much to the Christian influence. The decisive influence on the comprehensive religious revitalization agenda was Vaishnava influence.[15] But Bhagat cult that characterized the new cultural revitalization movement, since about 1914, was different in nature. The difference has been misinterpreted by two renowned scholars, Herbert Risley and Sarat Chandra Roy. Whereas Risley did not find any originality in the Bhagat phenomenon and confused it with the traditional Oraon religious customs,[16] Roy considered the movement as a mere continuation of the earlier Bhagat cult devoid of any political motif.[17] But B.B. Chaudhuri had proved that Tana Bhagat Revitalization Movement (collectivist in orientation and organization) was different from the earlier Bhagat cult (essentially oriented to spiritual uplift of a small number of Oraons) and not its continuation. The most significant difference was that the new movement was part of a wider social protest movement.

According to Joseph Marianus Kujur, Gandhian thought had a lot of resemblance with the Adivasi belief system that helped them to understand his ideology as well as his philosophical thought process. He said that, Gandhian faith resonates well with the belief system of the Adivasis, especially in the Adivasi belt of Bihar. Gandhi, like the Adivasis, is a theist. For Gandhi, God's existence is a matter of personal faith. According to the Adivasi world view, the Supreme Being exists very concretely in their midst. In the Gandhian cosmology, there is an orderly world, but the Divine is of a higher order to which the natural order is subordinate. Adivasis believe in the hierarchy of beings: there are the natural and the supernatural realms. It is Gandhi's conviction that the practice of moral living is possible only for the individual in relation to other human beings. Ahimsa or non-violence is the basic law of love, which, according to Gandhi, should govern all human affairs and all interpersonal relations. Adivasis have a very similar ideology where morality is part and parcel of their social framework. Religion thus becomes a way of life for them.[18]

K.S. Singh had analysed how the new religious movement of the Oraons merged with their protest movement. In doing so, he had downplayed the role of religion that affected the organization of the movement and said that the Tana Bhagats lacked appropriate organization uptill about 1921-2, when the Gandhian Non-Cooperation movement provided it. He said,

> Tribal politics in the pre-1920 phase could be described in terms of a series of revolts, sporadic, isolated and spontaneous. . . . Inspired by the primeval dream of freedom these movements aimed at the total reconstruction of the primitive system which was breaking down under the impact of the colonial economy. . . . They were violent, and ruthlessly crushed. . . . The phase of tribal politics which began after 1920 was free from such episodes and was marked by movements which could be sustained only by organization and through external stimuli. The latter were provided by the nationalist struggle which came to the tribal world in the 1920s through the message and personality of Mahatma Gandhi.[19]

Singh's views seem contradictory because Congress workers only occasionally visited the Oraon villages.[20] No local unit of the Congress involving the Oraons was set up. In fact, it was the Oraon participation in the Non-Cooperation movement that had broadened its base. Not only that, without an organization how come the Oraon protest movement could disseminate so rapidly to a wide area? So, when Singh is saying that the movement was local, sporadic and spontaneous, it is going against the fact. K.K. Datta has documented that, Gandhi symbolized to them an infallible power that was potent enough to replace the British authority before long. A local report wrote of a 'rumour that the Tana Bhagats have asked Gandhi to visit them'.[21]

In 1915, British reports began to mention the Tana Bhagat disturbances among the Oraons of Chota Nagpur. It was initially called as *Kurukh Dharam* (true religion) and from their continuous chanting of *tana baba tana* (pull out, father, pull out) and it came to be termed as Tana Bhagat. According to Stephen Fuchs,

> About the latter part of 1915 these local movements began to converge to one large and powerful messianic movement which went under the name 'Tana Bhagat Movement'. It spread practically over the whole of Chota Nagpur wherever Oraon villages could be found. Members of other tribes rarely joined this movement. The message of this Tana Bhagat Movement—called tano or tana (to pull, or pulling) from the frequent use of this word in their hymns—was that God (whom they called Dharmes, the 'Just', or Bhagwan, the 'Bountiful') would send a most powerful and beneficient delegate down to earth to redeem the Oraon from their misery.[22]

The Tana Bhagat movement may be said to have developed in two phases: the first phase was that of eradication of existing beliefs and practices or a programme of cleansing and purging, and the second phase had a constructive programme. British intervention in Chota Nagpur, their administrative arrangements and agrarian legislations only intensified the already prevalent hierarchies in the Oraon community. They were forced to provide free labour for construction work and had to work as coolies at any other worksites by the British. So, the opposition to the world of spirits and ritual celebrations and a resistance to the landlords-moneylenders and the British Raj—were thus interlinked.[23] The Oraons were mobilized by their charismatic leader Jatra Oraon, who convinced the Oraons that the Oraon Raj was soon to be established. He asked them to refuse to pay rents to the landlords and to meet the oppressive demands made by the local police. Jatra Bhagat formulated a rule of conduct and said that, the Oraons have to give up worshipping of the spirits and instead worship the Kurukh Dharam; they have to give up animal sacrifice, meat-eating, liquor consumption, song and dance, visiting to the dormitories, wearing colourful clothes or jewellery or tattoo, and witchcraft practicing. He declared that the Oraons had to lead an ascetic life free from extravagance and luxury. The Oraon ought, further, to stop tilling the fields and paying rents to their landlords and to refuse to engage themselves as labourers to any non-Oraons.[24] The movement spread like wildfire and the British police eventually arrested and imprisoned him. But the idea of non-payment of taxes or non-cooperation with the British became so popular that the movement did not die down so easily. Gradually, the rumour of the advent of a Messiah started spreading everywhere in the Oraon region of Chota Nagpur. Some more disciplinary conducts were introduced during this time, e.g. Thursday was chosen as a Sabbath day for rest and prayer meetings, daily bath became mandatory, inter-caste dining and inter-caste marriage were banned.[25]

Having said that, it is also needed to be mentioned that the Oraons were well aware that mere religious revitalization would not help them in bringing the Oraon Raj. Thus it was from 1919 onwards that the Tana Bhagat movement developed political overtones. By January 1919, the fire of the Tana Bhagat movement became widespread and met with severe police repression. The leaders such as Shibu, Maya, Sukra, Singhia, Debia, were arrested and convicted.[26] In the autumn of 1920, the extremist section of the Tana Bhagats, led by Shibu Bhagat, let loose their cattle and, taking with them only such cash as they had, started for the Sat Pahari Hill in the neighbouring district of Hazaribagh, 'where they expected the advent of a Saviour or Deity who would bring back the good old days of prosperity to the Oraons'.[27] Then the leadership was handed over to Turia Bhagat and Jitu Bhagat, who vigorously launched the campaign for non-payment of Chaukidari tax and no-rent campaign against the zamindars. These resolutions were immediately supported by the leadership of the Congress.[28] From 1915 the movement started lacking the support of many among the Oraon community; coercion was one of the methods adopted to bring members to the faith. Those who did not comply with the regulations of the Tana faith were forbidden the use of wells, their wives were declared to be witches, and their fowl and pigs killed. What was particularly resented was the renunciation of the faith by erstwhile Tanas who now chose to revert to their former customs.[29]

A widespread rumour that British rule would soon end, deeply influenced the Oraon political perception at that time. They believed British rule could be replaced, with German help, by an independent Oraon Raj. Far more powerful was the image of Gandhi as a political authority alternative to the British Raj.[30] Gandhi's visit to Bihar generated enthusiasm and expectations amongst the people and proved valuable for the movement. The aura of divinity surrounding him also helped in the mobilization process. A large number of rumours were also getting associated with him. For example, rumours were afloat that the Tana Bhagats had got exclusive rights to some of the villages, and that transfer of the lands of these villages in Tana Bhagats' name would be recognized with the advent of Gandhi's Raj.[31] The Non-Cooperation movement built up slowly in Chota Nagpur, even though efforts were made to spread the movement from November 1920 onwards. It was only in late January 1921 that non-cooperators succeeded in establishing contact with the Tana Bhagats in Ranchi.[32] The Tana Bhagats responded in large numbers to the appeals made by the non-cooperators and their association with the Non-Cooperation movement gave fillip to their unrest. The movement amongst the Tana Bhagats primarily brought forth their animosity against the landlords and trading community.[33]

As already mentioned, the turning point in the Tana Bhagat movement was a visit by Mahatma Gandhi himself to Ranchi. Gandhi observed the Tana Bhagats and wrote about them as follows:

From Chakradharpur to Chaibasa is a pleasant motor ride over a very good road. It was at Chaibasa that I made the acquaintance of the Ho tribe—a most interesting body of men and women, simple as children, with a faith that it is not easy to shake. Many of them have taken to the charkha and khaddar. Congress workers began the work of reformation among them in 1921. Many have given up eating carrion and some have even taken to vegetarianism. The Mundas are another tribe whom I met at Khunti on my way to Ranchi. . . . Among these tribes there is quite a colony of them called Bhaktas, literally meaning devotees. They are believers in khaddar. Men as well as women ply the charkha regularly. They wear khaddar woven by themselves. Many of them had walked miles with their charkhas on their shoulders. I saw nearly four hundred of them all plying their charkhas assiduously at the meeting I had the privilege of addressing. They have their own *bhajans* which they sing in chorus.[34]

Needless to say when Gandhi announced the Non-Cooperation movement, non-payment of tax and rents were an integral part of his programme which was first introduced by the tribals of Chota Nagpur and was already proved to be successful. Therefore, the Tana Bhagats could easily relate their desire for Oraon Raj to the Gandhian vision of self-rule and started imbibing the ideology propagated by him during the non-violence Non-Cooperation movement against the British. In 1921, when Gandhi launched the Non-Cooperation movement the Tanas went into underground to gain importance. They felt a strange affinity between their own aims and Gandhi's movement. Gandhi rejuvenated the millenarian zeal of the movement and gave it a fresh but brief life. With the brutal police repression, the fire of the extremist strand eventually died down and the moderate Tanas who remained loyal to the Gandhian non-violence ideology succeeded in maintaining their existence though just as a mere sect.[35] To quote from Vinita Damodaran,

> By the 1920s the Tana Bhagat movement had acquired 'disturbing' links with the Congress movement in the rest of Bihar. Gandhi's non-cooperation struggle resulted in renewed agitation in Chota Nagpur, and protesters intensified their demands for low rents, restoration of rights to the jungle, and abolition of forced labour.[36]

The Oraons had long been bitter with the local law courts and consequently readily responded to Gandhi's call for boycotting them and setting up instead village panchayats for arbitration of village disputes. Abstinence from liquor drinking, included in Congress rural programmes, was an essential part of their revitalization movement. Familiarity with the Bhagat tradition made it easier for them to comprehend the idioms in which Gandhi spoke to people.[37] They began to wear Gandhi caps and carrying Congress tricolour flags as a mark of protest against the colonial masters. Emma Tarlo has said that, Gandhi cap, despite its visual consistency, was used by different groups to represent their own interests. The Santhals wearing Gandhi caps would confront and attack the police believing that they were immune from bullet wounds as they were wearing Gandhi Maharaj's caps. To them the Gandhi cap had taken on the role of a talisman, capable of protecting its wearer.[38] Gandhi cap became a symbol of *swadeshi* and *swaraj*. According to Sangeeta Dasgupta, from 1921 fresh injunctions were added to the Tana tenets; followers were to carry the Congress *jhaṇda* (flag), wear *khaddar* (home-spun cloth) and take vows in Gandhi Maharaj's name. Lores, myths and rumours grew around Gandhi, his *charkha* (spinning wheel) and *swaraj* (self-rule). In subsequent years, the campaign of the Tanas was narrated as part of another history in which their interest was shown to have merged with that of the nation striving for independence.[39]

According to S.P. Sinha, the liaison between the Tana Bhagats and the Gandhian movement was established by band of devoted workers both Hindu and Muslim who were operating from Ranchi. By the start of 1921 these leaders and workers had reached the interior spreading the message of Gandhi.[40] According to Sachchidananda, this leads us to the conclusion that the Tana Bhagats were more susceptible to the impact of the Non-Cooperation movement than the other Adivasis and it is they who responded to the call in huge numbers. The Deputy Commissioner of Ranchi admitted that the Non-Cooperation movement had revitalized the Tana Bhagat movement.[41] He said, 'the Tana Bhagats, who have already got a grievance, are being gradually taught to believe that government is a bad government and is responsible for their troubles. Rumour also played a crucial role in spreading the Non-Cooperation movement in Ranchi. There was a rumour that the Tana Bhagats had asked Gandhi to visit them, which caused serious concerns for the police. Probably this is but a rumour, nevertheless, it gives an indication as to the trend of affairs.[42]

The two political developments—British reverses in the war and the emergence of Gandhi's charismatic leadership—more directly impinged on the rise of political radicalism. The Tana Bhagats started attending the Congress meetings (both open and secret), processions and strikes organized in Ranchi in large numbers comprising not only of Oraons, but also Mundas, Bhuians, Ghashis, and so on. According to a report submitted by the SP (Superintendent of Police), Ranchi on the issue of Non-Cooperation movement among the Oraons and other tribals of Ranchi from 31 January to 13 February 1921, it is evident that in these 13 days, 18 meetings were organized (especially in the Tana Bhagat areas, i.e. Mandar, Kuru, Lohardaga and Bero Police Stations) where the tribals outnumbered the non-tribals.[43] The Tana Bhagats were in touch with the national leadership of the Congress party and Rajendra Prasad, Mazrul Haque, Motilal Nehru—all paid visit to different districts of Chota Nagpur starting from Dhanbad, Hazaribagh, Jharia, Chatra and of course Ranchi. Under the influence of these great leaders, the Tana Bhagats started boycotting foreign cloth and anti-liquor agitation which was again an integral part of their own programme. They also started using *khadi.*[44] Sarla Devi, a niece of Rabindranath Tagore, visited several districts of Chota Nagpur in October 1921 advocating *khadi* and *charkha.*[45] According to Louis Fisher, Patel and Gandhi both had a profound influence on the Tana Bhagats. The latter also threw themselves heart and soul in the midstream of the *satyagraha* and were jailed.[46]

As far as the temperance movements amongst the tribals are concerned, it had two aims, first was to save them from impoverishment as it caused the indebtedness for the illiterate tribals and lost their lands to these wealthy liquor-dealers-cum-landowners; and the second reason was to enhance the status of the tribals as in Brahmanical Hindu culture abstinence from alcohol is considered a great virtue. So, liquor boycott was not only fuelled in part by resentment against the colonial liquor laws but was also part of radical tribal cultural reform movements for upward mobility. According to Lata Singh, with the emergence of Gandhi in Congress after 1918, the temperance activities of the middle-class were linked to the anti-liquor movements of the masses.[47] In 1921, Gandhi gave his blessings to a campaign to picket liquor and toddy shops. As a result, the sale of drink decreased significantly in many areas.[48] The liquor boycott was one of the most effective actions in Chota Nagpur. Liquor boycott during the Non-Cooperation movement was most intense in Hazaribagh. The non-cooperators had considerable success in stopping drinking and in many places the liquor shops were not opened since the beginning of the official year 1921.[49] Another strong belt in Chota Nagpur was Chakradharpur, where the volunteers were very well organized and posted at different shops for picketing. The liquor sale in Chakradharpur went down considerably.[50]

Yet another activity related to liquor protest that was very popular in this region was 'illicit distillation of liquor'.[51] It might seem contradictory to the anti-liquor campaign among the tribals of Chota Nagpur. But it has a very close link with it. Illicit distillation of liquor was a manifestation of dissatisfaction against the colonial excise policy. Under the new excise policy, the government had banned private distillation of liquor. Such protest flouted the government policy. The non-cooperators made strong efforts to prevent the settlement of excise liquor shops.[52] In October 1921, in the Santhal Parganas and Hazaribagh, a rumour had spread that everybody was empowered by Gandhi to distil liquor as they pleased.[53] Often in some parts of Chota Nagpur, a strong rumour was prevalent that *swaraj* was imminent that led to rampant distillation of 'illicit' liquor, because *swaraj* meant to them that they are no longer compelled to abide by the British law. Thus illicit distillation bore the tone of infringing British law and exercising the customary rights of the Adivasis. Adivasis did not consider 'illicit' distillation a crime; rather it was taken to be an order of Gandhi.[54] There was a widespread belief in Ranchi that Gandhi had been invested with divine attributes and enthroned as a king and that the consumption of meat and alcohol would be forbidden under Gandhi Raj.

Tana actions, however localized in its expression, were seen to be in consonance with Congress and Gandhian ideals. In February 1921, many tribals from the northern parts of Ranchi district rushed to the markets and disposed of their goats and sheep at very low prices.[55]

> They carried the idea of non-violence to the extent of abjuring eating anything red, because blood was red. When they heard that Mahatma had arisen and was asking the people to stick to non-violence they felt that the rearing of goats which would ultimately go to the slaughterhouse was against the creed of non-violence and therefore, drove out their goats from their houses to the jungles and abandoned them not knowing that they would become victims

to wild animal and to men who were even wilder. . . . They gave up red chilies, because they looked red. The song which they sang had the refrain that even an ant has life just as a man has and so should not be hurt.[56]

After the suspension of the Non-Cooperation movement, the Tana Bhagats maintained what Gandhi instructed before his incarceration and engaged themselves in constructive work like spinning of *khadi*. In December 1922, AICC held its Gaya session where Chittaranjan Das, Hakim Ajmal Khan, Motilal Nehru, Sarojini Naidu, Srinivas Iyengar, C. Rajagopalachari, Vallabhbhai Patel, and Kasturba Gandhi participated and was also attended by a large number of Tana Bhagats. Later in September 1925, Gandhi during his visit to Ranchi, to attend the Bihar Provincial Conference, came across 400 Tanas who regularly plied the *charkha* and habitually wore *khadi*. During the visit of Simon Commission in 1928, the Tana Bhagats took part in a black flag demonstration. On 29 January 1930 there was a huge procession of the Tana Bhagats in Ranchi. Later in the year, according to the police report, almost 2000 Tanas had enlisted themselves as members of Congress and under the leadership of Bhuka Bhagat also participated in salt *satyagraha* and immediately after that in the Civil Disobedience movement of 1930. Salt *satyagraha* was in full swing in Manbhum and Ranchi, the forest laws were violated in Singhbhum and Palamu and picketing before liquor shops in Lohardaga districts of Chota Nagpur.[57]

Besides, it is also interesting to note that Gandhi passed through Chota Nagpur visiting Hazaribagh and Gomia while returning from Assam in April 1934. At Gomia, where the Santhals had taken active part in Civil Disobedience movement, he started his constructive and ameliorative programme as he had been doing for the Harijans elsewhere[58] which attracted 400 Tana Bhagats from Ranchi and Palamu. Gandhi's tour of Chatra, Hazaribagh, Gomia, Barmo, Jharia, Jamshedpur and Chakradharpur in 1934 drew an overwhelming response from the Adivasis, who revered him as an 'incarnation of God'. At times he was getting mobbed by the crowds who were trying to touch his feet and have his blessings.[59] They were hoping that Gandhi would help them get rid of heavy rents, but all their hopes were dashed when Gandhi spoke of inter-dining with Harijans only. The Bhagats later said that since their fathers had not taken food with Harijans, they also would not do so. The district administration was overjoyed that Gandhi's visit had 'done good in dashing the mounting hopes of the rump of the Tana Bhagat movement'.[60] On his way to Orissa from Patna, Gandhi spent four busy days at Ranchi from 29 April to 3 May 1934 discussing the political issues with Congress leaders. Gandhi's visit to Bermo and Gumia inspired the Santhal men and women which led to an anticipation of a revival of the Santhal movement backed by the Congress in February 1935 with the passing of a resolution requesting government to remit rents in consideration of the low agricultural prices. But the resolution did not mention any follow-up action.[61]

One of the greatest incidents in the Chota Nagpur region's history was the holding of the Congress session at Ramgarh in Hazaribagh district in 1940. A large number of Adivasis including Tana Bhagats, followers of the Sanatan Adivasi Mahasabha and Momins (largest Muslim community in Chota Nagpur) and others attended the Congress session. Some of the Adivasis acted as volunteers of the Congress. The main gate at the venue of the session was named after Birsa, leader of the Adivasi uprising 40 years ago. Stories of his life were also written and published in the souvenir. The Adivasis were attracted to the Congress movement in a big way.[62]

It is interesting to note that the Tana Bhagats adopted the Gandhian ideology of vegetarianism and severe austerity to strengthen their fight against the non-tribal landlords. But at the same time, they were also keen to produce their own brand of culture and modernity. Thus, Vinita Damodaran has rightly observed,

> It can be argued that the movement's appropriation of the symbols of the national movement helped promote a feeling of solidarity with a wider struggle against an oppressor state. Gandhi was also understood in terms of the people's own religious consciousness. The Chota Nagpuri world was filled with divine and semi-divine beings, and Gandhi was considered a divine force of this type, with powers to mediate between the local communities and nature.[63]

So, the Tana Bhagat movement was a spirited protest against the prevailing social order. To quote Sachchidananda, their 'simplicity became a value all the more because of the impact of the social movement under the leadership of Mahatma Gandhi'.[64]

Did the Tanas recede to the background because their movement had chalked for itself a trail beyond that of Congress politics? Or, was their faith in the efficacy of the 'Gandhi Raj' somewhat shattered? According to Sangeeta Dasgupta, the paths of the Congress and the Tanas had crossed, moments had been shared, a history was enacted together and separately—and yet the cherished dream of *swaraj* remained undelivered. The Tanas withdrew, and, except for stray incidents reported in 1942, government reports are silent on their participation. Tanas spread their messages in Gandhi's name in order to ensure their objectives and interpreted the Gandhi Raj in many different ways, but expressing in the name of Gandhi their demands, dreams and aspirations. In Tana perception, both Jatra and Gandhi expressed God's spirit in human flesh; their making reflected the ways through which the Tana Bhagats related to the divine world and to their everyday world.[65]

SAPHA HOR MOVEMENT OF SANTHALS

Another type of messianic movement was called the Kherwar or Safahor (pure men) movement, since *kherwar* (villager) was the original name of the Santhal. Its aim was the return of the Santhal to their original culture and religion. It was announced that their present oppression was a divine punishment for abandoning the worship of God and for venerating the spirits. Deliverance could come only through a radical change of heart.[66]

The word *kherwar* derives from the word *khair* which means man. *Kherwar* is an ancient term of the Santhals. To them Kherwar movement denotes adoption from the dominant Hindu culture for the betterment of their own. They truly believed in the golden past and dreamt of a Santhal Raj. Though the Santhal movement was brutally suppressed in 1856, the desire for a separate Santhal Raj was not done away with from the Santhals' mind. So, the movement was continued again and again in 1860, 1871, 1874 (under the leadership of Bhagirath Manjhi) and in 1880 (under the leadership of Dubia Gossain). In all these, movements, the Hindu element was getting more and more prominent. Later on when the Census Reports of 1911 and 1921 were revealed, it was found that the idea of Kherwarism did not die down but instead had prospered. The Kherwar movement split into three sects—the Sapha Hor, Samra and Babajiu.

Bangam Manjhi of Hazaribagh with the assistance of Opan Manjhi, started another reform movement among the Santhals of Gumia on the line of Dubia Gossain during the Gandhian Civil Disobedience movement. He termed the movement as Gandhi *ulghulan*. He stressed on the use of *khadi* and a purification drive. Many Gandhian leaders were attracted by his movement who worked hard among the tribals to channellize the movement on the Gandhian line. If Bangam Manjhi symbolized the revivalist trends in the Santhal culture, then Opan Manjhi merged it with the Congress as well as Gandhian ideology. Top Congress leaders like Vallabhbhai Patel and Rajendra Prasad were invited in their meeting at Gumia. Both the leaders, Bangam and Opan, were arrested and ruled to rigorous punishments.[67] After that the flames of Kherwarism led to the outbreak of the Sapha Hor (clean Santhal) movement in 1939.

The Sapha Hors form a reformed section of the Santhals and Paharias. The process of Sanskritization or Hinduization was completed in the Sapha Hors. They vowed to lead a purified life, abstaining from alcohol, meat, animal sacrifice and indulged in planting *tulsi* trees, chanting the name of Ram, and so on. Monotheism, wearing sacred thread and a sandal paste mark on the forehead—all are the distinctive rituals in Vaishnavism. Therefore, the cultural revitalization movement among the Santhals involved rejection of the vital aspects of the Santhal tradition, and a sharp break with the old Santhal lifestyle and culture. One of the striking evidences of Vaishnava cult on this religious revitalization movement was that caste system of Hinduism had no place in the Adivasi reform agenda.[68]

Tanika Sarkar has recorded the forgotten history of Jitu Santhal who in 1924, emerged as the leader of a local anti-landlord movement among the Santhal sharecroppers in Malda. The creation of the district of Malda was effected by taking parts of Purnea, Dinajpur and Rajshahi and later included in Bhagalpur Division. He had also come in contact with the local Swarajists (Indian nationalists/Gandhians) and had visited Faridpur Congress session. By 1926, he had been converted to Hinduism by a Swarajist leader. In 1928, he conducted a crop looting movement and in 1932 he led a large band of Santhals to occupy the historic Adina mosque at Pandua and resisted the colonial police for some time until they killed him. For the colonial government, the linkup between a grass-roots local Adivasi leader and the Congress organization was very worrisome. Jitu and Arjun Santhal are referred as *sannyasi baba.* Jitu represented the local face of the Congress, Hinduizing national populism that was particularly active in Bihar/Bengal regions. On 3 December 1926 Jitu along with his followers occupied the ruins of the mosque and proclaimed himself as Gandhi, and gave *darshana* (sight) to his followers, sitting at the spinning wheel in a Gandhian fashion. He proclaimed that *ram-rajya* (rule of God) had arrived. This was the first time that Jitu had invoked Gandhi's name. But by then, links with Gandhians and Santhals were already established.

In 1927, Jitu declared complete Swaraj. Tanika Sarkar has further stated that the greater the distance between the mainstream Gandhian movement and the subaltern one, the more likely it would be that plural and diverse groups would associate, in a protean manner, with Gandhi's name. There was a sudden inflation of horizon, in the form of Gandhi's *ram-rajya* and Adivasi Raj (or Jitu's *desh*), that made Jitu a representation of Gandhi, who regarded the colonial state as their last enemy and wanted to reconcile both the spaces.[69] But the fact is that whereas Gandhi employed an asymmetrical resistance by non-violence, the pattern adopted by Jitu was evidently a symmetrical one. Later, although Jitu attempted at taking recourse to condign power against condign power, he was vanquished by a superior instrument wielding more power.[70]

In 1931, Jitu started collecting subscriptions from people of the locality ostensibly to establish the Gandhi Bank. Subsequent inquiries indicated that Jitu was collecting money to procure and distribute *charkhas* (spinning wheels) to the tribals. This was in pursuance to the call given by Gandhi to take to the *charkha.* Jitu himself had started wearing *khadi* by that time. The collection went in the name of Gandhi and the prospect of getting interest-free loan was a lure to the cultivators. In effect, the programme was a necessity for the tribal leadership to keep the flame of resilience alive.[71]

Calcutta's Hindu Mission, leaders of Forward Block and many other nationalist leaders were engaged in carrying on political, social and spiritual activities among the Santhals of Chota Nagpur. The Sapha Hors were disheartened due to various reasons, chiefly socio-economic. With the gradual tightening grip of the national movement among the tribals, they also took part in the Quit India movement of 1942 for the eradication of socio-economic evils. Their adherence to Hinduism and abhorrence for Christianity gave birth to a constant hatred against the British and a constant urge for self-rule. According to Dhiren Baske, the Adivasis of Bihar and Chota Nagpur had the opportunity to work with the Forward Block and Congress leaders. These two all-India organizations had their district level centres and many members joined from Chota Nagpur and Santhal Parganas. The most important factor had been good roads and better connectivity with the towns.[72]

On 25 August 1942 a group of people comprised mostly by the Sapha Hor Santhals and Paharias under the leadership of P.C. Patnaik and Shri Krishna Prasad, set fire to Dak Bunglow and the Forest Guard's quarters at Alubera and later Dumarchi, which caused immense damages. On 30 August, under the leadership of Lal Hembrom, they planned further destruction of bridges, culverts, telegraph lines, etc. The Sapha Hor Santhals 'inspired by revolutionaries from Bihar and Bengal, joined not only the demonstrators but committed many acts of violence. They burnt police stations and government houses and many liquor shops, destroyed bridges and roads, severed telegraph lines and tampered with railway lines. For these acts of sabotage many Sapha Hors had to go to jail'.[73] During an attempt to burn down liquor shops at Palasai in Rajbandh, the Sapha Hors confronted with the military force which opened fire, killed some of them and injured many. The repression operation on the part of the British became more brutal; several were arrested and awarded rigorous punishments. The confrontation of the Sapha Hors with the police continued till the end of 1943.[74]

The freedom movement, especially the propaganda of the Congress among the Adivasis in the 1930s and 1940s, aroused sky-high expectations among the Kherwars that their oppression would soon to be ended and their land and forest rights were going to be restored. But after Independence, the Kherwars got very little relief in the form of the abolition of *zamindari* system and protected forests. They felt betrayed and launched a forest *satyagraha* under a Bhagat party during the mid 1950s. In this forest movement the Kherwars articulated some new-fangled ideas.

> Mahatma Gandhi had told us, . . . cultivate barren lands, produce cotton, spin the charkha, manufacture clothes, wear them and beat drums. But where is the Kisan Raj? How can we eat unless we cultivate and grow food. You should shout slogans so that they may reach Delhi. We feel that the Britishers have not gone as yet. We think the Zamindari is as it was before. . . .
>
> Gandhiji had told us, . . . tillers will be owners of land. But we are laboring hard and dying and others are merry making. Big persons have snatched away our claims. Why should they snatch our lands? . . . We do not accept this Government. We will establish our own Bharat Raj.[75]

These forest *satyagrahas*, however, failed to achieve its goals, which elude them to this day.

HARIBABA MOVEMENT OF THE HOS

Kolhan, in Singhbhum district, was once described by the British administrators as the 'Tibet of Chota Nagpur' because of its total inaccessibility to outsiders.[76] When the British annexed Kolhan the Ho tribals were peacefully settled down. According to Sanjukta Das Gupta, except the Revolt of 1857, where a small section of the Hos participated, there were no such well-organized movement launched by the Hos unlike the Tana Bhagat movement of the Oraons, the Sapha Hor movement of the Santhals or the *ulghulan* of Birsa Munda.[77] In 1907, a religious reform movement spread among a section of the Hos, called as the Satya Dharam or the Punya Dharam movement. The followers of this movement gave up drinking of rice beer, traditional dancing and other customs and became vegetarians. By 1918 the adherents numbered around 300.[78] Not only in the field of religion, social customs of the Adivasis were also under the wave of reform movements led essentially by the educated middle-class Hos. Therefore, many of the social customs, like drinking, dancing, sexual behaviour and the like, which were regarded as degenerating, became the targets of the Hindus.

By August 1921, the Non-Cooperation movement had acquired a strong hold amongst the Hos. The Hos even called themselves 'chelas' of Gandhi'.[79] They danced about shouting 'Mahatma Gandhi ki jai'. Phulchand Dusadh, an influential person from Chittimitti, showed the villagers picture of Mahatma Gandhi and Kasturba Gandhi and told them that Gandhi was their Raja. He even distributed pamphlets and pictures of Gandhi and Bharat Mata to the villagers. He asked the people to obey Gandhi's orders.[80] He said:

> If the people do not obey Gandhi's orders *rakshasas* and devils will come and eat them, people will get no food or drink, worms will eat them, they will become lame. . . . People should not take any flesh. The English are leaving the country and the few Englishmen who are left behind, are hiding in Chaibasa and will run away in three or four months' time. 40 crore of Habsi, who are the soldiers of Gandhi, will come to Chaibasa and fight with the sahibs. The sahibs will run away to their own country. All the pupils are leaving the Zila and Mission schools in Chaibasa. Oriya language will be spoken in the Kolhan. New schools will be constructed with the order of Gandhi and the government schools will be abolished. No school fees should be paid. The *cutcheries* should be closed. In Gandhi's Raj, no rents will be paid. There will be only a poll tax of two pieces per head, of which one piece will go to the Manki and the other piece to the Munda.[81]

The special emphasis on temperance in order to purify tribal life was partly influenced by the Gandhian movement and became more vivid during the Haribaba movement, a religious movement of 1930-2. Haribaba movement also bore a political message which was considerably shaped by the Gandhian plan of action. The image of Gandhi in the Adivasi thought had a crucial role in creating the radical political temper of the Hos. For the Hos, Gandhi was the symbol of an alternative social and political order to the British

Raj. In September 1923, Gandhi came on a tour of the tribal region where he was impressed with Tana and Birsaite Bhagats, 'the colony of bhaktas, who believed in khaddar and nearly four hundred of them plied their charkhas most assiduously and sang their *bhajans* in chorus'[82] as he described them. He exercised the tribal's imagination. The Mundas did not fail to establish the link between Gandhi and their culture hero, Birsa. The Mahatma crept into the gamut of the tribal bhagats' prayers and mantras. New words were in the air: Gandhi Raj, non-payment of taxes etc. The tribals seized upon the new idioms to express their urge for freedom, equality and status.[83]

After the failure of the Non-Cooperation movement, Gandhi's constructive programme became the sole objective to pursue. The constructive programmes were quite popular in Chota Nagpur. In 1924 when Gandhi was released from jail because of his deteriorating health condition, C.F. Andrews requested him to come to Jamsedpur where he was leading a labour union. Later Gandhi persuaded the Tatas to recognize the labour union. In 1929, All India Trade Union Congress Session was held at Jharia. In 1925 Gandhi visited Jamsedpur along with Dr Rajendra Prasad and from there he went to Chaibasa, the Ho heartland.[84] The Hos styled themselves as the disciples of Gandhi and used to recite *Angrez Bahadur Noy* (No More British) *Gandhi Mahto Ki Jai* (Victory to Gandhi Mahto) and thus promoted Gandhi as a tribal functionary. At the same time it is also true that Gandhi's temperance movement became popular among the Hos because it coincided with their own reform programme. But before that, during Gandhian Non-Cooperation and Civil Disobedience movement in 1920s and 1930s, Congress was quite actively propagating the ideology of non-violence among the Hos. They actively took part in the forest *satyagraha*[85] and no-tax campaign at the local weekly markets by chanting 'Gandhi ki jai'.[86] Hos started considering Gandhi Raj as an alternative to the British Raj.

Towards the end of 1928 or the beginning of 1929, one Bonga Manjhi of Horobera (Hazaribagh) proclaimed himself a religious teacher, a *chela* of Gandhi, and exhorted his people to eschew meat and alcohol and wear a sacred thread like the Hindus: he predicted that Gandhi Raj would replace the British Raj. This brand of indigenous movement (bongaism) spread, and a large number of Santhals were converted to the new religion. A political dimension emerged: they refused to pay *chowkidari* tax, and displayed and danced under the Congress flag. Manjhi was arrested on 4 July 1930 on the charge of inciting people against the British government, which, according to him, caused them misery and deprived them of their means of subsistence. The Raj was doomed, and he declared in a typical Birsaite vein, the bullets of the soldiers would be harmless like water, and Gandhi Raj would bring ease and comfort. He was convicted and later released in March-April 1931. This was a setback to the movement, but the Santhals continued to wear the sacred thread and became ardent supporters of the Congress in Hazaribagh in the 1930s.[87]

In the early 1930s, a major religious reform movement began among the Hos. The movement was led by one Duka Ho, who called himself as Haribaba. In spite of being primarily a religious movement, Haribaba also had a political motive. Haribaba movement swept through northern parts of Singhbhum and the whole of the Ranchi district. Though originally he hailed from Siriapos village in Seraikela estate, Haribaba erected his *ashram* in the forest at Jamrogara, near Chitpil which was located twelve miles north-west of Chakradharpur. The principal object of the movement was to purify Ho culture by eliminating all alien elements from its society, especially Hindus. The Hos realized that their gods are not responding to their call and for some reason they were displeased.[88] So, their religion required cleansing, purification and reform. The movement was thus against the evil practices of the Hos themselves, for example, witchcraft, black magic, blind faith on the *bongas* or malevolent spirits, etc.[89] Everything suspected of being *bonga* was discarded. The Haribabaites worshipped Hanuman and wore the sacred thread. Binay Bhushan Chaudhuri has noted one significant difference between the Birsa *ulghulan* and the Haribaba movement. According to him, Birsa ignored the *sarna* (sacred grove), the traditional mode of worship. But the Haribabaites restored the *sarna* tradition. The *sarna* concept became a construct used for uniting the Adivasi groups.[90]

The Haribaba movement, like the other movements discussed here, bears a resemblance to the Gandhian Temperance movement. Taking bath in sacred water and the performance of specific rites were stressed upon to ensure absolute cleanliness. Eating beef was strictly prohibited and vegetarianism was adopted. The followers of Haribaba were instructed to worship the *tulsi* plant and wear the sacred thread (*janeu*) like the Hindus.[91] Haribaba's wife Nani Kui, widely known as Harima, used to sprinkle holy water (*haripani*) on the followers on payment of a nominal fee. According to a highly practised ceremony among tribes, the father in a family would collect some rice and a few pice, make them up into three packets, one each for Gandhi, Kali and Durga, leave these packets by the side of a tank for a short while, throw Gandhi's packet into water and pick up the other two remaining packets; no explanation of this strange practice could be obtained.[92]

According to Mathew Areeparampil, the Haribaba movement was an attempt at Sanskritization. He has also highlighted the impact of the Hindu caste system on the Haribabites.[93] However, B.B. Chaudhuri pointed out that, there is no specific record as to the implications of caste system that it introduced caste hierarchy among the Haribabites.[94] This cannot be denied that there was a huge amount of influence of Hindusim on the Haribaba movement, but at the same time, this is also true to say that these cultural features were used to make the Ho identity stronger and purer, because there was no attempt to transform the Hos into Hindus or to integrate them to the Hindu fourfold caste system. Instead, the movement was very much against the *dikus*, who were mostly Hindus.

In September 1925, Gandhi finally visited the Chota Nagpur region from Purulia to Hazaribagh in course of which he was introduced to the Hos at Chaibasa and the Mundas at Khunti and also met many of the prominent leaders of the Hos. The Gandhian programme had a far-reaching impact on the reform movements like the Haribaba movement among the Hos. Gandhi's tour encouraged the Adivasis and the Congress leadership in organizing *khadi* exhibitions and popularized the use of *khaddar*. In 1927, Gandhi visited Chota Nagpur again and addressed a number of public meetings. He was pleased to see the Christian missionaries running the schools. Nevertheless, he wanted the Christian missionaries to render humanitarian CLA service without the ulterior motive of proselytization.[95]

Again, vegetarianism for Gandhi was more than a fad. Yet he was not a puritanical vegetarian (like the vegans who avoid even milk and milk products and honey). His reasons for vegetarianism was that one does not kill plants in the sense animals are killed. Gandhi was vegetarian by conviction on moral and religious grounds.[96] He was a careful reader of books on the philosophy of vegetarianism which by the end of the nineteenth century had claimed its allegiance to 'true civilization'. He read *The Perfect Way in Diet* (1881) by Anna Kingsford and *The Ethics of Diet* (1881) by Howard Williams which claimed vegetarians were the pioneers of a 'true civilization'.[97] However, he wished at the same time that every Indian were a meat-eater, and he declared that he looked forward to being one openly some day and to enlisting others in the cause. He tells the reader that after reading Salt's book, *Plea for Vegetarianism*, he became a vegetarian by choice.[98] At another point in his autobiography, he writes that his views on vegetarianism were not influenced by any religious texts.[99] According to Nishikant Kolge, though he practised very strict vegetarianism, it was a personal commitment for him rather than a matter of religion or caste.[100]

After Gandhi's visit the nationalist fervour impacted the Haribaba movement which, in its next stage, gained a political overtone along with its religious purification goals. Despite Gandhi's deep rooted ideological implications on the Hos, Haribaba movement was primarily a Ho cultural movement and remained the same till the end; Gandhi's teachings had a very short-term effect on the overall Ho culture. In the beginning Duka Ho had no direct connection with the Congress activities of which Chakradharpur was an important centre. It has been recorded that on 19 July 1931 Haribaba went to the Congress headquarters for the first time. According to a police report, only after his visit he launched the no-rent campaign and the use of *khaddar*, a fact that was later rejected by Haribaba himself.[101] Initially Haribaba was so impressed by Gandhi that he proclaimed that he would organize a grand gathering where Gandhi would arrive before the Hos and replace British Raj with the Gandhi Raj. He also promised to his followers to bring back the golden past. The advent of the reign of Gandhi was celebrated with dances and feasts and chanting 'Haribol, Haribaba ki jai, Gandhi Mahato ki jai'.[102] Many Christian tribals willingly participated in the movement.[103]

Duka Ho visited Tarachand, another tribal leader, to exchange ideas. Though Tarachand asked him to keep off his sphere of influence, the two leaders were fused in popular imagination: Tarachand became a 'satellite' of Haribaba. Gandhi became a symbol of the tribals' aspirations. Through the slogans of 'Gandhi Raj' and *swaraj* and through protest actions like the non-payment of rent, the tribals expressed their aspiration to be independent. Haribaba declared that if the Hos followed his teachings and worshipped according to his instructions, they would be able to achieve *swaraj* and regain their traditional rights.[104] Haribaba also promised that a great meeting attended by himself, Tarachand and Gandhi would be held on some hill near Jamshedpur, and that the state of things as existed before the British Raj would be restored. Haribaba was one of the most intimate disciples of Gandhi: his parting message was that the reign of Gandhi had begun. According to the missionaries' reports, this happy advent was to be celebrated with dancing and feasts. But to establish it on a firm basis, the Mahatma needed 'money and prayers' while Haribaba himself required some clothes.[105]

The British authority kept a close watch on the movement. With the developing political agenda the movement was inevitably under the scanner of the British government. On the evening of 27 July 1931 Haribaba himself was arrested on charges of sedition. After Haribaba's imprisonment, his wife Nani Kui set up her own *ashram* at Nandpur near Manoharpur and preached Haribaba's spiritual purification teachings. She tried to keep the movement confined to the religious activities. According to K.S. Singh, several lesser 'Haribabas' came up to propagate the new religion. One Jojo Tamaria called himself a disciple of 'God Hari' in Chota Nagpur and preached on the lines of Duka Ho. The Deputy Commissioner of Singhbhum visited six villages in the area on 18 January 1932 and broke up the bamboo fences and huts. The Haribaba movement was declared illegal. A few Hos in Manoharpur instigated the people not to pay rent and they were arrested as were Hari Ma along with Jojo Tamaria.[106] The movement, in fact, caused great hardship to the ordinary people. The Settlement Report of 1932 mentioned that,

> Some persons have exploited the movement for their own benefit and the country has been emptied of fowls and black goats. It was explained that the fowls and black goats were primarily for offerings to the spirits of the village and as such offerings were no longer necessary it was no use keeping them. The idea caught the imagination of the people to such an extent that the local hats were for some weeks simply flooded with fowls and black goats which were sold at ridiculously low prices. People are already finding it difficult to pay for salt and other minor necessaries, many of which they used to get by the sale of fowls and goat.[107]

The political aspect of the movement was soon receded to the back burner and the religious reformatory character of it became the sole objective. Eventually, the British repression succeeded in quelling the movement and the new religion of Haribaba gradually disappeared into oblivion.

RAJ GOND MOVEMENTS OF GONDS

The Gonds did not have a tradition of militant struggle waged in defence of their right in land and forest. The Gond zamindars, however, spearheaded the 1857 rebellion in their region like the zamindars elsewhere, but the Gond peasants as a whole were not involved in any movement. From the 1940s, there have been instances of the Gond's resistance to encroachment on their rights in the forests. In the Census of 1911, L.S.S. O'Malley reports the presence of Gonds in Chota Nagpur. In Chota Nagpur, the Gonds speak Sadari, a mixture of Magahi, Bhojpuri and certain tribal dialects. The Singbhum Gonds remember fondly that their place of origin was Madhya Pradesh where they locate three landmarks, Gondwana, a large area, Gondki, a river, and Gondsila, a hill. They migrated to Singbhum in the thirties of the nineteenth century.

Most of the Gonds claim to be Rajgonds and trace relationship with the ruling chiefs of Mayurbhanj and Keonjhar in Orissa. The Dhuria Gonds are lower in status and are confined to the Dalbhum subdivision of the Singbhum district. The Gonds of Ranchi belong to two broad subdivisions, viz., Rajgond and Popa Gond. Singbhum Gonds are divided into two endogamous divisions, viz. Rajgond and Dhuria Gonds.[108]

In the pre-colonial period, the Gonds were also adversely affected by the increasing Hindu population in their territories. The tension between the Gonds and the Hindu *dikus* gave birth to severe hostility amongst them, which led to the outbreak of some messianic movements in their country. The Gond movement in Chota Nagpur was the most revolutionary in nature. Gonds of Bonai state of Chota Nagpur and contiguous of Kolhan of Singhbhum, rebelled in 1888 against an unfair rate of revenue. It can be assumed that with the growing influence of reformist movements among the other tribal communities, like Kherwars or Oraons, the wave of Hindu reformism flooded the Gond land as well. In 1929 a certain Bhausingh Rajnegi of Balaghat district began to reform them to Hinduism. In the late 1936 another Raj Gond reformer propagated similar rules of reforms. Another such movement was started in summer 1945 or 1946, which was called the Mahua Deo cult, mainly in today's Chhattisgarh, which was then a part of Chota Nagpur plateau. They all emphasized on the ritual purity, such as prohibition on beef eating, animal sacrifice and liquor consumption. Women's movement was also restricted. Initially these restrictions were obeyed by the simple Gonds, but when they found that these taboos had failed to meet their grievances, they realized that the Hindu culture was not meant for them as tribals are not vegetarian nor their women are treated like the Hindu middle-class women with *purdah.* Moreover, liquor, songs and dance had always been an integral part of their custom. Needless to say, all these movements were inspired by India's Independence movement if not Gandhian ideology of temperance and severe austerity and both of which were highly Hinduized in nature. This impact was realized later when in 1951 another Gond movement, led by Raj Mohini Devi in Surguja district, openly admitted the influence of Mahatma Gandhi and in the last days after its failure engaged itself into welfare activities. Raj Mohini Devi's reform, inspired by Gandhi, left a deep impression on the Gonds for many years.[109]

There are many versions of Raj Mohini Devi's conversion to Hinduism. One version relates that Raj Mohini went one day into the jungle to collect fruits and tubers to still her hunger. When she failed to find anything edible she felt very miserable and started weeping. She was resting on a rock when suddenly she had a vision. She saw a 'Mahatma' (saint) who consoled her and promised her that all her troubles would vanish if she started to lead a pious life. According to another story, narrated in the official Constitution of 'Bapu Dharma Adivasi Seva Mandal' under which name the movement was propagated, Raj Mohini went on 10 July 1951 to the jungle in search of edible fruits and roots. Not finding anything she laid down on a rock weeping bitterly. Then and there she received enlightenment about the life and teachings of Mahatma Gandhi! This consoled her greatly. After her enlightenment Raj Mohini sat down on the rock—today her *ashram* stands on the rock. On the way back home she went on a fast for 21 days. Her prayer was granted, rain fell, peace and prosperity returned to her people.[110]

She started preaching and advised the people to give up liquor, meat and to stop telling lies. They should follow the path of truth. In short, she asked them to follow the Hindu religion which she declared was the supreme way of life. She began to tour the neighbouring areas and on her preaching tours she went as far as Bihar and Uttar Pradesh. Wherever she went she was received with great enthusiasm and reverence. She later formed an association, legally registered as the 'Bapu Dharma Sabha Adivasi Mandal' (Association of Aboriginals following Gandhi's way of life). The aims and objectives of this society were:

1. to create the feeling of universal brotherhood;
2. to preach the principles of Mahatma Gandhi and to perform all kinds of national service;
3. to wean the tribals from eating meat and drinking liquor, to spread the idea of cleanliness, to raise their economic standard, and to lay emphasis on leading a simple and truthful life;

4. to propagate the Hindu religion, to sing Hindu hymns (*havans* and *kirtans*); and
5. to eradicate all social and communal evils. Thus her movement—once a messianic movement—gradually turned into a welfare association.[111]

Raj Mohini Devi appeared to have been influenced greatly by Gandhian ideology. Her great respect for Gandhi had percolated down even to her followers in the interior areas. The procession of the Bhagats used to start and end with the slogan 'Mahatma Gandhi ki Jai'. There was a temple dedicated to Ram in Govindpur Ashram where her followers worship during Dusserah, Magh Purnima, Ramnavami and Janmashtami. There was no statue of any god within the temple; instead, pictures of Gandhi, Vinoba Bhave and Sardar Patel were hung on the walls. The principal teachings of Raj Mohini Devi as contained in the official constitution of the Mandal are as follows:

1. Follow true religion and love God.
2. Wear *khaddar*, spun and woven by *charkha* and *kargha.*
3. Do not sell *mahua* in the market, nor ferment it in the *bhathi* (liquor distillery).
4. Liquor is the dirt of the world, abandon it.
5. Do not chew tobacco but save money (for domestic purpose).
6. Keep away from *dewar* (magico-medicine men) and cheats, get rid of the fear of ghosts and witches.
7. Take bath everyday and keep your body, mind and house clean.
8. Venerate the cow, do not afflict her.
9. Love your neighbours, becoming the children of one mother.
10. Do not kill any animal, give up eating meat and fish.
11. Follow the path of Gandhi Baba and become a real *swaraji.*
12. Birth and religion are one, keep away from cheating.
13. Do the work of the nation, society and home, maintain the honour of the group (of Bhagats).
14. Plough the land, cultivate it and worship the cow and the Goddess of wealth (Lakshmi).[112]

In the Gond region proper, a tribal organization was set up as early as in 1950 with its headquarters at Chanda, which promoted activities for the welfare of the tribals, mainly Gonds. First, Dharma Das and Lal Shyam Shah, who were influenced by the freedom movement and had participated in the rural reconstruction programme launched by Gandhi, led the movement. Hira Singh founded an organization called Adibasi Kalyan Samiti in the late 1950s. He claimed that he had stayed with Gandhi and confabulated with Nehru 'who had given him the Gond Raj'.[113]

EVALUATION

Thus, between 1944 and 1947, the activities of the Adivasis of Chota Nagpur were confined to the constructive programme of Gandhi, such as to promote *khadi* and *charkha*. When the nationalist movement was at its peak in the Gandhian era, the Adivasis of Chota Nagpur neither claimed a separate state nor fought against the Hindu outsiders as Gandhi always wanted a unified freedom struggle that would not be divided by caste, creed or religion. The Hindu *dikus* had in fact always been the close associates of Gandhi. The Adivasis, especially Santhals, in this time did not even think of establishing Santhal Raj. They fully integrated themselves with the national movement. Gandhi, thus, perhaps unknowingly, produced a communion between tribal interest and national interest.[114] Though the actions of the Adivasis were framed in terms of what was popularly regarded to be just, fair and possible, they derived and insisted on deriving the legitimacy for all their actions from the supposed orders of Gandhi. There was a popular tendency to look upon Gandhi as an alternative source of authority. Everything that was unjust, cruel and oppressive was fought against in Gandhi's name, who emerged as the symbol of their hopes and aspirations. The tribals looted bazaars, distilled 'illicit' liquor, burnt liquor shops on Gandhi's order and gave slogan in Gandhi's name. In fact, during the entire phase of the Non-Cooperation movement, it was Gandhi, and not Congress, whose name was frequently invoked. The organizational structure at the local level was not so strong. It was Gandhi who emerged as a phenomenon and an aura was getting created around him. Lots of rumours centred round Gandhi and he was elevated to a higher moral pedestal and divinity. In actuality, Gandhi emerged as an alternative power vis-à-vis the British.[115]

According to K.S. Singh, the influence of Mahatma Gandhi in the process of the mobilization of the tribals during India's Independence movement could be seen at two levels. First, Gandhi's personality and his message seemed to carry forward and deepen the process of Sanskritization started by the tribal Bhagats in the latter half of the nineteenth century. In fact, it is among the members of the Bhagat sects, already sensitized to Vaishnavism, that Gandhi made the greatest impact. Followers of Gandhi sprang up among the Bhils, Gonds and Hos. At another level, the Gandhian reconstruction programme initiated the process of politicization of the Adivasis, nurtured a generation of Adivasi leaders, and provided a common political platform for both the Adivasis and non-Adivasis, thus bringing the first into the mainstream of national politics. Evidence of tribals' participation in the local level action organized by the Congress came in from Bihar, Central Provinces and Bombay.[116] He has further stated that,

> The Bhil Bhagats, the Tana Bhagats, and the Sapha Hors among Santhals, the Haribaba movement . . . saw in the freedom movement led by Gandhiji an opportunity for the recovery of their Raj and their rights as agrarian communities which they had lost, for continuing social reforms such as temperance and purification and education, and for seeking social uplift and establishing an equation with peasant castes. Most of these Bhagat sects in their origin antedated the freedom movement. They received a fresh lease of life through Gandhiji's reconstruction programme.[117]

The participation of the Adivasis in the Gandhian movements evinces two things: first, of all, the Adivasis shared a similar kind of nationalist sentiments against colonial imperialism like the other Indians and took part in the mainstream nationalist struggle for independence. Second, they tried to utilize the time of the crisis of the British Empire for negotiating with the moneylenders, landlords, British officials and liquor shop owners. This class struggle was conducted without any instigation from outside; rather the Adivasis themselves were quite conscious about their exploitative character that was the sole reason of their poverty and indebtedness.

It is interesting to note that while the neo-literate Adivasis were demanding a separate state for the Adivasis, the Tana Bhagats, Sapha Hors and Haribabaites were constantly supporting Gandhian ideology of non-violence, non-payment of taxation, idioms of purity, temperance and vegetarianism, constructive programmes like *khadi* and *charkha*, *swaraj* or Gandhi Raj and came out as one of the strongest political force behind Indian nationalism. While Western education was a factor behind the rise of an articulate tribal leadership, its uneven diffusion combined with growing agrarian crisis, social development among Christian converts and urbanization to produce certain side effects. These effects found expression in the Tana Bhagat movement coexisting with the Chota Nagpur Unnati Samaj and a lesser known Hari Baba movement of early 1930s. The leaders of these movements addressed the impoverished semi-Hinduized tribals, whose hope for relief from their dismal condition was pinned on the millenarian powers.[118] The recourse they sought was not in the new avenues opening before them, but in self-purification with some ingredients of Vaishnavism. It is this section to whom Gandhi appealed to establish a perennial connection with the Indian National Congress from 1920.[119] The next chapter will shed light on the movement of the neo-literate Adivasis of Chota Nagpur.

NOTES

1. K.S. Singh, 'Tribal Land Organisation in Chota Nagpur and its Development', in *Proceedings of the National Seminar on Trends of Socio Economic Change in India 1871-1961*, ed. K. Choudhuri, Shimla: Indian Institute of Advance Study, 1969, pp. 547-58.
2. K.S. Singh, 'Colonial Transformation of Tribal Society in Middle India', *Economic and Political Weekly*, vol. 13, no. 30, 29 July 1978, pp. 1221-32.
3. K.S. Singh, 'Transformation of Tribal Society: Integration vs Assimilation', *Economic and Political Weekly*, vol. 17, no. 33, 14 August 1982, pp. 1318-25.
4. *Harijan*, 15 February, Quoted in the *SWMG*, Chapter 80, vol. VI, 'From the Voices of Truth', Ahmedabad: Navajivan Press, 1942, p. 38.
5. D.G. Tendulkar, *Mahatma: Life of Mohandas Karamchand Gandhi*, New Delhi: Publication Division, Government of India, new edn., vol. 7, 1962 (revised), p. 34.

6. N. Kumar, 'District Gazetteer', Ranchi, Patna: Gazetters Branch, Revenue Department, 1970, pp. 583-4.
7. Ibid., p. 584.
8. P.C. Roy Chowdhary, 'District Gazetteer', Santhal Parganas, 1965, p. 663.
9. K.S. Singh, *Birsa Munda and his Movements 1874-1901*, Delhi: Oxford University Press, 1983, p. 9.
10. K.S. Singh, *Tribal Society in India*, Delhi: Manohar, 1985, pp. 131-2.
11. S.P. Sinha, *Conflict and Tension in Tribal Society*, New Delhi: Concept Publishing Company, 1993, p. 390.
12. Nirmal Kumar Bose, *The Structure of Hindu Society*, New Delhi: Orient Longman Limited, 1996, pp. 53-4.
13. Sarat Chandra Roy, *Oraon Religion and Customs*, Delhi: Gyan Publishing House, 1999, pp. 339-50.
14. Virginius Xaxa, *State, Society and Tribes: Issues in Post-Colonial India*, New Delhi: Pearson Education India, 2008, pp. 52-3.
15. Binay Bhushan Chaudhuri, 'Revaluation of Tradition in the Ideology of the Radical Adivasi Resistance in Colonial Eastern India, 1855-1932: Part II', *Indian Historical Review*, 37 (1), 2010, pp. 39-62.
16. H. Risley, *The Tribes and Castes of Bengal*, vol. I, Kolkata: Harvard Library, Bengal Secretariat Press, 1891, pp. 91-2.
17. Sarat Chandra Roy, *Oraon Religion and Customs*, Delhi: Gyan Publishing House, 1972, Chapter VI.
18. Joseph Marianus Kujur, 'Gandhian Thought vis-à-vis Indigenous Ideology: Some Reflections for an Integral Humanism in the Third Millennium', in *The Meaning of Mahatma for the Millennium*, ed. Kuruvilla Pandikattu, Washington DC: The Council for Research in Values and Philosophy, 2001, pp. 83-93.
19. K.S. Singh, op. cit., pp. 157-8.
20. 'Judgement in the Oraon Case', Proceedings No. 280-1, June 1916, p. 3.
21. An official report quoted by K.K. Datta, *History of the Freedom Movement in Bihar*, vol. I, Patna, 1957, p. 335.
22. Stephen Fuchs, 'Messianic Movements in Primitive India', *Asian Folklore Studies*, vol. 24, no. 1, 1965, pp. 11-62.
23. Sangeeta Dasgupta, 'Constructing a Tribe: A Case Study of the Oraons and the Tana Bhagats in Late Nineteenth and Early Twentieth Centuries', in *Changing Tribal Life: A Socio-Philosophical Perspective*, ed. Padmaja Sen, New Delhi: Concept Publishing, 2003, pp. 15-30.
24. Phillip Ekka, 'Revivalist Movements among the Tribals of Chota Nagpur', in *Tribal Situation in India*, ed. K.S. Singh, Shimla: Indian Institute of Advanced Studies, 1972, p. 426.

25. R.O. Dhan, 'The Problems of the Tana Bhagats of Ranchi District', *Bulletin of Bihar Tribal Welfare Research Institute*, Ranchi, vol. 2, 1960, pp. 136-8.
26. Letter dated 15 October 1919 from Commissioner of Chota Nagpur to Government of Bihar, Ranchi. Cited in S.P. Sinha, *Conflict and Tension in Tribal Society*, op. cit., pp. 261-2.
27. Binay Bhushan Chaudhuri, 'Ideology and Organization of Millenarian Protest Movements in the Tribal World of Colonial Eastern India', in *Organizational and Institutional Aspects of Indian Religious Movements*, ed. J.T.O'Connell, Shimla: Indian Institute of Advanced Study, 1999, pp. 152-79.
28. R.O. Dhan, op cit., p. 169.
29. Bihar and Orissa Government, Police Department, Abstract of Intelligence, vol. V, Palamau, 11 April 1916; Bihar and Orissa Government, Police Department, Abstract of Intelligence, vol. V, Palamau, 15 May 1916.
30. Binay Bhushan Chaudhuri, 'Revaluation of Tradition in the Ideology of the Radical Adivasi Resistance in Colonial Eastern India, 1855-1932': Part I, *Indian Historical Review*, 36(2), 2009, pp. 273-305.
31. Bihar and Orissa Political Special File no. 50/21, 'Note by the Chaukidari Magistrate of Ranchi Showing the Attitude of the Tana Bhagats, Commissioner, Ranchi, to Chief Secretary, 1 April 1921'.
32. Fortnightly Report of Bihar and Orissa for the second half of January 1921, Government of India, Home Department (Political), File no. 42/1921, NAI.
33. Bihar and Orissa Political Special File Nos. 50/1921, 51/1921 and 219/1921.
34. Quoted in K.K. Datta, *Writings and Speeches of Gandhiji Relating to Bihar from 1927 to 1947*, published by the Government of Bihar, Patna, March, 1967, pp. 181-2
35. J. Reid, *Final Report on the Survey and Settlement Operations in the District of Ranchi, 1902-10*, Patna; File no. 86 of 1919, Political Department, *Special Section*, Government of Bihar and Orissa; File no. 313 of 1920, Political Department, Government of Bihar and Orissa; File no. 75 of 1921, Political Department, *Special Section*, Government of Bihar and Orissa, 1926.
36. Report of the Commissioner of Chota Nagpur, 12 May 1921, Political/Special/1921, cited in Vinita Damodaran, 'Indigenous Forest Rights, Discourses, and Resistance in Chota Nagpur, 1860-2002', in *Ecological Nationalisms: Nature, Livelihoods, and Identities in South Asia*, ed. Gunnel Cederlof and K. Sivaramakrishnan, Delhi: Permanent Black, 2005, pp. 115-50.

37. Binay Bhushan Chaudhuri, 'The Story of a Tribal Revolt in the Bengal Presidency: The Religion and Politics of the Oraons: 1900-26', in *Aspects of Socio-Economic Changes and Political Awakening in Bengal: From the Eighteenth Century to Independence*, ed. Adhir Chakravarti, Calcutta: State Archives of West Bengal, Education Department, Government of West Bengal, 1989, pp. 30-57.
38. Emma Tarlo, *Clothing Matters, Dress and Identity in India*, New Delhi: Penguin, 1996, p. 100.
39. Sangeeta Dasgupta, 'Reordering a World: The Tana Bhagat Movement, 1914-19', *Studies in History*, 15: 1, 1999, pp. 1-41.
40. S.P. Sinha, B.N. Sahay and B.K. Srivastava, 'Gandhi's Impact on Tribals of Chota Nagpur 1920-30', *Gandhi and the Social Sciences*, 1970, pp. 151-6.
41. Sachchidananda, 'The Bhagat Movements in Chota Nagpur', in *Indian Movements: Some Aspects of Dissent, Protest and Reform*, ed. S.C. Malik, Shimla: Indian Institute of Advanced Study, 1978, pp. 159-90.
42. Bihar and Orissa Political Special File no. 5011921, 'From Deputy Commissioner, Ranchi, to Commissioner, 3 February 1921'.
43. K.K. Dutta, *History of Freedom Movement in Bihar*, Patna: Government of Bihar, 1957, p. 336.
44. S.P. Sinha, B.N. Sahay and B.K. Srivastava, op. cit., pp. 151-6.
45. K.K. Dutta, *History of Freedom Movement in Bihar*, Patna: Government of Bihar, 1957, p. 394.
46. Fisher, Louis, *The Life of Mahatma,* UK: Granada Publishing, 1982, p. 326.
47. Lata Singh, *Popular Translations of Nationalism Bihar, 1920-22*, New Delhi: Primus, 2012, pp. 128-9.
48. Judith Brown, *Gandhi's Rise to Power: Indian Politics 1915-22*, London: Cambridge University Press, 1972, pp. 315-16.
49. Fortnightly Reports of Bihar and Orissa for the first half of May 1921, Government of India, Home Department (Political), File nos. 63/June/1921, NAI.
50. Bihar and Orissa Political Special File no. 478/1921.
51. Fortnightly Reports of Bihar and Orissa for February and March 1921, Government of India, Home Department (Political), File nos. 42/1921, 43/1921, 65/1921 and 45/1921, NAI.
52. Bihar and Orissa Political Special File no. 153/1921.
53. Fortnightly Reports of Bihar and Orissa for the first half of October 1921, Govt. of India, Home Department (Political), File nos. 18, October 1921, NAI.
54. Fortnightly Reports of Bihar and Orissa for the second half of April 1921,

Government of India, Home Department (Political), File nos. 13, June 1921, NAI.

55. *Bihar and Orissa Annual Administration Report 1921*, Patna: The Bihar and Orissa Secretariat Book Depot, pp. 148-9.
56. R. Prasad, *Mahatma Gandhi in Bihar*, Bombay: Prabhat Prakashan, 1949, p. 131.
57. For detail see, J.C. Jha, 'The Tribals of Bihar and the Indian Freedom Movement', *Indian Historical Review*, vol. XII, no. 1-2, 1986, pp. 291-2; S.P. Sinha *Conflict and Tension in Tribal Society*, op. cit., p. 230; K.K. Dutta, *History of Freedom Movement in Bihar*, vol. II, Published by Government of Bihar, 1957, p. 198.
58. J.C. Jha, 'The Tribals of Bihar and the Indian Freedom Movement', *IHR*. vol. XII, no. 1-2, 1986, p. 62.
59. Political Department, special section, K.W. (DIG-CID), Hazaribagh, 30 April 1934, quoted in Papiya Ghosh, *The Civil Disobedience Movement in Bihar (1930-1934)*, New Delhi, 2008, p. 216.
60. Police Department, Special Section, Confidential, No. 104C, Ranchi, 4 May 1934.
61. P.K. Shukla, 'The Adivasi Peasantry of Chota Nagpur and the Nationalist Response (1920-1940s)', *Social Scientist*, vol. 39, no. 7/8, July-August 2011, pp. 55-64.
62. J.C. Jha, 'The Tribals of Bihar and the Indian Freedom Movement', *IHR*. vol. XII. no. 1-2, p. 62, cited in 'Political Consciousness in Jharkhand, 1900-1947' by L.N. Rana, *Proceedings of the Indian History Congress*, 1996, vol. 57 (1996), 1986, pp. 467-84.
63. Vinita Damodaran, 'Indigenous Forest Rights, Discourses, and Resistance in Chota Nagpur, 1860-2002', in *Ecological Nationalisms: Nature, Livelihoods, and Identities in South Asia*, ed. Gunnel Cederlof and K. Sivaramakrishnan, Delhi: Permanent Black, 2005, pp. 115-50.
64. Sachchidananda, 'The Bhagat Movements in Chota Nagpur', in *Indian Movements: Some Aspects of Dissent, Protest and Reform*, ed. S.C. Malik, Shimla: Indian Institute of Advanced Study, 1978, pp. 159-90.
65. Sangeeta Dasgupta, 'Mapping Histories: Many Narratives of Tana Pasts', *The Indian Economic and Social History Review*, 53(1), 2016, pp. 99-129.
66. Stephen Fuchs, 'Messianic Movements in Primitive India', *Asian Folklore Studies*, vol. 24, no. 1, 1965, pp. 11-62.
67. S.P. Sinha, *Conflict and Tension in Tribal Society*, New Delhi: Concept Publishing, 1993, pp. 217-22.
68. Binay Bhushan Chaudhuri, 'Revaluation of Tradition in the Ideology of the Radical Adivasi Resistance in Colonial Eastern India, 1855-1932: Part II', *Indian Historical Review*, 37 (1), 2010, pp. 39-62

69. Tanika Sarkar, 'Rebellion as Modern Self Fashioning: A Santhal Movement in Colonial Bengal', in *The Politics of Belonging in India: Becoming Adivasi*, ed. Daniel J. Rycroft and Sangeeta Dasgupta, New York: Routledge, 2011, pp. 65-81.
70. A.B. Chaudhuri, *State Formation among Tribals: A Quest for Santhal Identity*, New Delhi: Gyan Publishing House, 2013, p. 132.
71. Ibid., pp. 140-3.
72. Dhiren Baske, *Gana Andolane Santhal Samaj*, Calcutta: Maitreyi Prakasani, 1996, p. 22.
73. Stephen Fuchs, *Rebellious Prophets: A Study of Messianic Movements in India*, Bombay: Asia Publishing House, 1965, p. 58.
74. S.P. Sinha, *Conflict and Tension in Tribal Society*, op. cit., pp. 217-22.
75. K.S. Singh, 'A Forest Satyagraha', in *Tribal Movements in India*, vol. II, ed. K.S. Singh, New Delhi: Manohar, 2015, pp. 187-95.
76. C.P. Singh, *The Ho Tribes of Singhbhum*, New Delhi: Classical, 1978, p. 11.
77. Sanjukta Das Gupta, *Adivasis and the Raj*, New Delhi: Orient Blackswan, 2011, p. 313.
78. D.M. Panna, 'Note on the Hos', in A.D. Tuckey, *Final Report on the Re-settlement of the Kolhan Government Estate in the District of Singhbhum*, 1920, p. 128.
79. J.C. Jha, 'The Bihar Tribal and the Indian National Movement', in *Bihar: Past and Present*, ed. P.N. Ojha, Patna: Kashi Prasad Jayaswal, Research Institute, 1987, p. 225.
80. Bihar and Orissa Political Special File no. 478/1921, 'From District Magistrate, Singhbhum, to Lyall, Commissioner of the Chota Nagpur Division, 2 September 1921'.
81. Ibid.
82. Quoted in K.K. Dutta, *History of the Freedom Movement in Bihar*, vol. I, 1957, pp. 473-6.
83. K.S. Singh, 'Haribaba and his Movement: Changes in Chota Nagpur', *Tribal Transformation in India*, vol. III [Ethnopolitics and Identity Crisis], in *Tribal Studies of India Series*, ed. Buddhadeb Chaudhuri, New Delhi: Inter India Publications, 1992, pp. 344-57.
84. Shushil Rajgarhia, *The Tribal Soldiers of Mahatma Gandhi 1920-1947*, New Delhi: Satyam Publishing House, 2010, p. 168.
85. Annual Progress Report tin Forest Administration of the Province of Bihar and Orissa, 1921-2, Ch. 2, para. 13, Go&O Rev. (Forest) Progs., no 1-7, November 1922, OIOC, p. 11152.
86. Lewis to Lyall, Commissioner of Chota Nagpur, demi-official letter no. 149—TC, 17 August 1921, para 2, Government of Bihar & Orissa, Pol. (Special) Progs, File no. 465, 1921, BSA.

87. K.S. Singh, 'Haribaba and his Movement: Changes in Chota Nagpur', op. cit., pp. 344-57.
88. Deputy Commissioner of Singhbhum has commented about this in his report, R.P. Ward to Tuckey, Confidential D.O. No 132/C, 30 July 1931, para. 8, GoB&O, Pol. (Special) Department, File no. 57, 1931, BSA.
89. Areeparampil Mathew, 'Socio-cultural and Religious Movements among the Ho Tribals of Singhbhum District of Bihar', in *Continuity and Change in Tribal Society*, ed. Mrinai Miri, Shimla: Indian Institute of Advanced Studies, 1993, p. 399.
90. Binay Bhushan Chaudhuri, 'Revaluation of Tradition: Part II', *Indian Historical Review*, 37 (1), 2010, pp. 39-62.
91. L.O. Skrefsrud, 'The Santhal Parganas', *The Englishman*, 16 June 1932.
92. K.S. Singh, 'Haribaba and his Movement: Changes in Chota Nagpur', op. cit., pp. 344-57.
93. Areeparampil Mathew, op. cit., p. 402.
94. B.B. Chaudhuri, 'Society and Culture of the Tribal World in Colonial Eastern India: Reconsidering the Notion of Hinduisation of Tribes', in *Perspectives on Indian Society and History: A Critique,* ed. Hetukar Jha, New Delhi: Manohar, 2002, p. 65.
95. K.K. Datta, ed., *The Writings and Speeches of Mahatma Gandhi in Bihar: 1917-47*, Patna: Government of Bihar, 1960, p. 182.
96. T.N. Khoshoo and John S. Moolakkattu, *Mahatma Gandhi and the Environment: Analysing Gandhian Environmental Thought*, New Delhi: Teri, 2017, p. 28.
97. Anthony Parel, ed., *Gandhi: Hind Swaraj and Other Writings*, Cambridge: Cambridge University Press, 2009, p. xlvi.
98. M.K. Gandhi, *An Autobiography or the Story of My Experiments with Truth*, tr. Mahadev Desai, London: Penguin Classics, 2001, p. 59.
99. Ibid., p. 297.
100. Nishikant Kolge, 'Was Gandhi a "Champion of the Caste System"? Reflections on His Practices', *Economic and Political Weekly*, vol. LII, no. 13, 1 April 2017, pp. 42-50.
101. R.P. Ward to Tuckey, Confidential D.O. No 132/C, 30 July 1931, para. 4, GoB&O, Pol. (Special) Department, File no. 57, 1931, BSA.
102. G. Vanhoutta, 'Haribaba', Chota Nagpur Mission Letter, no. 11, November 1931, pp. 236-9.
103. C. Vanhoutta, op. cit., pp. 238-9.
104. Areeparampil, Mathew 'Socio-Cultural and Religious Movements', op. cit., 1993, pp. 396-436.
105. K.S. Singh, 'Haribaba and his Movement: Changes in Chota Nagpur', op. cit., 1992, pp. 344-57.

106. K.S. Singh, 'The Haribaba Movement in Chota Nagpur 1931-2', *Journal of Bihar Research Society*, vol. XLIX, pts. I & IV, 1963, pp. 284-96.
107. F.E.A. Taylor, *Final Report on the Revisions: Settlement of Porahat Estate, District Singhbhum 1928-32*, Bihar, Patna: Supt. Govt. Print, 1938, p. 31.
108. Sachchidananda, 'Tribe-Caste Continuum: A Case Study of the Gond in Bihar', *Anthropos, Bd. 65, H. 5./6.*, 1970, pp. 973-97.
109. William Ekka, 'Reform Movement of Raj Mohini Devi', ASI Seminar, cited in 'Transformation of Tribal Society: Integration vs. Assimilation', by K.S. Singh, *Economic and Political Weekly*, vol. 17, no. 34, 21 August 1982, pp. 1376-84.
110. S.L. Kalia, 'The Raj Mohini Devi Movement in Surguja', *Bulletin of the Tribal Research Institute*, Chhindwara, vol. 2, no. 1, June, 1962, pp. 49-61.
111. Stephen Fuchs, 'Messianic Movements in Primitive India', *Asian Folklore Studies*, vol. 24, no. 1, 1965, pp. 11-62.
112. William Ekka, 'Reform Movement of Raj Mohini Devi', *Tribal Movements in India*, vol. II, ed. K.S. Singh, New Delhi: Manohar, 2015, pp. 209-21.
113. K.S. Singh, 'The Gond Movements', *Tribal Movements in India*, vol. II, ed. K.S. Singh, New Delhi: Manohar, 2015, pp. 177-85.
114. Shushil Rajgarhis, *The Tribal Soldiers of Mahatma Gandhi 1920-1947*, New Delhi: Satyam Publishing House, 2010, pp. 192-3.
115. Lata Singh, *Popular Translations of Nationalism Bihar, 1920-1922*, New Delhi: Primus, 2012, pp. 193, 235-6.
116. K.S. Singh, 'From Ethnicity to Regionalism: A Study, in Tribal Politics and Movements in Chota Nagpur from 1900 to 1975', in *Dissent, Protest and Reform in Indian Civilisation*, ed. S.C. Malik, Shimla: Indian Institute of Advanced Study, 1977.
117. K.S. Singh, 'The Freedom Movement and Tribal Sub-movements 1920-1947', in *Essays in Modern Indian History*, ed. B.R. Nanda, New Delhi: Oxford University Press, 1980, p. 149.
118. Letter from L. Van Hoeck, Rector, Manresa House, Ranchi to C. Van den Driessche dated Ranchi 17 August 1916, *Correspondence on the Tana Bhagat Movement*; 'Hari-Baba', *The Chota Nagpur Mission Letter*, November 1931, pp. 236-7.
119. S.P. Sinha, 'Gandhi's Impact on the Tribals of Chota Nagpur 1920-30', in *Gandhi and Social Sciences*, L.P. Vidyarthi et al., op. cit., 1970, pp. 147-63.

CHAPTER 3

Conflicting Forces behind the Jharkhand Movement: Gandhi and Jaipal Singh

The Adivasis endorsed nationalist political ideology preached by Gandhi and participated in the nationalist struggle headed by him, but they did not forget their own demands. *Swaraj* for them not only meant freedom from foreign yoke, it was also from the oppression of the *dikus*, moneylenders and zamindars. Once Victor Das stated that, the main inspirations behind the Jharkhand movement were the Tana Bhagat movement among the Oraons during First World War, the Kherwar uprising among the Santhals in 1871 and the Birsa *ulghulan* among the Mundas during 1895-1900 in Bihar. All these movements were millenarian and prophetic in nature and sought the attainment of Adivasi independence through regaining of ancestral lands grabbed by immigrant non-Adivasi landlords. The present Jharkhand movement too may be regarded in the same light.[1] N. Datta-Mazumdar attributed this growth of new political consciousness among the tribals to the rising national movement of that period.[2] The leaders of these reform movements later took to political activities and became the spokesmen of their communities.[3]

Christian missionaries came with the mission of civilizing the people of India along with the colonizers, the British. On the one hand, they brought education, health facilities, jobs and economic well-being, but on the other, the activities of religious conversion gave rise to discontent at every corner of the society. Needless to say, this was one of the principal reasons of the Santhal *hul* in 1855. The Christian missionaries also started taking interest in the land issues of the tribals after Munda *ulghulan* of 1900 and later contributed in raising political consciousness in Chota Nagpur. The spread of Western education produced an Adivasi elite-Christian and developed a pan-tribal sentiment in the region as well. Chota Nagpur was exposed to the operation of many interests. The Bengalis formed a sizeable professional and landowning community, and the Muslims were a significant trading and professional interest. The Bengali-Bihari controversy over employment in the late 1930s and the Muslim League politics also affected the development of the tribal separatist movement.[4] Some educated Christian tribals of Lutheran Mission (Germans) and Anglican Mission (SPG) established the Chota Nagpur Improvement Society in Ranchi in 1913.[5] The aim of this organization was to make the tribals self-dependent and prepare them to take up government jobs for protecting their interests by themselves. Thus a class of educated and sophisticated tribal elite emerged that later reorganized it. In 1928, Chota Nagpur Improvement Society was renamed as Chota Nagpur Unnati Samaj.

The interplay between discourses of resistance, social justice and anti-communalism form some of the remarkable features of the Adivasi movement in the new state of Jharkhand which emerged in November 2000. The beginning of the tribal autonomy movement in the form of a separate statehood can be traced back to the period prior to the end of colonial rule. It was articulated way back in the 1920s, though in an incipient form. The tribal leadership in Jharkhand had raised the issue during the visit of the Simon Commission in 1928.[6] So, this has been one of the longest fought battles and has gone through many historical ups and downs. The movement had also undergone considerable transformation in its nature, planning, organization and people's participation during the 1930s. Later from the 1970s onwards the ethnic character of the movement was converted into a regional one. The ingrained cultural disparities and unequal development between the Adivasis and the non-Adivasis made the Jharkhand movement successful.

In the wake of the electoral setback in 1937, except the Tana Bhagats and Congressite tribals (because by 1936 Tana Bhagats had become a staunch supporter of Congress), all the tribal organizations of Chota Nagpur, viz. Chota Nagpur Unnati Samaj, Catholic Sabha and Kisan Sabha merged to form the Adivasi Mahasabha on 31 May 1938, under the leadership of Theodore Surin, Rai Saheb Bandi Ram Oraon and Paul Dayal. Surin and Ram Oraon were elected as president and vice-president respectively.[7] The purpose of the organization was to demand for a separate state for the tribals of Chota Nagpur. During the elections of 1937, it was strongly believed that the Congress party had little to offer the tribals of Chota Nagpur and was a party of *dikus* and had little respect for the tribal cause. As Biswamoy Pati has correctly observed, inclusive politics of Gandhi did to a certain extent see the involvement of tribals in his mass movements over the 1920-43 periods and his strategy of leaving *swaraj* largely undefined meant that the tribals could relate to it on the basis of many of their unresolved problems. But the bourgeois leadership of the Congress party which had strong links was not interested in a resolution of the problems affecting the tribals. Consequently, the tribal movements continued.[8] So, when Chota Nagpur Unnati Samaj was reorganized as the Adivasi Mahasabha in 1937, it was very much opposed to Congress politics and remained loyal to the British. It, therefore, remained outside the so-called mainstream nationalist politics. This was the reason why the party gained even the support of the Muslim League.

Gandhi by then did not take much interest in Adivasi affairs. He was, however, soon pushed towards a more active engagement with the issue through fear that the Adivasis might develop their own separatist sentiments. The formation of the Adivasi Mahasabha proved to be an organization mostly for the Christian converts. Its links with the Muslim League against the Congress was even a bigger jolt for him. Gandhi was worried that under Christian mission influence the Adivasis would become 'de-Indianized'—as he put it—and that the Congress needed to provide a strongly Indian counter. He encouraged his followers to work amongst the Adivasis: 'They provide a vast field of service for Congressmen'.[9] An Adivasi Seva Mandal was established as a counter to the Adivasi Mahasabha; the president of this body was B.G. Kher, who had been Prime Minister of Bombay in the Congress ministry of 1937-9. Gandhi also added the topic of 'service of Adivasis' to a manifesto for the constructive programme—it had previously been absent.[10] The term 'Adivasi' was coined in Jharkhand and popularized by the Adivasi Mahasabha. Thakkar Bapa seized on it and became a major advocate of its use. Gandhi, who then began to apply the term himself, even believed that Thakkar Bapa had coined it.[11] In the late 1920s, Thakkar Bapa had written in Gujarati that the Bhils, Santhals, Gonds, etc., were *asal vatani* (original inhabitants) of India. His close associate Lakshmidas Shrikant once said that Thakkar Bapa had learnt the term 'Adivasi' from a political leader from southern Bihar who was himself an Adivasi. Many Hindu nationalists, however, opposed him as they believed that it would seem as the Hindus had displaced these original inhabitants from their lands. They even claimed that the Adivasis are backward Hindus. But Gandhi continued to use the term until his death by rejecting all criticisms.[12]

Gandhi was afraid that Adivasis would follow the path of the Muslim League and demand for a separate state. He anticipated that this would happen if the caste Hindus continued to exploit the Adivasis. So, he wanted the Congress workers to go to the tribal areas and work among them selflessly. He also instructed that if they were obstructed by the British government from going there they should court arrest and be ready to go to jail. During the last days of his life Gandhi admitted that tireless work was needed amongst the Adivasis to win them over and he also made a point of channelling Congress funds in that direction.[13]

The second conference of Adivasi Mahasabha was held on 20 January 1939, where Jaipal Singh (*Marang Gomke* or the supreme leader), a Munda by birth, was elected as the President.[14] Jaipal Singh was the son of a *sarpanch* of Takra village and was only 36 year old. He had studied in St. Paul's School, Ranchi, and later in 1919-20 he went to Darlington, England for pursuing higher study. His allegiance to the Anglican Mission also inspired him to study at Augustine College, Canterbury. He was a brilliant hockey player and led the Indian hockey team to its golden trail in the 1928 Olympic Games. From 1922-6 he was at St. John's College, Oxford.[15] Jaipal Singh had a bright career and was also politically ambitious. On 21 January 1939 Jaipal Singh delivered his first presidential address before hundreds of thousand Adivasis of Chota Nagpur. He said,

> . . . The Adivasi movement stands primarily for the moral and material advancement of Chota Nagpur and the Santhal Parganas, for the economic and political freedom of the aboriginal tracts and, in sum, for the creation of a separate Governor's province comprising roughly Chota Nagpur and Santhal Parganas, with a government and administration appropriate to its needs. It is conceded everywhere that Chota Nagpur suffered by being tagged on to Bihar. . . . We have waited patiently and silently long enough for others to help us, we have trusted others in vain to help us march forward along the path of progress and improvement. Thank God, we have learnt our lesson in time. We must help ourselves. Our great future is in our own hands.[16]

The above-mentioned speech clearly demonstrates Jaipal Singh's anti-Congress attitude. The worsening political situation in Chota Nagpur led the Congress Working Committee to entrust Dr Rajendra Prasad to enquire into the causes of the Adivasi unrest in Chota Nagpur and make a report on it. Prasad sought suggestions in redefined form to redress the Adivasis' grievances from Jaipal Singh for consideration and necessary steps.[17] Jaipal promptly submitted to him the demands of Adivasis which included: appointment of a Minister and a Parliamentary Secretary from the aboriginal communities on recommendation of the Adivasi Mahasbha; adequate representation to Adivasis in the government, legislature, services, etc., in proportion to their numbers; posting of officials well acquainted with the aboriginal's problems in the partially excluded areas; opening of a degree college at Ranchi, nomination of Adivasis to various committees and District Boards, etc.[18] He impressed upon Rajendra Prasad that he too wanted *purna swaraj* and that even the Adivasi Mahasbha was in full harmony with Gandhi's principles. He wanted Chota Nagpur and Santhal Parganas to be constituted into a Congress Province, separated and redeemed from Bihar and the question of a Governor's Province for Jharkhand to be studied and implemented from within the INC. He described his movement as thoroughly democratic and aimed at securing a place of honour in the national life of India.[19]

According to a secret West Bengal Police Report, when Subhas Chandra Bose visited Jamshedpur on 3 December 1939 to enlist support of the labourers against the war efforts of the British government, Jaipal Singh met Netaji and an address on behalf of the Adivasis was submitted to him by him demanding constitution of Chota Nagpur and Santhal Parganas into a separate Congress province. In December 1939 while addressing an Adivasi meeting presided over by Jaipal Singh, Netaji advised the Adivasis to join Congress and capture the Congress machinery instead of nurturing hatred and separatism.[20] Shortly after that Jaipal, who was not expected to receive this advice, held a meeting at Ranchi 'in favour of a separate province for Chota Nagpur, drink, dancing and the British government'.[21] He busied himself in explaining to the Adivasis that the Congress government, which had already resigned, was the worst they could ever have had.

Jaipal Singh urged to form a separate state for the Adivasis and demanded a thorough investigation of the misdeeds of the Congress Ministry in Bihar. After the ministry's resignation in 1939, Jaipal Singh supported the British in the Second World War.[22] He himself played a key role in recruiting tribals for the British Army.[23] His loyalist image was criticized by many.

The INC held its 53rd session on 19 and 20 March 1940 at Ramgarh under the Presidentship of Maulana Abul Kalam Azad. It stirred the Adivasi politics of Chota Nagpur. Jaipal Singh planned an Adivasi rally at Ranchi during the Adivasi Mahasabha session to be held from 14 to 16 March, 1940, a little before the Congress session, and appealed to Jawaharlal Nehru and Rajendra Prasad to visit his rally or hear a delegation of the Adivasi Mahasbha at the Congress session and to assure them that the Congress would consider their claim for separate recognition. In reply, Jaipal Singh was requested to send a delegation to Ramgarh to represent the Adivasis' case. He was also invited to join the anti-compromise conference to be held during the Congress session. Hurt at this, Jaipal decided to go with his plan of holding Adivasi rally at Ranchi as scheduled. Before delivering his Presidential address, Jaipal moved a resolution of loyalty to the Crown. The INC was requested in one resolution to take steps towards the creation of an Adivasi

Province and to institute enquiries into malpractices of the Bihar Congress ministry.[24]

Jaipal Singh's anti-Congress attitude led him to establish links with the Muslim League. At the same time, it is also true that Muslim League manipulated Jaipal Singh and his platform of Adivasi Mahasabha for its own interest, i.e. to prevent Adivasis being considered as backward Hindus and thus weaken the political influence of Congress, which was regarded as chiefly a Hindu organization. The Muslim League leaders also tried to popularize the idea of Adivasisthan—Pakistan Confederacy and planned to incorporate Chota Nagpur into the Eastern Pakistan. Jaipal Singh was fed up of the ideology of *ram-rajya*, propagated by Gandhi and instead prepared to fight for the Muslims.

But when he witnessed the gruesome riots during the Direct Action Day, he realized the actual aim of the Muslim League and withdrew his support. About this time Jaipal Singh was elected to the Constituent Assembly and was mostly engaged in Assembly work at Delhi and had very little time for the Adivasi movement of Chota Nagpur. His close association with the top brass of Congress changed his attitude about Congress. He later said that he was not in favour of Pakistan and did not like to boycott the Assembly. He even invited Nehru, Vijay Lakshmi Pandit and Jagjivan Ram to attend a meeting of Adivasi Mahasabha.[25] According to K.S. Singh,

> Behind the separatist movement in Chota Nagpur there were influences of many kinds: a high level of literacy and political consciousness, the role of the Christian missions, Bengali-Bihari controversy over employment, and Muslim League politics. The Chota Nagpur Improvement Society formed in 1916 demanded employment for educated tribals, reservation in the services and legislative bodies and the formation of a sub-state joined to Bengal or, Orissa. In 1938, a militant phase started with the formation of the Adivasi Mahasabha, which demanded not the formation of a sub-state but complete separation from Bihar. But by 1947, militancy had failed. The Sabha was routed by the Congress in the first elections held in 1946. The link with the Muslim League was broken, and the Bengali-Bihari controversy tapered off. This movement also stimulated a mini renaissance among the Chota Nagpur tribes; discovering or inventing scripts, revival of the forms of art and literature were all part of a movement to define and assert tribal identity.[26]

Jaipal Singh and the Adivasi Mahasabha supported the British during the Second World War and also recruited soldiers from the tribal areas with the expectation that it would make the British sympathetic towards the Adivasi demands.[27] Many Gandhians went to work in Adivasi areas in the late 1940s and early 1950s, in some cases as a reaction to the successful Communist Party mobilization of particular Adivasi communities. It is also true to say that Congress failed to ameliorate the condition of the tribals in Chota Nagpur. Adivasi Mahasabha contested the elections of 1946 and won three seats in Bihar Assembly. But Jaipal Singh was defeated by a Congress candidate. During the time of the formation of Congress ministry in Bihar in 1946, it was insisted that a genuine inhabitant of Chota Nagpur should be included in the Cabinet. On these lines, a memorandum was placed before Gandhi, Patel and Maulana Azad.[28] The nature of the relationship between the Congress and the Adivasi Mahasabha can be gauged by the violence which erupted during the elections in 1946. In these elections fights broke out in the region between them at various polling stations. In Khunti district, five Adivasis were killed and several injured in the violence, generating widespread condemnation.[29]

On 13 December 1946, Jawaharlal Nehru moved the Objectives Resolution in the Constituent Assembly of India. The debate on the Objectives Resolution went on for a whole week. Among the speakers were the conservative Hindu Purushottam Das Tandon, the right wing Hindu Shyama Prasad Mukherjee, the scheduled caste leader B.R. Ambedkar, the liberal lawyer M.R. Jayakar, the socialist M.R. Masani, a leading woman activist, Hansa Mehta, and the communist Somnath Lahiri. Jaipal Singh rose to speak, 'as a jungli, as an adibasi',

> I am not expected to understand the legal intricacies of the Resolution. But my common sense tells me that every one of us should march in that road to freedom and fight together. Sir, if there is any group of Indian people that has been shabbily treated it is my people. They have been disgracefully treated, neglected for the last 6,000 years. The history of the Indus Valley civilization, a child of which I am, shows quite clearly that it is the newcomers—most of you here are intruders as far as I am concerned—it is the

newcomers who have driven away my people from the Indus Valley to the jungle fastness. . . . The whole history of my people is one of continuous exploitation and dispossession by the non-aboriginals of India punctuated by rebellions and disorder, and yet I take Pandit Jawaharlal Nehru at his word. I take you all at your word that now we are going to start a new chapter, a new chapter of independent India where there is equality of opportunity, where no one would be neglected.[30]

Just after his defeat Jaipal Singh came out with the slogan 'we shall take Jharkhand'. He declared that Jharkhand was the land of the Adivasis, and the non-Adivasis had exploited the Adivasis economically and politically, and there was little hope for their regeneration unless the intruders quit Jharkhand. During this period, Jaipal Singh even preached violence to oust the intruders and achieve the goal of separate statehood. The educated Adivasi youth plunged into the movement against the non-Adivasis.[31] Once Jaipal Singh as the President of the Adivasi Mahasabha spoke to the Adivasis as follows:

Arise and wake up, recognize yourself, you all who had been toiling and sweating under the exploiting wolves for the last hundreds of years . . . get this firmly nailed down in your heads that you have not been destined to cut grass and draw water for the *dikus* all your lives. You have to take your place in the society on the basis of equality with others. So wake up, you are not inferior to anyone. Assert yourselves, and fight for your rights.[32]

In May 1947, the Adivasi Sabha of Jamshedpur wrote to Nehru, Gandhi and the Constituent Assembly urging the creation of a Jharkhand State out of Bihar. 'We want Jharkhand Province to preserve and develop Adivasi Culture and Language', said their memorandum, 'to make our customary law supreme, to make our lands inalienable, and above all to save ourselves from continuous exploitation'.[33] The Constituent Assembly appointed a sub-committee headed by A.V. Thakkar to go into the tribal problems of the excluded and partially excluded areas of the provinces (other than Assam) and recommend remedial measures to be suitably incorporated in the Constitution. Jaipal Singh and Phulbahan Saha were appointed its members. When the sub-committee visited Chota Nagpur in September 1947, the Adivasi Mahasabha and other tribal organizations submitted a memorandum demanding creation of a Jharkhand Province. The visit was marked by huge demonstrations and 'Jharkhand Alag Prant' slogan rented the air. Jaipal Singh held out hopes to his supporters that Jharkhand would soon be created,[34] though he knew well that the sub-committee was not concerned with that. A.V. Thakkar, chairman of the sub-committee, wanted the constitutional safeguards to be provided to non-Christian tribals only,[35] who were markedly less advanced than their Christian brethren. Jaipal Singh disagreed with him and ultimately no such provision could be incorporated in the constitution.

In February 1948, Jaipal Singh delivered the presidential address to the All-India Adivasi Mahasabha. He spoke of how, after Independence, 'Bihari imperialism' had replaced 'British imperialism' as the greatest problem for the Adivasi. He identified the land question as the most crucial, and urged the speedy creation of a Jharkhand state. Simultaneously underlined was his commitment to the Indian Union by speaking with feeling about the 'tragic assassination of Gandhiji', and by raising a slogan that combined local pride with a wider Indian patriotism: 'Jai Jharkhand! Jai Adivasi! Jai Hind![36]

The Adivasi Mahasabha was in fact the first full-fledged regional political party in Chota Nagpur which transformed itself into the Jharkhand Party on 5 March 1949.[37] Jaipal Singh became the president of the Jharkhand Party and Ignes Beck was appointed its Secretary. With the formation of the Jharkhand Party, the tribal movement in Bihar evolved into a modern political organization.[38] It will be a travesty of truth, however, to regard the Jharkhand movement of Jaipal Singh simply a continuation of the Kherwar movement, as understood by Fuchs.[39]

The subsequent period witnessed a gradual decline in the popularity of Jaipal Singh and the Jharkhand Party. According to S. Bosu Mullick, the formation of Jharkhand Party went against the popular aspiration of the recovery of the right to self-determination. Therefore, the leaders took resort to lies to mobilize the people under the banner of their new organization. It was said that Jaipal Singh, the most charismatic leader of the party, in his speeches delivered in the countryside used to talk about the glorious *hul* and *ulghulan* and promised to fulfil the dreams of the people of establishing their own *raj*. People believed in this and in the first general elections, Jharkhand Party had a landslide victory. The movement apparently reached another phase of 'conflict' and was about to become really so but the leadership was neither ideologically nor morally prepared for it.[40] Actually since 1930s, 'tribal' politics shifted from 'millenarian, messianic' movements based in the countryside, to party politics based on a more urbanized leadership. It changed from violent upheavals to electoral struggles, and from a politics that looks wholly inward and was exclusively 'tribal' to a politics of coalitions with 'tribal' leaders seeking political allies.[41]

During the 1957 general elections, Minoo Masani, a Parsee unknown to the tribals of Chota Nagpur, was invited by Jaipal Singh to fight the election from the prestigious Ranchi seat as Jharkhand Party candidate. The news of his victory was received with suspicion by the tribals. Many of them suspected transaction of money between Jaipal Singh and Minoo Masani for allowing the latter to fight the election as a Jharkhand Party candidate. The final betrayal came from Jaipal Singh when on 20 June 1963 he joined Congress party with all the elected members of his party under the persuasion of Pandit Binodanand Jha, the then chief minister of Bihar, without holding a public meeting to obtain the opinion of his brethren about the merger.[42]

As a reward for the merger, Jaipal Singh was accommodated as cabinet minister in the Bihar government in 1963 and all the other important leaders were appointed to various districts and state level boards.[43] Vinita Damodaran said that, in the 1962 elections the Jharkhand Party was reduced to 20 seats in the Bihar Assembly and it appeared that it could no longer maintain itself as a viable political organization. The merger of the Jharkhand Party with the Congress was thus a natural corollary to these events. Jaipal Singh accepted a portfolio in the Bihar cabinet and many of his supporters never forgot this betrayal.[44] After 1967 election Jaipal Singh's eclipse was complete. There was also some talk of reviving the Adivasi Sabha but nothing concrete took place. Jaipal Singh is said to have told N.E. Horo shortly before his death in 1970 that he felt cheated by Nehru who had not created a separate state of Jharkhand.[45]

Amit Prakash said, later Jaipal Singh recorded a Minute of Dissent against the Interim Report of the Excluded and Partially Excluded Areas (other than Assam) Sub-Committee where Manbhum, Hazaribagh and Palamau districts were recommended to be descheduled. In this Minute of Dissent he argued against the descheduling of the districts of Manbhum, Hazaribagh and Palamau.[46] He pointed out: 'I cannot see how I can agree to demolition of the economic, geographical and ethnic unity and entity of the Chota Nagpur Division. It is not right that we should give an ex parte verdict and change the status quo of these three districts.'[47] His statement also carried a strong undertone to consider the needs, opinions and aspirations of the tribal people. In some ways, Jaipal Singh was utilizing the same arguments that the nationalist had advanced to the British administration. He was emphasizing the same rationalist arguments for recognition of the tribal community as the campaigners for popular government had done vis-à-vis the British rule.[48] Jaipal Singh again recorded a Minute of Dissent in the final report on the lines of the one in the interim report arguing against the descheduling of certain areas in south Bihar. However, what is pertinent here is the fact that the chairperson of the sub-committee, A.V. Thakkar, decided to record a Note of Comment on this Minute of Dissent.[49] This expressed the view that '"Scheduling" has a certain special meaning which was not explained to nor known by the witnesses at all, not even to Dr Sachchidananda Sinha. Therefore, they could not distinguish between Scheduled and non-Scheduled areas in which tribes reside. . .'[50]

According to Amit Prakash, Jaipal Singh differed on a number of issues. In the debates on the Draft Constitution on 24 August 1949, Jaipal Singh raised the issue of the existence of a politically conscious tribal community in Jharkhand, albeit in a nascent form. He emphasized the unity of India and at the same time emphasized necessity to reserve seats for the tribal people and thus, implied that the tribal identity was a part of the Indian identity and yet separate from it. The claim of the 'sub-national' identity in

Jharkhand for political recognition was, thus, underway. Jaipal Singh also outlined, though not in detail, the existence of an identity amongst the tribal peoples as different from the non-tribal population.[51] He pointed out that:

> It does not lie in the mouth of those people to tell Adibasis what democracy. . . . In Adibasi society all are equal, rich or poor. Everyone has equal opportunity and I do not wish that people should get away with the idea that by writing this Constitution and operating it we are trying to put a new idea into the Adibasi society. . . . Adibasis are the most democratic people and they will not let India get smaller or weaker. . . . I would like the members . . . [to] not be so condescending.[52]

He further stated:

> . . . the backward groups in our country should be enabled to stand on their own legs so that they can assert themselves. It is not the intention of this Constitution . . . that the advanced communities should be carrying my people in their arms for the rest of eternity. All that we plead is that the wherewithal should be provided . . . so that we will be able to stand on our own legs and regain the lost nerves and be useful citizens of India. . . .[53]

In the debates on 5 September 1949, Jaipal Singh was also critical of the envisaged advisory role of the Tribes Advisory Councils and not an actively political one (as had been recommended by the Joint Sub-Committee on Tribal Areas).[54]

However, the demand for a separate province for the tribals in the region was mooted for the first time by the Adivasi Mahasabha under Jaipal Singh during its second session in 1939. Curiously enough, after the merger of the Jharkhand Party with the Congress in 1963 Jaipal Singh himself expressed doubt over the practicability of a separate state of Jharkhand 'as we could not provide even five engineers from amongst ourselves'.[55] Jaipal Singh, who was instrumental in the disappearance of the Jharkhand Party and became a minister in the Bihar cabinet for a couple of months, too became frustrated soon. Increasing factionalism and mutual bickering among the leaders followed the merger. The resultant confusion as well as the difference between pro- and anti-merger factions gave rise to a number of splinter groups in the region none of which could however fill the vacuum created by the merger.[56] Congress government was extremely hesitant to grant any level of regional autonomy to the Adivasis of Jharkhand. Rather, the national elites advocated an affirmative action policy, of reservations of certain Scheduled Tribes and certain lands, to prompt integration and 'social cohesion' whilst recognizing the cultural diversity and impoverishment of many Adivasis.[57] Yet the idea of Adivasi minority identity was not just the product of negotiations between the 'fathers' of the nation, Jawaharlal Nehru and M.K. Gandhi, and early representatives, notably Jaipal Singh of the Adivasis and B.R. Ambedkar of the Dalits. In fact, the idea of Adivasi collectivity and related claims to autonomy, whilst gaining some foundational clarity and certainty via the de-colonization process, refers in Jharkhand more directly to the conflicts between Adivasi insurgents and British rulers in the nineteenth century.[58]

The difference between Ambedkar and Jaipal Singh was that while the former saw through the deleterious effect on the Scheduled Castes' position exercised by the politics of the Congress and thus disassociated himself from it. Jaipal Singh led the Jharkhand Party into the embrace of the Congress. The result of these different courses was that while the movement of the Scheduled Castes retained sufficient autonomy to allow self-expression of its people to go through the stages of *achhoot* (untouchable) to Harijan (named by Gandhi) to Dalit (oppressed), the self-consciousness of the tribals under Jaipal Singh remained passive. The perceptive British civil servant, John Hubback, remarked, 'Jaipal Singh's prowess on the hockey field was not necessarily combined with sound political judgment'.[59]

The more recent trend is the internalization of other national movements by the Adivasis as a way to reflect on the meanings of de-colonization and Adivasihood in contemporary India. For example, they internalize Quit India movement and later Rajmahal Pahar Bachao Andolan in Jharkhand which can be viewed as a combination of the legacies of both the Santhal *hul* and the Gandhian movement. At the same time, it is also crucial to note that the Adivasis are not accepting any kind of imposition of Gandhian ideologies uncritically to interpret their indigenous past activism. We may conclude the chapter by quoting Daniel Rycroft, who has vividly described the pan-Indian Adivasi identity in the context of de-colonization,

> Keeping in view later discourses of de-colonization, which in a Gandhian spirit promote parallel popular notions of political sovereignty, such as gram sabhas (village councils) and panchayats (local councils), one can begin to see how in the Adivasi context, the two divergent subject positions may be conflated. A hardening of a pan-Indian Adivasi identity occurred during the early years of national de-colonization when national elites upheld the social minority 'paradigm' as a social fact and as a potential instrument of empowerment and development. In contemporary India, Adivasi assertiveness is largely entangled in the practices of the state, i.e. it is instrumental and democratic, despite a preponderance of idioms and images, especially in the state of Jharkhand, signifying insurgency.[60]

NOTES

1. Victor Das, 'Jharkhand Movement: From Realism to Mystification', *Economic and Political Weekly*, vol. 25, no. 30, 28 July 1990, pp. 1624-6.
2. N. Datta-Mazumdar, *The Santhals: A Study in Cultural Changes*, Calcutta: Government of India Press, 1956, p. 62.
3. S.C. Panchbhai, 'The Jharkhand Movement among the Santhals', in *Tribal Movements in India*, ed. K.S. Singh, vol. II, New Delhi: Manohar, 2006, p. 34.
4. K.S. Singh, 'Transformation of Tribal Society: Integration *vs.* Assimilation', *Economic and Political Weekly*, vol. 17, no. 34, 21 August 1982, pp. 1376-84.
5. S.P. Sinha, *Conflict and Tension in Tribal Society*, op. cit., 1993, p. 282.
6. N. Sinha and L. Singh, *Jharkhand, Land and People*, Delhi: Rajesh Publication, 2009.
7. Ibid., p. 283.
8. Biswamoy Pati, 'Introduction: Situating the Adivasis in Colonial India', in *Adivasis in Colonial India: Survival, Resistance and Negotiation*, ed. Biswamoy Pati, New Delhi: Council of Historical Research, Orient Black Swan, 2011, pp. 1-27.

9. 'Notes: Adivasis', *Harijan, CWMG,* vol. 81, 18 January 1942, p. 419.
10. David Hardiman, *Gandhi in his Time and Ours,* New Delhi: Permanent Black, 2016, pp. 150-1.
11. 'Constructive Programme: Its Meaning and Place', *CWMG,* vol. 81, 13 December 1941, p. 369.
12. David Hardiman, *Gandhi in his Time and Ours,* op. cit., pp. 150-2.
13. Speech at Prayer Meeting, *CWMG,* vol. 95, 12 June 1947, p. 266. See also Speech at AICC Meeting, *CWMG,* vol. 95, 14 June 1947, p. 281; Speech at Congress Workers' Conference, *CWMG,* 89, 5 January 1946, p. 178; see, for example, Gandhi to S.R. Das, *CWMG,* vol. 89, 8 December 1945, pp. 13-14, and Gandhi to Chimanlal N. Shah, *CWMG,* vol. 93, 21 January 1947, p. 305. For detail, see also David Hardiman, *Gandhi in his Time and Ours,* op. cit., pp. 152.
14. R.K. Tiwary, *Jharkhand Ki Roop Rekha,* Ranchi: Shivangan Publications, 2012, p. 185.
15. Ibid., p. 284.
16. P.G. Ganguly, 'Separatism in the Indian Polity', in *Archaeology and Anthropology,* ed. M.C. Pradhan et al., London: Oxford University Press, 1969, p. 83.
17. Rajendra Prasad to Jaipal Singh, 18 May 1939; Valmiki Choudhary, ed. *Dr. Rajendra Prasad: Correspondence and Select Documents,* New Delhi: Allied Publishers, vol. III, 1984, p. 82.
18. Jaipal Singh to Rajendra Prasad, 24 May and 14 June 1939, ibid., pp. 97, 128.
19. Ibid.
20. S.P. Sinha, *Conflict and Tension in Tribal Society,* op. cit., 1993, p. 288.
21. *Political Proceedings of the Home Department,* Government of India (PPHD), 18/12/39-1939 (NAI).
22. Sewak Ram, *History of Bihar between Two World Wars, 1919-39,* New Delhi: Inter India Publications, 1985, p. 69.
23. Mathew Areeparampil, *Struggle for Swaraj: A History of Adivasi Movements in Jharkhand—From the Earliest Times to the Present Day,* Chaibasa: Tribal Research and Training Centre, 2002, p. 240.
24. L.N. Rana, 'The Adivasi Mahasabha (1938-49): Launching Pad of the Jharkhand Movement', *Proceedings of the Indian History Congress,* vol. 53, 1992, pp. 397-405.
25. S.P. Sinha, *Conflict and Tension in Tribal Society,* op. cit., 1993, p. 292.
26. K.S. Singh, 'Colonial Transformation of Tribal Society in Middle India', *Economic and Political Weekly,* vol. 13, no. 30 July 1978, pp. 1221-32.

27. Upjit Singh Rekhi, *Jharkhand Movement in Bihar*, New Delhi: Nunes Publishers, 1988, p. 143.
28. Memorandum dated 18 April 1946. Submitted by Adivasi Congressmen of Chota Nagpur to Mahatma Gandhi.
29. See *Indian Nation*, 8 March 1946, and *Sentinel*, 10 March 1946. Cited in Vinita Damodaran, 'Indigenous Forest Rights, Discourses, and Resistance in Chota Nagpur, 1860-2002', in *Ecological Nationalisms: Nature, Livelihoods, and Identities in South Asia*, ed. Gunnel Cederlof and K. Sivaramakrishnan, Delhi: Permanent Black, 2005, pp. 115-50.
30. *Constituent Assembly Debates*, vol. I, pp. 143-4, cited in 'Adivasis, Naxalites and Indian Democracy' by Ramachandra Guha, *Economic and Political Weekly*, vol. 42, no. 32, 11-17 August 2007, pp. 3305-12.
31. K.L. Sharma, 'Jharkhand Movement in Bihar', *Economic and Political Weekly*, vol. 11, no. 1/2, 10 January 1976, pp. 37-43.
32. K.L. Sharma, 'The Question of Identity and Sub-Nationality: A Case of Jharkhand Movement in Bihar', in *Continuity and Change in Tribal Society*, ed. Mrinal Miri, op. cit., 1993, pp. 463-73.
33. Memorandum dated 1 May 1947, in Subject File 37, C. Rajagopalachari Papers, Fifth Instalment, NMML.
34. Ignes Kujur, *Jharkhand Dumuhane Par*, Ranchi: Sudarshan Press, 1955, p. 40.
35. K.S. Singh, *Tribal Society in India*, New Delhi: Manohar, 1985, p. 189.
36. Ram Dayal Munda and S. Bosu Mullick, eds., *The Jharkhand Movement: Indigenous Peoples' Struggle for Autonomy in India*, Copenhagen: IWGIA, 2003, pp. 2-14. Cited in Ramachandra Guha, *India After Gandhi: The History of the World's Largest Democracy*, London: Picador, 2008, pp. 266-7.
37. L.N. Rana, 'Party Politics in Chota Nagpur 1937 to 1987', PhD Thesis, Ranchi University, 1991, pp. 134-67. Also see his article 'Political Consciousness in Jharkhand 1900-47', *Proceedings of Indian History Congress*, 1996, p. 476.
38. Sashishekhar Jha, 'Tribal Leadership in Bihar', *Economic and Political Weekly*, vol. 3, no. 15, 13 April 1968, pp. 603, 605, 607-8.
39. Stephens Fuchs, *Rebellious Prophets*, op. cit., 1965, p. 58.
40. S. Bosu Mullick, 'The Jharkhand Movement: A Historical Analysis', in *Continuity and Change in Tribal Society*, ed. Mrinal Miri, op. cit., 1993, pp. 437-62.
41. Myron Weiner, *Sons of the Soil: Migration and Ethnic Conflict in India*, Princeton, NJ: Princeton University Press, 1978, p. 120.
42. Victor Das, 'Jharkhand Movement: From Realism to Mystification', *Economic and Political Weekly*, vol. 25, no. 30, 28 July 1990, pp. 1624-6.

43. Asha Mishra, 'Indigenous Movements for a Separate State: Jharkhand during the Twentieth Century', in *Tribal Movements in Jharkhand: 1857-2007,* ed. Asha Mishra and Chittaranjan Kumar Pati, New Delhi: Concept Publishing, 2010, pp. 169-84.
44. Vinita Damodaran, 'Environment, Ethnicity and History in Chota Nagpur, India, 1850-1970', *Environment and History*, Cambridgeshire: White Horse Press, vol. 3, no. 3, October 1997, pp. 273-98.
45. Rekhi, op. cit., p. 167.
46. Amit Prakash, 'Contested Discourses: Politics of Ethnic Identity and Autonomy in the Jharkhand Region of India', *Alternatives: Global, Local, Political*, vol. 24, no. 4, 1999, pp. 461-96.
47. *Interim Report of the Excluded and Partially Excluded Areas (other than Assam) Sub-Committee*, New Delhi, 1949, Appendix D, Minute of Dissent, 19 August 1947.
48. Amit Prakash, 1999, op. cit.
49. Amit Prakash, 'The Politics of Development and Identity in the Jharkhand Region of Bihar (India), 1951-91', Thesis submitted for the degree of Doctor of Philosophy, School of Oriental and African Studies University of London, 1998.
50. Note by the Chairman on the Minutes of Dissent by Shri Jaipal Singh, 25 September 1947 in Final Report of the Excluded and Partially Excluded Areas (Other than Assam) Sub-Committee, September 1947, New Delhi, 1947, para 2, reproduced in B. Shiva Rao, vol. III, op. cit., pp. 763-70.
51. Amit Prakash, op. cit.
52. *Constituent Assembly Debates*, 24 August 1949, New Delhi, 1949, pp. 653-4.
53. Ibid., p. 654.
54. Amit Prakash, 'Decolonisation and Tribal Policy in Jharkhand: Continuities with Colonial Discourse', *Social Scientist*, vol. 27, no. 7/8 July-August 1999, pp. 113-39.
55. *Hindustan Times*, 23 April 1987.
56. Arunabha Ghosh, 'Ideology and Politics of Jharkhand Movement: An Overview', *Economic and Political Weekly*, vol. 28, no. 35, 28 August 1993, pp. 1788-90.
57. G.C. Rath, 'Introduction', in *Tribal Development in India: The Contemporary Debate*, ed. G.C. Rath, Delhi: Sage, pp. 15-26; G.C. Rath, 'Nehru and Elwin on Tribal Development', ibid., 2006, pp. 65-91.
58. A. Prasad, 'Unravelling the Form of "Adivasi" Organization and Resistance in Colonial India', *The Indian Historical Review*, vol. 33, no. 1, 2006, pp. 225-44.

59. Arvind N. Das, 'Jharkhand Aborted Once Again', *Economic and Political Weekly*, vol. 33, no. 45, 7-13 November 1998, pp. 2827-9.
60. Daniel J. Rycroft, 'Beyond Resistance: Idioms and Memories of Insurgency in the Adivasi Movement in Jharkhand', in *Narratives from the Margins, Aspects of Adivasi History in India*, ed. Sanjukta Das Gupta and Raj Sekhar Basu, Delhi: Primus Books, 2012, pp. 255-74.

CHAPTER 4

Disillusionment and Disappointment: Evaluation of the Role of Gandhi in Consolidating Adivasi Movements in Chota Nagpur Region

Adivasis selflessly contributed to the national cause and added immense strength to the mass character of Gandhi's movement, but did Gandhi convey adequate respect to their cause? The fact is that Gandhi hardly 'devoted any great intellectual or political energy to their problems'.[1] The tribals all over the country were heavily influenced by the Non-Cooperation movement. They stopped paying taxes, resisted taking over lands, took up the *charkha*, and wore *khadi*, and so on. The extent, however, was negligible. It was up to this point that the Adivasis remained within the confines of the Gandhian way of resistance. Gandhi's way was passive resistance, *satyagraha* to be more precise, and essentially asymmetrical. According to J.K. Galbraith,

> The most notable cases of asymmetry in the exercise of countervailing power were those of Mohandas K. (Mahatma) Gandhi in contending with British authority in India. . . . Against the foregoing element of British rule Gandhi offered his powerful personality and a substantial organization, and from both of these came social conditioning on the right of the Indians to rule themselves. But he did not proceed, as would have been expected, to build an armed force in opposition to that of the British—to bring condign power to bear on condign power. Instead he restored to non-violence passive resistance to the exercise of British Rule, including at various times resistance to the collection of taxes or the functioning of the Courts, refusal to obey police orders, and other specific acts of civil disobedience. This departure from the accepted design was a source of infinite wonder, so deeply is symmetry

assumed. Nonetheless, the Raj would have dealt in a matter of hours with any army Gandhi might have assembled, while in dealing with this asymmetrical resistance, it was recurrently at a loss and, in the end, defeated.[2]

It is interesting to note that Non-Cooperation movement continued in Singhbhum long after Gandhi called it off in early 1922 following the Chauri Chaura incident. Though the movement was organized around local issues, the Adivasi and non-Adivasi population were bound together in a common cause. While local grievances undoubtedly made for the success of the movement, a broader political vision was present among the section of Ho leaders involved. This is proved, among other things, by the fact that local movements were organized in the name of Gandhi and Gandhi Raj was held before the people as a viable political alternative to the British Raj.[3]

Gandhi's soldiers like Amritlal Thakkar and Jugatram Dave were engaged in Adivasi predicament in Gujarat but other parts of India remained beyond the touch of his affection. The only instruction that Gandhi gave to his soldiers was to stay away from any type of forceful imposition of Hindu religion and culture on the Adivasis. He said:

> As regards taking our message to the aborigines, I do not think I should go and give my message out of my own wisdom. Do it in all humility. . . . What have I to take to the aborigines and the Assamese hillmen except to go in my nakedness to them? Rather than ask them to join my prayer, I would join their prayer.[4]

Social scientists and historians have paid a very little attention to the role of Gandhi's ideas in the mobilization of the Adivasis during national movement. The movements—national or local—did not influence the course of the tribal movement to a great extent. The tribals drew upon their traditions and were bent on creating a Raj for them when the yoke of the foreign rule was shaken off. To them Gandhi was a name to conjure with and they had invoked the name of Gandhi Raj ascribing suzerain power to him. To them the days of the British Raj were at an end, and Gandhi Raj would dawn on any of the days. The tribals of Chota Nagpur drew their inspiration from Gandhi like other Hindus of our country. Among the tribals the great wave of the national movement created a deep impression. Yet they perceived the programme in the light of their comprehension. In the semi-conscious mental recesses, the image of Gandhi was too high and the adoration for him matched the spirit of the tribal sense or greatness; emulation came automatically. It was the British Raj replaced by Gandhi Raj that had fascinated the tribals. They mixed up the streams of movement and conceived their own ideas and programmes. Movement went in the name of Gandhi.[5]

Adivasis participated in the Civil Disobedience movement in large numbers and violated different forest laws, which was termed as the 'forest *satyagraha*'. But Gandhi refused to sanction such action, on the grounds that he was ignorant of forest regulation. Ironically, when Gandhi was sent behind the bars, the Congressmen led the Gonds and Korkus to start forest *satyagraha* and cut the grass to violate the forest laws in government forests of central India. From 1930 onwards the Adivasis went through massive police repression and gradually their movement was quelled.[6] Gandhi's response to the revolutionary violence or terror of the Adivasis had been captured in *Hind Swaraj*:

> If you will give the matter some thought, you will see that the terror was by no means such a mighty thing. . . . We are not to assume that the English have changed the nature of the . . . Bhils[7] . . . I should prefer to be killed by the arrow of a Bhil than to seek unmanly protection. India without such protection was an India full of valour. Macaulay betrayed gross ignorance when he libelled Indians as being practically cowards. They never merited the charge. Cowards living in a country inhabited by hardy mountaineers, infested by wolves and tigers must surely find an early grave . . . our agriculturists sleep fearlessly on their farms even today, and the English, you and I, would hesitate to sleep where they sleep. Strength lies in absence of fear, not in the quantity of flesh and muscle we may have on our bodies. Moreover, I must remind you who desire Home Rule that, after all, the Bhils are our own countrymen.[8]

There were limitations in Gandhi's fetish of *ahimsa*. For the Dominion of India, that was established in 15 August 1947, he accepted *himsa* (violence) as the first postulate among the incentives of its citizens. He did not, therefore, recommend the abolition of the police in the administration of this state. He took it for granted also that the Indian Dominion might become the target of attacks from aggressive states. The army, the navy and the air force were therefore accepted by him without question as the indispensable limbs of this new state. He did not preach or practise pacifism in such a manner as to prescribe the annihilation of the defence departments. Both in internal and external affairs the utility of arrangements to deal with violence by methods of violence was recognized in his creed of non-violence in no questionable manner.[9]

Moreover, the role of religion was ignored by the Gandhian leaders. Adivasi religion was equalled with superstitions which in actuality had a profound bearing on their state of consciousness. The fact is, all religion consists of folk beliefs and that is why they have a mass appeal. But for the Gandhian leaders, religion was either hegemonic ideology imposed from above or a political weapon used by their indigenous leaders to manipulate the Adivasis for their own interest. What the Gandhian leaders forgot was that Adivasi consciousness is inherently religious.[10]

The Adivasis of Chota Nagpur were conscious about their peasant identity too, they were conscious about the goal as well as a Raj for themselves. This consciousness was necessarily suffused with religion. As long as the tribals maintained their contact with the Non-Cooperation movement, they were having the benefit of an asymmetrical movement initiated by Gandhi. But when other communities parted company, and the tribes adopted the line of tribal revivalism, they reverted to the process of symmetrical opposition—arms against arms, condign against the condign. The rationale of an asymmetrical process of resistance was beyond the comprehension of the Santhal. In the psyche of the Santhal, power is irretrievably associated with the condign, an invariable attribute of the king who also controls land as a source of income. To this goal—to attain power by having their own Raj—the Santhals have ever been proceeding. Insurgency was no more than a point in the life of the Santhal peasants. The stream of consciousness about the final goal—a Raj unto themselves—has ever been flowing underneath and urging them to find new channels to achieve it. Insurgency was means to that end.[11]

Gandhi's engagement with the Adivasi movements was not out of his own will, but was pre-planned by the Congress workers in the Adivasi areas like Chota Nagpur. This can be proved by the fact that the Congress leaders spread different rumours regarding Gandhi's arrival as well as his supernatural powers. These rumours spread like wildfire and created a kind of stir among the Adivasis who wrongly dreamt of a free Adivasi country under Gandhi Raj and sacrificed their own causes for the independence of India. Another example may be the Bhumij movement of Chota Nagpur which took place during 1921. In that year, rumour spread that a new king had appeared on earth who was the incarnation of God himself. He told the Bhumij to give up taking liquor, fish and meat. The movement spread like wildfire and so did the rumour. The Bhumijs started disposing of their hens and goats. Within a few years they witnessed a very good harvest which made them believe that their decision was right. A few years later the name of the king was revealed as being that of Mahatma Gandhi.[12]

We may site another example here. The Devi movement among the Dang Adivasis of south Gujarat had many features similar to that of Tana Bhagat. Gandhi arrived at Bardoli in early December 1921 to launch a land-tax refusal campaign under the Civil Disobedience movement. By then the nationalists failed to win the Adivasis' heart. Gandhi ordered them to go to the Adivasi villages. Kunvarji Mehta, on behalf of Gandhi, persuaded Adivasis by a speech which was replete with myths and stories of miraculous powers of Gandhi. He said:

> . . . The gods travelled all over India, but they could not find a suitable person. At last they went to South Africa where they found one of our countrymen who was working in the same manner as themselves. . . . The name of this man was Mahatma Gandhi. . . . In our country Ram and Krishna were avatars. Gandhi is such an avatar. He has come to uplift us.[13]

After this speech, the Adivasis started believing that Gandhi was a god and would be able to grant boons. But when Gandhi came to know about this he told Kunvarji that he was no god, but a human being like any other, and ordered him to stop making such false speeches. Soon after this Gandhi was arrested and in March

1922 was jailed by the British. But the stories never died down, rather popularized his name among the Adivasis all over the region. The Adivasis had a vague understanding that Gandhi would somehow 'free' them from oppression.[14] Inspired by Gandhi's charisma, Salabai, the great goddess of the Devi movement, told her Adivasi followers to take vows in the name of Gandhi, wear *khadi* and attend nationalist schools. Salabai was seen as an ally of Gandhi and a proponent of the nationalist cause. Rumours were heard that spiders were writing Gandhi's name in cobwebs. It was said that Gandhi can be seen in the well and people began peering into wells in the hope that they might receive Gandhi's *darshan*. Gandhi was also said to be seen in the roof, where the sun comes through the tiles. Some also said that they could see a vision of Gandhi on a white cloth spinning in the sun. It was also said that Gandhi had fled from jail and could be seen sitting in a well side-by-side with Salabai, spinning his *charkha*.[15]

Even Gandhi's Constructive Programme interpolated Adivasis as the last segment, i.e. 14th number. There Gandhi wrote,

> The term Adivasi, like raniparaj, is a coined word. Raniparaj stands for kaliparaj (meaning black people, though their skin is no more black than that of any other). It was coined, I think by Shri Jugatram. The term Adivasi (for Bhils, Gonds, or others variously described as Hill Tribes or aboriginals) means literally original inhabitants and was coined, I believe, by Thakkar Bapa.
>
> Service of Adivasis is also a part of the constructive programme. . . . Our country is so vast and the races so varied that the best of us cannot know all there is to know of men and their condition. As one discovers this for oneself, one realizes how difficult it is to make good our claim to be one nation, unless every unit has a living consciousness of being one with every other.
>
> The Adivasis are over two crores in all India. Bapa began work among the Bhils years ago in Gujarat. In about 1940 Shri Balasaheb Kher threw himself with his usual zeal into this much-needed service in the Thana District. He is now President of the Adivasi Seva Mandal.
>
> There are several such other workers in other parts of India and yet they are too few. Truly, 'the harvest is rich but the labourers are few'. Who can deny that all such service is not merely humanitarian but solidly national, and brings us nearer to true independence?[16]

It was Thakkar Bapa who actually convinced Gandhi to include Adivasis in his constructive programme. Later Gandhi cleared his conscience by stating that,

. . . The complaint is just, many other causes are included in the constructive programme by implication. But that cannot and should not satisfy such a humanitarian as Thakkar Bapa. The Adivasis are the original inhabitants whose material position is perhaps no better than that of Harijans and who have long been victims of neglect on the part of the so-called high classes. The Adivasis should have found a special place in the constructive programme. Non-mention was an oversight. . . . The Christian missionaries have been more or less in the sole occupation of the field. Great as his labour has been it has not prospered as it might have because of his ultimate aim being the Adivasis' conversion to his fold and thus becoming de-Indianized. . . . They provide a vast field of service for Congressmen. . . . Anyways, no one who hopes to construct *swaraj* on the foundation of non-violence, can afford to neglect even the least of India's sons. Adivasis are too numerous to be counted among the least.[17]

When Independence came and lands remained largely unrestored, in spite of the laws enacted by the Congress government, disillusionment set. K.S. Singh said that the non-Adivasi Congress leaders told to the Adivasis that,

If people abstained from drinking alcohol and killing cows, if they plied the spinning wheel and introduced the panchayat system for settling disputes they would attain *swaraj* and get rid of the white people. The Gandhi Raj would usher in the tribal millennium. A few of the social workers even went about the Munda country telling the tribals that Gandhi was none other than Birsa Bhagwan risen from the dead. Gandhi was a god or demi-god, who was going to drive and establish a *dharam raj* (the kingdom of righteousness). Possessed of supernatural powers, he could walk through fire and water unharmed; walls could not imprison him. The Mahatma had even saved a child by throwing it into a cauldron of boiling water. *Swaraj* meant not only the expulsion of the English but also the aliens (*dikus* to the Mundas and *khattakhurus* to the Oraons) from their land. Christian tribals had already got *swaraj* from the British because they no longer rendered any service to the landlord. The *swaraj* for non-Christian tribals was not far off.[18]

It is quite evident that the Adivasi problem did not attract the attention of the nationalists till the 1920s. Gandhi initially saw the tribal people through the prism of non-violence. Speaking in a different context, about what one could do for the tribal people of the north-west, Gandhi said, 'I would accept a challenge of conquering tribal areas, but as a non-violent man I would not bribe them nor kill them: I would serve them. Have not the missionaries allowed themselves to be eaten by cannibals?'[19] In contrast, he asked, 'Why have the Congressmen been unable to reach these tribes and make them proof against blandishments of those who would exploit their traditional violent tendencies, so-called or real?'[20] Gandhi's appeal to the nationalists was to involve the tribals both in his *sarvodaya* and nationalist project. The endorsement of the Congress position on class collaboration has been severely criticized by Pandey because it presumes that *swaraj* implied 'the simple physical eviction of the British from Indian soil'. He contends that the idea of *swaraj*,

> . . . whether articulated by a Gandhi . . . or a Nehru . . . or by the humblest nationalist sympathizer . . . had built into it the dream of 'a new heaven, a new earth'—increased participation by all in the making of the decisions that affected them, reduced burdens (of rents and other taxes and imposts), an end to oppression.[21]

The fulfilment of such a dream, according to Pandey, would greatly depend on the alignment of the forces involved in the struggle for *swaraj*. He argues that the insistence of the Congress on a united front of land lords and 'peasants' (tenants) was 'a statement in favour of the status quo and against any radical change in the social set-up when the British finally handed over the reins of power'. As a consequence, he points out, the victims of oppression were implicitly required to perceive 'landlords and princes' as 'trustees in the economic sphere', while the Congress piloted the struggle for political independence.[22]

Adivasis responded to Gandhi's call for non-violence Non-Cooperation movement without any hesitation or without any doubt. Their uncounted sacrifices gave his movement the mass character and made it a success. But did Gandhi on his part do justice with the Adivasi movement when it came to him? The answer is no. Gandhi's response towards Adivasi movements was neither unbiased nor selfless. A powerful protest movement was developed among the Bhils in the border region between Gujarat and Rajasthan, called the Ekki movement. The movement, headed by Motilal Tejawat, a Baniya of Mewar state, revealed various dimensions and contradictions of the Non-Cooperation movement. The Ekki was not restricted to the Bhils alone; it was a common forum for tribals and non-tribals. It provided an opportunity for greater interaction between the two. Through this organization, Tejawat initiated social reforms among the Bhils. He asked them to abhor drinks, abstain from meat-eating, abandon *dapa* (bride price) and lead a pious life.[23] Tejawat identified himself with Gandhi to a degree where he was treated by his Bhil disciples as a 'holy emissary of Gandhi', a fact that caused panic among the British authorities. They too considered Tejawat a 'disciple' of Gandhi. Tejawat gradually acquired for the masses a messianic personality. The Bhils in thousands would worship him and offer coconuts as a mark of respect to him. He would issue instructions to the Bhils under a *sogan* or oath and any one defying him was considered to be a sinner against religion. Punishment was inflicted on them by out casting the individuals or by imposing penalties on the villages.[24] Tejawat considered the movement as being a part of the wider independence struggle led by Gandhi which was then at a very ripe phase. In speeches he stated that once 'Gandhi Raj' was established they would only have to pay one anna in the rupee to their rulers. Some of his followers also used to wear Gandhi cap. Gandhi was not aware of the movement.[25]

Tejawat and the Bhils also did not adhere to the ways of nonviolence. For instance, in December 1921, he along with a large number of Bhils beat up three revenue officials in the Jhalore *thikana* (Mewar) while they were collecting revenue. He snatched away from them the amount they had collected. Similar acts of violence took place in the surrounding areas. The Bhils inhabiting Panurwa Jawas and Para and numbering several hundred became ready for a confrontation and refused to pay state revenue. They gave a call to their brethren in the adjoining areas to undertake similar actions by sending them bangles of lac and arrows, which was their traditional means of communication. In 1922, hundreds of thousands of Bhils led by Tejawat took up arms like bows and arrows and went on a progress around the villages of that region. There were a very small encounter with the aggressive policemen and officials who were beaten by the Bhils.

So far as the politics of violence is concerned, the Bhils were no exception. The other tribal movements too present the same story of deviation from the Gandhian path of non-violence.[26] The Gonds in offering resistance to the forest laws broke the barriers of non-violent politics. The Koyas and Jatapus of the Rampa region adopted the same course. Alluri Sita Rama waged guerilla warfare. Raju, clad in *khadi*, in a meeting of the local officials, expressed his high regards and admiration for Gandhi, yet he maintained that violence was necessary.[27]

The Bhils did not kill anyone and protested in a completely non-violent way. But when Gandhi heard that about this, he wrote an article in *Young India* disowning the Bhils and their leader, he wrote: 'none has authority to use my name save under my own writing . . . nobody has any authority from me to use any arms, even sticks, against any person.' He also warned that if the Bhils resorted to violence then 'they will find everything and everybody arrayed against them and they will find themselves heavy losers in the end'.[28] Later Gandhi sent Manilal Kothari, a leading nationalist worker to investigate the matter in detail. Kothari was impressed by the Bhil movement and gave a favourable report to Gandhi. Motilal was so identified with the nationalist Gandhian movement that Gandhi's concern about the violent activities indulged in by Motilal created an impression among the officials, to their natural satisfaction, that Motilal was disowned by Gandhi.[29] The British authorities therefore felt encouraged to arrest Motilal. Gandhi observed: 'Assuming that Motilal has been at fault in some matters, both the rulers and the subjects are likely to benefit if this is overlooked and the state takes advantage of the good effect of his work among the Bhils and, pays attention to improving their condition'.[30]

But he got really disheartened when he came to know that Gandhi had disowned the movement by publishing an article in the *Young India*. After that, troops were sent to quell the movement in which indiscriminate firing took away hundreds of thousand Bhils' lives.

Motilal succeeded in escaping but by 1922 the movement was crushed by the British. In Panch Mahals area, the leader of the Bhil movement was Govind who became an opponent of the Gandhian ideology during the Non-Cooperation movement. Govind was ditched by the nationalist leaders and got arrested by the British.[31] These two incidents withered away all possibilities for the Gandhians to gain the support of the Bhils in the nationalist movement. In south Gujarat, Gandhians were quite successful in winning confidence of the tribals. In the movement of 1922, Gandhi was projected as a divine figure by the Adivasis. They were persuaded by the Gandhians to give up liquor and meat, to wear *khadi* and remain clean.

Laxman Naiko who played an active role in the 1942 movement in Malkangiri was influenced by Alluri Sita Rama Raju's rebellion in the Rampa area. It was in this phase that he came into contact with Ramchandra Kutia, a Koya youth, who had led the *fituri*, and learnt to use a gun. He had the opportunity of going around this place and understanding the problems which affected the people. Laxman was appointed as the President of the Congress Primary Committee of Mathili, which was formed by Radhamohan Sahu. This had a considerable effect on Malkangiri. The *charkha* penetrated the remotest areas of Malkangiri, many tribal supporters in this tract, like Laxman, gave up hunting and eating meat under the influence of Gandhi.[32] To the people he was the 'Gandhi of Malkangiri', and, as long as he was alive they used to follow him in crowds wherever he went. On 21 August 1942 the opium shop and the Revenue Inspector's office at Mathili were raided.[33] The 'crowd' was termed as a 'violent mob' which wanted to burn the police station, kill the officers and loot the Malkangiri treasury.

According to Biswamoy Pati, the revolt incorporated the messianic and millenarian legacy of the *fituri* tradition. The former was associated with some of the leaders of the movement like Laxman and Lal Raja, as well as Gandhi, who emerged as 'saviours from above' for the Malkangiri folk. The convergence of the dominant myths—Laxman Raj, Gandhi Raj and *swaraj*—united the Malkangiri folk and strengthened the revolt. The people in this tract related to Gandhi and *swaraj* through leaders like Laxman Naiko and Lal Raja. However, the destruction of liquor shops and the distillation apparatus suggest a departure from Gandhian methods of boycott and picketting. Laxman Naiko was hanged in the Berhampur jail on 29 March 1943.[34] Therefore, some deviations from the nationalists' programme and the tribals' refusal to acquiesce in non-violence do not make the tribal movements an isolated political episode. The masses followed the path of violent agitation and non-Gandhian ethics and yet did not hesitate to draw inspiration and succor from Gandhi's national image even for those non-Gandhian acts.[35]

Another very dangerous trend was that the Gandhians, after being accepted by the Adivasis, often tried to modify their course of movements. They used to give less importance to those aspects of the movement which they felt unnecessary and sometimes even avoid socially divisive and hence unhelpful activities for national integration. For example, in case of the Devi movement in South Gujarat the Dang Adivasis challenged the dominance of the Parsi liquor dealers. But the Gandhians like Vallabhbhai Patel and Kasturba Gandhi told the Adivasis not to boycott work, such as working in the liquor shops and tapping toddy trees.[36] They first tried to dilute the force of the movement by stressing on *atmashakti*, and then discouraging assertion. This can be easily understood that these leaders were actually conveying what Gandhi had to say because we know that Gandhi never wanted any class struggle. But the Dangs did not respond to the call of the Gandhian leaders and launched militant attack on the Parsis. Finally, Vallabhbhai Patel had to advocate violence openly against the Parsis.

Gandhi ignored some of the very serious issues as far as the Adivasi autonomy was concerned, such as, tribal land alienation by non-tribals, Sanskritization, self-determination and so on. For example, Nagas had always been outside the fold of the Congress-led national movement. There had been no *satyagraha* here, no civil-disobedience—in fact, not one Gandhian leader in a white cap had ever visited these hills. In 1946, a group of educated Christian Nagas formed Naga National Council (NNC).[37] After Independence, Naga delegates met Nehru with the demand of independence from India, but Nehru told them that they could have autonomy but not independence. They then called Gandhi in a meeting.[38] Gandhi said that, 'Personally I believe you all belong to me, to India. But if you say you don't, no one can force you.' He then advised the Nagas that a better proof of independence was economic self-reliance; they should grow their own food and spin their own cloth. 'Learn all the handicrafts', said the Mahatma, 'that's the way to peaceful independence. If you use rifles and guns and tanks, it is a foolish thing.'[39] Gandhi was against use of arms, but he did not oppose the Indian army's use of the arms. Surprisingly, when Naga delegation came to Delhi to meet Nehru and Gandhi, they also met Jaipal Singh who apprised them of the 'blunt fact' that 'the Naga Hills have always been part of India. Therefore, there is no question of secession.[40] David Hardiman said that,

> The Gandhian approach to Adivasis tended to focus on their education into citizenship. There was much less emphasis on the need to struggle for their rights within the polity through *satyagraha.* The process of education brought limited gains for a few Adivasis, but it failed to bring the more general emancipation that was hoped for. For most Adivasis, their experience since Indian independence was one of displacement, marginalization and exploitation. . . . This state of affairs can only be resisted through struggle. This has led some Adivasis towards violent resistance, as for example within the Naxalite movement. Others, however, have resisted non-violently under a leadership that is inspired, broadly, by the Gandhian tradition, as in the Chipko Andolan and Narmada Bachao Andolan.[41]

Swaraj, also known as Gandhi Raj, came to be seen as a regime where the peasants and tribals would have to pay no rent, tax or *haat* dues, and also forest resources would be their own. The impact of the Non-Cooperation movement was felt in some areas of Ranchi, amongst the Tana Bhagats, Kolhan, amongst the Hos, the Santhal Paragana and Palamau, amongst the Kherwars and Cheros. Tribals responded with their own grievances, bringing their local issues to the forefront. It is true that the Congress, whom local officials called 'outsiders', gave stimulus to their unrest but the tribals responded to the movement with their own beliefs, aspirations and desires. The action of peasants against the planters and tribes were framed by the Congress in terms of what was popularly regarded to be just, fair and possible. But, they derived and insisted on deriving the legitimacy for all their actions from the supposed orders of Gandhi. There was a popular tendency to look upon Gandhi as an alternative source of authority. Everything that was unjust, cruel and oppressive was fought in Gandhi's name. Gandhi became the symbol of their hopes and aspirations. The hailing of Gandhi became a militant avowal of the organized strength of peasant volunteers and a rallying cry for direct action. It was a cry with which an attack on a market was announced or burning of a factory initiated.

Thus, the enthusiasm which Gandhi generated among the Adivasis, the expectations he aroused and the attack he launched on British authority combined to initiate the process of defiance of authorities. It marked the inversion of power relations that were deemed inviolable. Apparently in 1925, Gandhi instructed the Hindus of Santhal Parganas to show a spirit of patience, sacrifice, and *satyagraha* in order to resist the colonial attempts at privileging the 'primitive' in that area. Yet when Gandhi called for a boycott of all that was white and some local Santhals ended up killing all their white poultry, this was ironically seen to 'prove' the Santhals' Hinduism and newfangled vegetarianism![42]

In most of the cases, the Gandhian leaders out and out denied the indigenous initiatives taken by the Adivasis themselves or relegated the initial discontent among the Adivasis to insignificance that was burst against the exploiters long before the arrival of Gandhi. For example, Jugatram Dave in his book (*Khadibhakta Chunibhai*, 1966) had claimed that Devi movement was inspired by the activities of Gandhi and ignored the fact that the Adivasis preached similar doctrine way before Gandhi entered the scene. Another Gandhian, Mahadev Desai in his book (*The Story of Bardoli*, 1929), tried to focus more on the success of the bourgeois social workers who went to the 'virgin' Adivasi region to 'uplift the tribals' and receded the Adivasis at the back stage by depicting them as mere 'collective mass' or 'crowd'. None the less, the primary sources have always proved that the Adivasis themselves initiated and carried on these movements.

Just as Gandhi's social and cultural programmes only marginally affected the 'purification' movement of the Adivasis of Chota

Nagpur, the ongoing nationalist agitation only provided additional forms of expression to a political engagement which remained essentially tribal in nature and outlook. The problem with Gandhi's ideal was that it did not work much among the Adivasis as he always believed that the subalterns could be won over through sympathy, compassion and *seva* or social service. The dialogue of *satyagraha* was conducted with the subaltern section of the society from a position of superiority, which was very much embedded in a Hindu upper caste hierarchal social order. He tried to incorporate subalterns into his politics and according to his understanding of politics. In doing this he had never tolerated any other alternative representation, be it of Dalits, Adivasis or Muslims. Gandhi has always had a paternalistic attitude towards the Adivasis which was intrinsically arrogant and unequal. This paternalistic attitude, he believed, of service through volunteers of mainstream agencies would continue till the rise of genuine leadership among tribals.[43] His constant rejection of the 'Other' made this section to think of their own alternative, which sometimes went through the claim of separate electorate, sometimes through separate statehood and eventually through partition. At the initial stage rumours played a vital role in popularizing Gandhian ideology, mobilizing masses and personifying Gandhi's charisma among the Adivasis, but his complete rejection of class-struggle gradually made them indifferent to the broader interest and thus initiated a new phase of Adivasi movement for separate statehood in eastern and north-eastern regions.

When we look back to Gandhi's South African days we can also say that Gandhi found himself within a social formation which demanded his affiliation with the oppressed or with the oppressors; and while it cannot be denied that Gandhi fought against the racial arrogance informing the Boer and British hegemonic practices, never did he challenge the allegedly natural bases upon which dominance and privilege could be legitimated. When confronted with situations which required affiliation with the victims of white supremacy, Gandhi discursively reproduced and elaborated the imperial project in relation to 'Coloureds', 'Negroes', 'Natives', 'Kaffirs', 'Aboriginals', 'coolies in the proper sense', 'Asiatics of a low type', and so on.[44]

NOTES

1. David Hardiman, *Gandhi in his Time and Ours*, New Delhi: Permanent Black, 2016, p. 146.
2. J.K. Galbraith, *The Anatomy of Power*, London: Hamilton, 1984, pp. 79-80.
3. Sanjukta Das Gupta, *Adivasis and the Raj: Socio-Economic Transition of the Hos, 1820-1932*, Delhi: Orient Blackswan, 2011, pp. 290-3.
4. 'Discussion on Fellowship', *Young India, CWMG*, vol. 31, 19 January 1928, p. 462.
5. A.B. Chaudhuri, *State Formation among Tribals: A Quest for Santhal Identity*, New Delhi: Gyan Publishing House, 2013, p. 111.
6. David Baker, ' "A Serious Time": Forest Satyagraha in Madhya Pradesh, 1930', *The Indian Economic and Social History Review*, vol. 21, no. 1, January-March 1984, pp. 75-82.
7. Bhils are an aboriginal tribe, found mostly in Gujarat and Rajasthan, numbering about 6,00,000 at the turn of the twentieth century.
8. Anthony Parel, ed., *Gandhi: Hind Swaraj and Other Writings*, Cambridge: Cambridge University Press, 2009, pp. 43-4.
9. Benoy Sarkar, 'Gandhi, Non-Gandhi and Anti-Gandhi in the Pattern of Indian Ideologies', *The Calcutta Review*, Calcutta: Taylor & Francis, Gandhi Number, 12 February 1948, pp. 11-25.
10. David Hardiman, *The Coming of the Devi Adivasi Assertion in Western India*, Delhi: Oxford University Press, 1987, pp. 7-10.
11. A.B. Chaudhuri, *State Formation among Tribals*, op. cit., 2013, p. 120.
12. Surajit Sinha, 'Bhumij-Kshatriya Social Movement in South Manbhum', *Bulletin of the Department of Anthropology*, Government of India, 8(2), July 1959, pp. 9-32.
13. Reported by Collector of Surat, J.R. Martin, 7 December 1921, BA, H.D. (Sp.) 584 of 1921-2. B.P. Vaidya, 1977, *Rentima Vahan*, Ahmedabad, pp. 165-6, cited in David Hardiman, *The Coming of the Devi*, op. cit., pp. 168-9.
14. David Hardiman, *The Coming of the Devi*, op. cit., pp. 170-1.
15. Ibid., pp. 3-4, 50-1.
16. M.K. Gandhi, *Constructive Programme: Its Meaning and Place*, Ahmedabad: The Navajivan Trust, 1945.
17. On train from Bardoli to Wardha, 9 January 1942, *Harijan, CWMG*, vol. 75, 18 January 1942, pp. 210-11.
18. *Confidential File*, Political (Special) Department, no. 75 of 1921; cited in K.S. Singh, 'Tribal Peasantry, Millenarianism, Anarchism and Nationalism:

A Case Study of the Tanabhagats in Chota Nagpur, 1914-25', *Social Scientist*, vol. 16, no. 11, November 1988, pp. 36-50.

19. P.K. Shukla, 'The Adivasi Peasantry of Chota Nagpur and the Nationalist Response (1920-40s)', *Social Scientist*, vol. 39, no. 7/8, July-August 2011, pp. 55-64. Also see D.G. Tendulkar, *Mahatma: Life of Mohandas Karamchand Gandhi*, New Delhi: Publication Division, Government of India, New Delhi: New Edition, vol. 8, 1962 (revised), p. 28.
20. D.G. Tendulkar, *Mahatma: Life of Mohandas Karamchand Gandhi*, op. cit., vol. 7, 1962 revised, p. 32.
21. Gyan Pandey, 'Peasant Revolt and Indian Nationalism: The Peasant Movement in Awadh, 1919-22', in *Subaltern Studies*, ed. Ranajit Guha, vol. I, Delhi: Oxford University Press, 1994, pp. 151-2.
22. Anand Chakravarti, 'The Unfinished Struggle of Santhal 'Bataidars' in Purnea District, 1938-42', *Economic and Political Weekly*, vol. 21, no. 43, 25 October 1986, pp. 1897-1909.
23. For Bijolia movement, see Shankar Sahay Saxena and Padmaja Sharma, *Bijolia Kisan Andolan ka Itihas* (1973). For further study on the movement, Ramnarain Choudhary papers relating to Bijolia lodged in Nehru Memorial Museum and Library are very useful.
24. *Foreign and Political Department*, confidential File No. 428-Political (Secret), 1923, Nos. 1-126, R.E. Holland, A.G.G. Rajasthan, to Johnwood, Political Secretary, no. 701, dated 29 September 1921.
25. David Hardiman, *Gandhi in his Time and Ours*, op. cit., pp. 139-40.
26. C.S.K. Singh, '"Bhils" Participation in Politics in Rajasthan in the 1920s', *Social Scientist*, vol. 13, no. 4, April 1985, pp. 31-43.
27. See K.S. Singh, 'The Freedom Movement and Tribal Sub-movement, 1920-47', in *Essays in Modem Indian History*, ed. B.R. Nanda, 1980; Sumit Sarkar, 'Primitive Rebellion and Modern Nationalism: A Note on Forest Satyagraha in the Non-Cooperation and Civil Disobedience Movements', *Proceedings of the Indian History Congress*, vol. 38, 1977, pp. 511-23.
28. 'Danger of Mass Movement', *Young India*, in *CWMG*, vol. 22, 2 February 1922, p. 315.
29. *Foreign and Political Department*, Confidential File No. 428, Political (Secret), 1923, Government of India, a note by J.P. Thomson, Officer on Special Duty dated 20 September 1921.
30. M.K. Gandhi, *Collected Works of Mahatma Gandhi*, vol. 22: 1921-2, New Delhi: Publication Division, Ministry of Information and Broadcasting, Government of India, 1966, p. 476.
31. David Hardiman, *Gandhi in his Time and Ours*, op. cit., p. 142.
32. S. Sanganna, 'Revolts in Orissa-Martyr Laxman Naik: A Hero of the Free-

dom Movement', in *Tribal Revolts*, ed. V. Raghavaiah, Nellore: Andhra Rashtra Adimajati Sevak Sangh, 1971, p. 249.

33. Mahtab and De, ed., *History of the Freedom Movement in Orissa*, vol. IV, Cuttack: Secretary State Committee for Compilation of History of the Freedom Movement, Orissa Publishing, 1957, p. 88.
34. Biswamoy Pati, 'Storm over Malkangiri: A Note on Laxman Naiko's Revolt (1942)', *Social Scientist*, vol. 15, no. 8/9, August-September 1987, pp. 47-66.
35. Kapil Kumar, '"Peasant's" Perception of Gandhi and his Programme: Oudh, 1920-1922', *Social Scientist*, February 1983, vol. 11, no. 2, pp. 16-30.
36. David Hardiman, *The Coming of the Devi Adivasi Assertion in Western India*, op. cit., pp. 192-3.
37. Ramachandra Guha, *India After Gandhi: The History of the World's Largest Democracy*, London: Picador, 2008, p. 264.
38. A.Z. Phizo, *The Fate of the Naga People: An Appeal to the World*, London: Privately published in July 1960.
39. *CWMG*, vol. 88, pp. 373-4.
40. *Constituent Assembly Debates: Official Report* (rpt. New Delhi: Lok Sabha Secretariat, 1988), vol. 4, pp. 947-8.
41. David Hardiman, *Gandhi in his Time and Ours*, op. cit., pp. 153-4.
42. Prathama Banerjee, *Politics of Time: 'Primitive' and History-writing in a Colonial Society*, New Delhi: Oxford University Press, 2006, p. 228.
43. Bina Kumari Sengar, 'Gandhian Approach to Tribals', *Proceedings of the Indian History Congress*, vol. 62, 2001, pp. 627-36.
44. J.H. Stone II, 'M.K. Gandhi: Some Experiments with Truth', *Journal of Southern African Studies*, vol. 16, no. 4, December 1990, pp. 721-40.

CHAPTER 5

Adivasi Movements after Gandhi: The Relevance of Gandhism in Twenty-first-Century Adivasi Movement—The Ideological Shifts

> In Gandhism, the common man has no hope. . .
> Under Gandhism the common man must keep on toiling
> ceaselessly for a pittance and remain a brute.
> In short, Gandhism with its call of back to nature,
> means back to nakedness, back to squalor,
> back to poverty and back to ignorance
> for the vast mass of the people.[1]
>
> B.R. AMBEDKAR

Right from the second half of the nineteenth century, Adivasis have gone through a process of forcible displacement, sometimes as coolies in the Assam tea gardens, and sometimes in the collieries. Their body symbolizes pure labour and only labour or perhaps potentially revolutionary labour. With the advent of modern capitalism, Adivasis spread across the country in search of work in mines and factories. Their untold history of dispossession and dislocation facilitated the big fat cats of capitalism to manipulate their labour for their own interests.

Adivasis have always been selectively added at the endnotes or in the appendix of the nationalist history writings. Their contribution remained at the periphery of the historical narrative of the great freedom struggle of the nation. This is a well-proved fact that Gandhi did not have direct contact with the indigenous people and there was no specific treatment of their problems in his writings either. There was, in fact, a dialectical relation between the Gandhian thought and indigenous ideology. In his autobiography, Gandhi wrote about his first encounter with the Adivasis in 1906 during his stay in Natal, South Africa. The black Zulus, Bachuanas, Basutos, Swazis and the like were the first who helped him to understand the ethnocentrism of white superiority and discrimination, brutality and merciless nature of the colonial rule against the innocence vulnerability of the Zulus. This innocence vulnerability later had a bearing on how Gandhi understood the Adivasis in India.[2]

In India, the Adivasi problem, as such, did not claim his attention until the early 1940s, but his missions and social movements were known through the welfare programmes implemented by a number of organizations. The Adivasis visit very frequently in the narratives of Gandhi's anti-liquor campaigns and later in large-scale arson and demolition of telegraph posts during the Quit India Movement of 1942. In fact, the leftist militant mass mobilization, for the first time, took the initiative of representing the radical agency of the subalterns or proletariats. The so-called 'tribal militants' have very often appeared as the principal force behind the leftist movement and also as a contrary to the capitalist modernity. Be it in Jharkhand (Dhanbad-based trade union group Marxist Coordination Centre) or in West Bengal (Naxalbari Uprising) or in Chhattisgarh (Maoist Movement) or in Andhra Pradesh (Srikakulam Uprising), Adivasi militant groups have always played a crucial role in bringing justice to the exploited through violent means. In an essay written in 1960, Che Guevara argued that in contrast to the Marxist-Leninist theory of revolution, which had to wait for the maturing of capitalism and the mobilization of the working class by a vanguard party, an elite few could catalyze the revolution through the use of force.[3] Confronted by violence, the government would, in all probability, intensify their oppression of the largely rural masses. The people would be left with no choice except to join the guerrillas. This by itself would ignite a revolution, validating the proposition that violence is the midwife of history. But Gandhian philosophy of non-violence did not accommodate this theory of militant Adivasi movement within its purview. Gandhi never acknowledged this radical political ideology of the Adivasis who stormed against the hegemony of the state, if not global capitalism.

According to Nivedita Menon, spontaneous violence against the structural violence of the state and of capitalist property, violence in self-defence, and even pre-planned violence as an act of desperation—these possibilities always seem just below the skin of normal society, and must be understood within the context of unrelenting, never-addressed injustice. Such acts are justifiable political violence—from the long history of Adivasi uprisings against state power, to violence on property during strikes, to the battered wife with an endlessly abusive husband, waiting for him to fall into a drunken sleep before stabbing him to death.[4]

The gist of Gandhi's philosophy for economics was worked out by J.C. Kumarappa. Kumarappa characterizes the modern capitalist economy as parasitic in nature—i.e. based on exploitation, and in the long term, unsustainable. Proper agriculture consists of 'local self-sufficiency in food production', and village self-reliance, rather than an increasing emphasis on cash crops and transporting food. Centralized production tends to reduce workers to a condition of enslavement. Machines and factories involve a basic inequality between the enslaved labour of those who mine the ore and make it into primary metal, and those they work for. As for exports, 'When ores are sent out of the country, the heritage of the people of the land is being sold out.'[5] Ramachandra Guha has categorically stated that,

> Ideologists may oppose Ambedkar to Gandhi; historians may know that Gandhi and Visvesvaraya disagreed on the importance of industrialization in economic development. Yet . . . our country today needs all three, for all were Indians of decency and integrity, all seeking sincerely to mitigate human suffering, all embodying legacies worthy of being deepened in our own age.[6]

National-territorial sovereignty and safety and survival of the nation: these are the two fundamental objectives on which political realism—both descriptive and normative—insists. These are also the two fundamental objectives of Gandhian nationalism. However, Gandhi insisted that these objectives be pursued through the techniques of struggle consistent with the principles of *satyagraha*, which he proposed as an alternative to an armed violence, to war, to guerrilla warfare, to terrorist action.[7]

According to Shiv Visvanathan, the *satyagrahi* as citizen was also challenged by a new figure that made the Gandhian theory of the city even more imperative. With Pol Pot and later with Mao, the idea of guerrilla warfare came to the forefront of revolutionary ideology that speaks about ruralizing every city through genocide. But in Gandhian ideology, once the revolution is over, the guerrillas become mere city dwellers and their revolutionary politics lapses into everyday life. For Gandhi, it is the *satyagrahi* who provides the rhythm of everyday resistance, which is both scientifically and politically innovative.[8]

Whether recourse to armed violence is morally justified or not depends, for Gandhi, too, on the situation and the alternatives available. This is why, throughout his life, he increasingly maintained that there were situations in which it was one's duty to resist the abuse of power, violent aggression and 'homicidal madmen'; and that, in these situations, if *satyagraha*, 'the non-violence of the strong', was not a realistic option, resource to armed struggle could be morally justified. But in what forms and proportions armed struggle should be used, have not been mentioned by Gandhi. In all events, he held, it is morally preferable to 'cowardly submission'.[9] In 1940, Gandhi stated that,

> Strictly speaking, no activity and no industry is possible without a certain amount of violence, no matter how little. Even the very process of living is impossible without a certain amount of violence. What we have to do is to minimize it to the greatest extent possible.[10]

Gandhi had a deep contempt for cowardice, 'unmanliness', 'effeminacy'. At times, he even expressed contempt for the weak; not in the sense of being unarmed, but for 'the weak in mind and spirit'.[11] On the other hand, he appreciated 'manhood' and 'manliness', and exalted courage, often that of the warrior, the brave soldier who risks his own life and has 'the courage to kill'. In a letter written in September 1917, he almost glorified 'the greatness of the man bearing arms . . . his determination and fearlessness in face of death'.[12] For a long time—at least until the end of First World War—he was apparently convinced that the practice of armed struggle, the life of a soldier on the frontlines, developed a number of qualities, 'martial values', which he appreciated deeply.[13] There were times when he even believed that warfare could turn 'savage' people into 'gentle' souls; 'And how many proud, rude, savage spirits has it not broken into gentle creatures of God?'[14]

In Gandhi's view, democracy should be the purest form of non-violence.[15] To meet all the shortcomings and problems of violence, Gandhi offered the radical panacea of non-violence in all its aspects—physical, social, economic, cultural and structural. 'To answer brutality with brutality,' said Gandhi, 'is to admit one's moral and intellectual bankruptcy'.[16] Gandhi continuously harped on the theme that non-violence aims at 'liquidating antagonism, but not the antagonists.'[17] He believed that the adversary should be converted, not coerced. Coercion can only hide away, postpone and preserve the opposition without dissolving it. *Satyagraha* should not entertain any ill will towards the opponent.[18] Nor should *satyagraha* resort to fraud, falsehood and untruth. According to Gandhism, violence should be turned into 'constructive, peaceful ways whereby differences of interests can be liquidated',[19] and consensus or compromise can be created. Gandhism attacks violence from another critical angle—violence brutalizes both the opponents in a conflict, the oppressor and the oppressed.[20] Gandhi responded that 'in reality, non-violence works directly and swiftly'. To those who, in their impatience for success, were willing to disregard and discount some amount of violence in the freedom struggle, Gandhi responded with absolute conviction and clarity—'I personally would wait, if need be, for ages than seek to attain freedom of my country through bloody means.'[21]

Pointing out that democracy and violence are incompatible, Gandhi said: 'Constitutional and democratic government is a distant dream so long as non-violence is not recognized as a living force, an inviolable need, not a mere policy.'[22] Violent revolution and civil war are antithetical to democracy. According to Gandhism, war leads to pure dictatorship while non-violence alone leads to pure democracy. Gandhi asserted that in its essence, democracy is the purest form of non-violence.[23] 'The method of non-violence,' said Gandhi 'is the swiftest the world has ever seen, for it is the surest.'[24]

But Gandhi always had a highly selective understanding of non-violence. Sumanta Banerjee has criticized Hardiman's views on Gandhian non-violence and said that, Gandhi shifted his stand on non-violence whenever it suited his political interests. He has quoted from an interview granted by Gandhi to Charles Petrasch of the French journal *Le Monde* on 10 February 1932. Petrasch asked Gandhi why during his negotiations with Lord Irwin he refused to seek pardon for the Garhwali soldiers (who responding to Gandhi's call for Non-Cooperation had refused to fire upon Pakhtun *satyagrahis* in Peshawar in 1930, and as a result had to face court martial). Following was Gandhi's reply:

> A soldier who disobeys an order to fire breaks the oath which he has taken and renders himself guilty of criminal disobedience. I cannot ask officials and soldiers to disobey; for when I am in power, I shall in all likelihood make use of those same officials and those same soldiers. If I taught them to disobey I should be afraid that they might do the same when I am in power. (reprinted in *Labour Monthly*, vol. 14, April 1932)[25]

According to Giuliano Pontara, Gandhi succeeded only partly in setting up and maintaining situations favourable to the spread of mass non-violent behaviour in the struggle for Independence. In the face of the cruel massacres that occurred during the Partition of India, he recognized that non-violence, as he understood it, had been a complete failure. What had been practised, he said, was 'the non-violence of the weak'.[26] W.H. Roberts has observed that,

> Gandhi's vision of a revolution to liberate three hundred million people, achieved not through war or violence but primarily through a moral regeneration, is surely one of the most magnificent that was ever opened to human aspiration. And it could not have been resisted by the most stupendous accumulation of materials of war. Had his people been capable, spiritually capable, of such a program as Gandhi demanded, they would have been irresistible, and no one could have denied them the spiritual leadership of the world.[27]

From 1980s onwards, the Adivasis are emerging as an effective site of a fundamental critique of the capitalist modernity which was accompanied with the emergence of a newly-formed political paradigm called environmentalism. This notion of environmentalism excoriates destructive development brought by industrial capitalism and advocates for more sustainable development. Adivasis are fighting for the sustainable development because their identity depends on the use and management of the natural resources. Large-scale displacement due to dam building, mining factories, real estate constructions, and industrial projects has endangered their life and livelihoods. Adivasis are not merely resisting industrial modernity, but they are struggling for their survival.

The tribal movements in post-Independence era represent the interests of the poor and exploited sections of the society. Gandhi's ideals were subverted much too soon. Shortly before his death, he had an exchange of letters with Nehru concerning a fundamental difference in their outlooks. For Gandhi, village life and industry, in the sense of self-sufficiency in producing one's own food, clothes and other needs, formed the core of civilized living. He thought that the rush towards machine-based industrialization and city life was making the human race rush headlong on a path to collective suicide.[28] Nehru's view was the opposite, though he did not deny the suicidal tendency in the industrial mode:

> A village, normally speaking, is backward intellectually and culturally. . . . I do not think it is possible for India to be really independent unless she is a technically advanced country. . . . There is today a tremendous acquisitive tendency both in individuals and groups and nations, which leads to conflicts and wars. Our entire society is based on this more or less. . . . You are right in saying that the world, or a large part of it, appears to be bent on committing suicide. That may be an inevitable development of an evil seed in civilization that has grown. I think it is so.[29]

In contrasts, Gandhi saw village life as healthier than city life and more sustainable. He saw the whole system of heavy industrialization as antithetical to freedom and to India's real independence, which he identified with village *swaraj*. Gandhi's last years were overshadowed by the betrayal of his vision of India's future, as Nehru pursued a policy of rapid industrialization. One of the first recorded instances of industrial pollution and protest in Orissa is a letter written to Gandhi in 1946 about pollution of the Ib River, near Sambalpur, by Birla's Orient Paper Mill, started in 1940. Even though he owned textile mills, Birla gave financial patronage to Gandhi's All India Hand Spinner's Association, believing that this spinning was of symbolic rather than practical significance. Gandhi passed on the letter to Birla, who was Gandhi's friend and supporter and who actually did nothing about it.[30] Notwithstanding, the Adivasi movements against various forms of displacement and exploitation kept the message of Gandhi's *ahimsa* alive and successful.

According to David Hardiman, non-violent method was always there in the pre-Gandhian era but it did not give rise to a politics of non-violence that was rooted in a state method, theory and vocabulary that served to link up protests from all over India, as was to be the case in the twentieth century. He has categorically maintained that, to have any useful analytical meaning, 'non-violent resistance' must entail a self-conscious choice by those involved, with the non-violent path being a clear strategic preference that is chosen over and above the other possible path that of violent resistance and this should be a consciously modern move. It is only in modern times that non-violence has thus become a strong informing ethos of many protest movements. Gandhi gave the concept a political dimension—meaning a refusal to harm another physically in any way.[31] This, however, was to be achieved through a non-violent refusal to cooperate, rather than through any counter-violence. In fact, it was better to accept death rather than retaliate with force.[32]

According to Ramachandra Guha, the life and work of Gandhi have had a considerable influence on the contemporary environmental movement in India. This movement truly began with the Chipko Andolan in April 1973; in one of the first printed accounts of Chipko, a breathless journalist announced that Gandhi's ghost had saved the Himalayan trees. Ever since Mahatma Gandhi has been the usually acknowledged and occasionally unacknowledged patron saint of the environmental movement. From the Chipko Andolan to the Narmada Bachao Andolan, environmental activists have relied heavily on Gandhian techniques of non-violent protest, and have drawn abundantly on Gandhi's polemic against heavy industrialization. Again, some of the movement's better-known figures, for example, Chandi Prasad Bhatt, Sunderlal Bahuguna, Baba Amte, and Medha Patkar, have repeatedly underlined their own debt of Gandhi.[33] Felix Padel has said that, when India gained Independence and Gandhi witnessed same patterns of injustice persisting in villages, with Indians exploiting Indians, he moved closer to the socialist tradition and took a strong stand against Western models of industrialization, arguing against Nehru that India would not achieve economic independence like this. His faith in India's village culture is alive in the present movements. These movements uphold a particular kind of lifestyle that accords closely with Gandhi's ideals of the self-sufficient village community, outlined in *Hind Swaraj* (1909) and with modern environmental awareness.[34]

By the 1990s onwards a new threat started emerging from the womb of capitalism and that is globalization. Massive explosion of media and modern technology put their life at stake. Initiatives are mostly taken on the direction of the preservation of Adivasi culture, art and craft, dance and music, and the like. The politics of reservation for the STs made them keener towards preserving their 'ethnic artifacts'. But the most unfortunate thing is that in doing this, the Adivasis are gradually losing their culture, the way of life. It is as part of this post-liberalization valourization of culture that the Adivasis are reclaimed by the national mainstream as primarily a cultural element, in need of preservation and promotion.[35] Like the city, the wilderness has no attraction for Gandhi. It is true that his practice of vegetarianism and non-violence oriented Gandhi towards a respect for all life, yet by all accounts he was hardly moved by the glories of un-spoilt nature. This might, perhaps be attributed to his severely practical temperament, for there was nothing of the romantic in Gandhi.[36]

In Gandhi's analysis basic prosperity is for everyone because world's resources, if carefully managed and fairly distributed, are sufficient to fulfil everyone's need, but not to fulfil any one man's hunger. He said,

That economics is untrue which ignores or disregards moral values. The extension of the law of non-violence in the domain of economics means nothing less than the introduction of moral values as a factor to be considered in regulating international commerce.[37]

According to me . . . everyone should be able to get sufficient work to enable him to make the two ends meet. And this ideal can be universally realized only if the means of production of the elementary necessaries of life remain in the control of the masses. This should be freely available to all as God's air and water ought to be; they should not be made a vehicle of traffic for exploitation of others. Their monopolization by any country, nation or group of persons would be unjust. The neglect of this simple principle is the cause of the destitution that we witness today not only in this unhappy land but in other parts of the world too.[38]

According to Felix Padel, Gandhi fought the exploitation of India under British rule, but saw that the situation would hardly improve with Independence, if the system of dispossession and exploitation remained in place. Why have economists failed to get to grips with understanding this? Eighty years, and no real development: the means of production are as alienated from the masses as totally as they were in the time of Marx or Gandhi. 'Real Development' would see an end to the exploitation, inequality and lies.[39] Prathama Banerjee has rightly observed that,

. . . Gandhi, despite his anti-modernist stance, sought to mobilize 'tribes' through the moral overtones of anti-liquor campaigns, directed against thriftless 'tribal' peoples, drinking, dancing, feasting their time away. The 'tribe' as culture and the 'tribe' as political thus remained in an irresolvable double-bind, continuing, till today, to plague movements of self-determination amongst Adivasis in India.[40]

According to B.D. Sharma, the tribal people are associated with a territory in their local parlance. There is a deep rooted symbolic relationship between the two. They never accept anybody's authority over them and this was the principal reason why the Tana Bhagats did not succumb in spite of losing the fight with the British. The Tana Bhagats did not change their stand even after the Independence. A law had to be passed in erstwhile Bihar exempting Tana Bhagats from payment of land revenue and restoration of confiscated land. The followers of Tana Bhagats in the southern fringe of larger Bihar Province before Partition—now Sundargarh of Orissa—were not lucky to have the benefit of the Bihar legislation declaring exemption from land revenue. Of interest is the case of Sunika Munda, the last amongst the vanishing tribe of the followers of Tana Bhagats, valiantly facing a notice from the revenue authorities—with a firm resolve 'Not to Yield'—received in February, 2010, to pay revenue overdue, assessed at Rs. 22,000. Along with the notice is a clear warning about being sent to civil jail in case of default. 'And his grandchildren shall not be issued ST certificate unless the arrears are cleared', is the Diktat of Tehsildar, the Chhota Raja (Junior Ruler) of the Grand Democratic Regime, that is India.[41]

Coming to the post-Gandhian era, the nature of the tribal unrest has gone under tremendous transformation. Both violent and non-violent movements are proved to be successful and ideologically taken by both the Adivasis and the state. The first set of violent protest movements sprang from the 1960s peasant struggle of Naxalbari and Srikakulam which also impacted a large part of tribal Chota Nagpur.

NAXALBARI MOVEMENT IN BIHAR

The tribal unrest in Naxalbari of 1967 is often regarded as the start of the Maoist movement. From Naxalbari village in West Bengal, Charu Majumdar and Kanu Sanyal led a violent uprising in which peasants attacked local landlords, forcibly occupied land, burnt records and cancelled old debts. The overall goal, as stated in the CPI (ML) programme of 1970, and reiterated again in the CPI (Maoist) programme of 2004, was to form liberated areas in rural zones and then encircle and capture the cities. This campaign was also initiated in the forested and hilly tracts of Srikakulam in Andhra Pradesh, Koraput in Orissa and in the plains of Bhojpur in Bihar and Birbhum in West Bengal. In these regions, the Naxalites tried to draw on histories of earlier peasant movements (for example, the 1940s communist movements of Tebhaga in West Bengal and the Telengana in Andhra Pradesh). Landlords were driven out of villages, people's courts were set up to redistribute land and deliver justice, and there were programmes to initiate the mass mobilization of the rural poor. These achievements went hand in hand with a form of class struggle that entailed the tactical strategy of 'annihilation of class enemies': the dissolution of what the Naxalites called 'the feudal classes', such as landlords, rich peasants, government employees, rival party members, as well as anyone suspected of being a police informer or agent. The massive state repression, which included the imprisonment of most of the Naxalite leaders, as well as factionalism within the Maoist ranks, meant that by 1973, Maoist activity in the base areas of Andhra Pradesh, Bihar and West Bengal had largely subsided. While different Maoist factions chose different methods, guerrilla warfare re-emerged in the late seventies in the forested areas of Burdwan in West Bengal, from which the movement spread in the 1980s to the central plains of Bihar, and into sociologically similar areas of northern Jharkhand. There is an 'uneasy marriage' between Maoist mass mobilization and armed action. The 1980s mobilization of the Dalits in Bihar was accomplished through the Maoist mass fronts, in particular, the MKSS (Mazdoor Kisan Sangram Samiti), whereas the 1990s saw a shrinking of the space for mass mobilization and an increasing reliance by the Maoists on armed actions.[42]

The recent people's movements, essentially of Adivasi in nature, are drawing heavily from Gandhian ideology and are holding the current of non-violence, often condemned as 'Maoist'. For example, the movement against Vedanta aluminium plant and bauxite mining in Niyamgiri or the withdrawal of the POSCO project as a result of a persistent campaign by the local Adivasi—both were guided by Gandhian principles of non-violence. In Narayanpatna in Koraput district of Orissa, a peaceful campaign to restore tribal land to the original owners, as per law, was suppressed and the Chasi Mulia Adivasi Sangh was banned and branded as a Maoist organization. The Niyamgiri Suraksha Samiti led by socialists and Gandhians have also been recently tagged as a front organization of the Maoists which indicates that Vedanta has now got even greater support from the central and state governments to pursue the project. The ashram of Himansu Kumar, a Gandhian worker, was dismantled in Jagdalpur in 2010 as his organization was accused of collusion with the

Maoists.[43] The voice of the Adivasis for their *swaraj* or the 'right to earth'[44] has been brutally gauged by the state sponsored violence and terror. According to Sumanta Banerjee,

> Some like the Maoists want to destroy the structure and strengthen the antagonistic movement against capitalism by leading these tribal populations in an armed struggle in confrontation with the state. . . . In the absence of any effective political guidance from the central leadership, most of the Maoist guerrilla squads are fast turning into roaming gangs of extortionists and criminals in areas like Jharkhand. This again suggests the failure of the leadership in educating the Maoist ranks in the basic ideology of Marxian socialism and humanism. Like their parliamentary counterpart—the CPI (M)—the Maoists are also facing a political crisis and a challenge to their moral credibility. In the light of their experiences of armed struggle during the last three decades or so, the Maoist leaders have to be self-critical, ask themselves whether the tactics of a protracted armed struggle (that was viable in China from the 1920s till the 1940s) can be replicated in 21st century India, and reformulate their programme for a radical change.[45]

The recent tribal scenario is replete with the Maoist activities. In most of the cases, the Maoists are championing the cause of the Adivasis. But there are exceptions as well. Having said that this is also pertinent to point out that the objective of the Maoists is to overthrow the state and become the state. The Maoists are well aware that the state would unleash counter-violence. But Adivasis are not ready to face the violence. On the question of the undifferentiated Adivasi-Maoist, there is much dissembling among middle-class supporters of the party. They argue, simultaneously, that the state is using the 'Maoist menace' as an 'excuse' to attack resource-rich tribal areas, but also that there is no difference between this party and the Adivasis. The non-differentiation between tribals taking up arms, 'Naxalites', and the CPI (Maoist) appears a pernicious conflation carried out by the mass media and the government and unknowingly by intellectuals of integrity—which suits the CPI (Maoist) very well. The same tactic is followed by local administrations of the state who brand all activists as 'Maoists'.[46]

According to Arundhati Roy, Adivasis, who are reeling under police terror, do not simply take instructions from a handful of ideologues that appear out of nowhere waving guns. Their decisions of what strategies to employ take into account a whole host of considerations: the history of the struggle, the nature of the repression, the urgency of the situation and the landscape in which their struggle is taking place. The decision of whether to be a Gandhian or a Maoist, militant or peaceful, or a bit of both (like in Nandigram), is not always a moral or ideological one. Quite often, it is a tactical one. Gandhian *satyagraha*, for example, is a kind of political theatre. In order for it to be effective, it needs a sympathetic audience which villagers deep in the forest do not have. When a posse of 800 policemen lay a cordon around a forest village at night and begin to burn houses and shoot people, will a hunger strike help? She has further raised question like, can starving people go on a hunger strike? And do hunger strikes work when they are not on TV? Equally, guerrilla warfare is a strategy that villages in the plains, with no cover for tactical retreat, cannot afford. Fortunately, people are capable of breaking through ideological categories, and of being Gandhian in Jantar Mantar, militant in the plains and guerrilla fighters in the forest without necessary suffering from a crisis of identity. The strength of the insurrection in India is its diversity, not uniformity.[47]

Adivasi movements against land grabbing, mining and so-called development projects are the cutting edge of anti-capitalist movements worldwide—an environmentalism of the poor that follows basic Gandhian principles of *ahimsa* or non-violence. Adivasi movements in post-Independence era have always been confused with the Maoist activities and deprived of the proper recognition of a non-violent movement which aims to maintain a sustainable lifestyle of them by resisting the invasion of mines, dams and factories. In many ways, as Gandhi realized, India's Independence was an illusion. Financial independence has been eroded, with key control exercise from London once again. All over the world, Gandhi is still an inspiring model of resistance to the multiple injustices of government repression and financial manipulation.[48]

With the changing nature of colonization the 'anti-colonial' movements have also changed their nature. During British period colonial policies regarding forest and forest resources, forced labour, railways, exploitation of the landlords, moneylenders, traders were some of the moot point on which tribal unrest occurred. But after Independence the nature of colonization has taken a new garb—internal colonialism. British imperialism has got transformed into neo-liberalism which systematically impoverishes the marginal Adivasis in the name of 'development' and 'growth'. Although the targets of the Adivasi movements have changed from aliens to the big corporate houses, the basic issues have remained the same and they are land, forest, water and human rights. Therefore, it is not wrong to say that, company still rules. In the colonial era it was East India Company and today they are numerous and more powerful. Besides the causes the methods of protest also have retained their past characteristics, like non-violence, people's marches, meetings, etc. Another aspect should also be paid attention to and that is the nature of repression. During the colonial times, police repression was immensely brutalized by the colonial administration and today even in an independent country the police still react in the same manner, open firing, mass arrest, arson, looting, raping, fake encounter of the innocent Adivasis on every small pretext.

Non-violence is always taken as a path of protest invented by Gandhi. But if we look at the Adivasi movements before the arrival of Gandhi, we will see that tribals were always non-violent while protesting against injustice perpetrated by the *dikus* and colonial masters. It was the indignation and hatred of the colonial rulers and the outsiders which forced them to resort to violent means in order to get their rightful rights back. Gandhi definitely advocated the path of non-violence, but did not invent it, rather popularized it, at least as far as the tribal situation is concerned. To quote Arundhati Roy,

> We have a living tradition of those who have struggled for Gandhi's vision of sustainability and self reliance, for socialist ideas of egalitarianism and social justice. We have Ambedkar's vision, which challenges the Gandhians as well as the Socialists in serious ways. We have the most spectacular coalition of resistance movements with experience, understanding and vision.[49]

Tribal movements in post-Gandhian era, thus, can be considered as a continuation of the previous movements not only in terms of their causes and courses, but also in terms of their methods of protest and the methods of suppression. Now let us discuss some of the movements very briefly.

KASHIPUR MOVEMENT AGAINST UAIL (2001)

Utkal Alumina International (UAIL), a joint venture with Hindalco of India, Alcan of Canada and Hydro, a Norwegian company (which has recently withdrawn from the project), the bauxite mining/processing company came on the scene of Kashipur in 1993. They offered cash compensation but the tribals of Kucheipadar village of Kashipur, Orissa refused to take it. Land was demanded from the Adivasis on the basis of the colonial land acquisition act of 1894 in the name of 'national interest'. Confrontation escalated in 1994 and with that government started arresting the innocent tribals. A strong movement was launched with the formation of an organization called The Prakrutika Sampad Surakshya Parishad (PSSP or Natural Resources Defence Council) in 1993 and the Bapla Mali Surakshya Samiti (The Bapla Mali Protection Society) in 1995. Panchayat Raj Extension to the Scheduled Areas Act or PESA (1996) or Samatha Judgement in Andhra Pradesh (1997) could not even save the Adivasis from the greed of the multinationals.

In 1998, the confrontation in Kashipur reached a new level. On 5 January police lathicharged and tear-gassed a roadblock at Kucheipadar, beating and badly injuring about 50 Adivasi protestors. Then the tribals of Maikanch village of Kashipur, launched a movement against Utkal Alumina Pvt. Ltd. in 2000. On 15 December, 2000 the Adivasis planned a wheel jam at Rapkona to block Kashipur main road. Police opened fire on an unarmed large crowd of Adivasi activists meeting opposing the project and killed three Jhoria Adivasi men. Several other tribals got severely injured. The police firing made international news. An enquiry commission was set up to investigate the police shooting in Maikanch on 20 January 2001.

On 18 September 2001 nearly 3,000-3,500 people with their traditional weapons participated in the block (Kashipur) *gherao* programme, conducted a meeting and presented a memorandum to the chief minister and district collector through the BDO. The main demands were cancellation of all bauxite mining projects in Kashipur-Luxmipur-Dasamantpur blocks, punishing responsible officers and politicians on Maikancha firing, withdrawing false police cases against the activists of PSSP, irrigation for each land by small check dams, provision for a health centre and a doctor with necessary medicines in each gram panchayat, provision for mobile health teams during rainy period, return of tribal land from land grabbers and punishment to the corrupt officials and others in misappropriation of all aid projects.[50] The movement came out successful as the Utkal Alumina was stalled by the commission which submitted its report in 2003 and since then every year villagers mark the anniversary with a commemoration of marches, meetings and dances.

On 1 December 2004, Adivasis numbring 300, mainly women were sitting in protest near the barrack site at Dom Karal, when they were ordered to disperse and then tear-gassed and lathicharged by about 500 police. In spite of that Utkal Alumina resumed its work soon and its construction is under way on a vast scale, though the land needed for the project is still not acquired due the protest. Thus Kashipur movement gained a reputation as one of the most important people's movements in India.[51] Not just in Kashipur, but in different parts of the state tribal communities are standing up and demanding that the state treat them as human beings and allow them to exercise their rights as human beings. They have asserted their right to local governance, and have taken up the challenge of entering into electoral processes to make this democracy work for them.[52]

LANJIGARH MOVEMENT AGAINST VEDANTA (2004)

The Sterlite Company wanted to acquire land of 12 tribal villages in Lanjigarh block of Kalahandi district, Orissa, to build a refinery. Most of the Adivasis refused to give their land. The Adivasis founded the Niyamgiri Surakshya Samiti (Niyamgiri Protection Society) soon. Two more organizations of the concerned citizens, i.e. Kalahandi Sachetan Nagarika Manch and Green Kalahandi have come up to join in the movement against Vedanta.[53] In December 2003, the Sterlite became Vedanta. The Refinery is operated by Vedanta Alumina Ltd. (VAL). The foundation stone for the Lanjigarh Refinery was destroyed by outraged villagers, but work started soon after constructing a boundary wall. Police rapidly started evacuating the place and brought the tribals, who accepted the compensation, to the new colony called Vedantanagar.

The process of acquisition has continued ever since. On 7 April, 2004 about 2000 adivasis took part in an Oath March from Belamba village to Lanjigarh town to strengthen resistance to the Vedanta project. The next day police arrested 15 people for setting fire to Sterlite machines. Vedanta started expanding and established many new smelters. Between November 2007 and January 2009, Orissa Pollution Control Board reported repeated violations by Vedanta of the environmental safeguards it had signed up. Bansdhara River is polluted, livestock and people have been poisoned, wildlife and tribals lost their lives and suffering from lung and skin diseases. Yet, in June 2009, Vedanta won a Golden Peacock Award for excellence in its environmental record. Opposition to Vedanta has been tagged as 'Maoists'.

KALINGANAGAR MOVEMENT AGAINST TISCO (2006)

With the advent of the neo-liberal era, the idea of Kalinganagar industrial complex emerged in 1990s. Industrial Development Corporation or IDCO was given the task of developing infrastructural facilities for the project. TISCO signed a deal with the Orissa government in August 1995. Prime Minister Narasimha Rao laid the foundation stone for Gopalpur Steel Plant on 30 December 1995. The factory threatened to displace about 25,000 people from 25 villages. Adivasis formed a Gana Sangram Samiti and women formed a Nari Sena. 6,000 armed police were sent to quell the resistance in August 1996 and arrested hundreds of Adivasis. In repeated lathi charges many women were injured and two died. Police invaded the area again in March 1999 and met strong resistance again, opened fire and injured four severely.

Kalinganagar is crowded with industries of corporate houses like

Tatas and Jindals. The more vigorously they have pursued their projects, the stronger has been the resentment of locals. The people of the state had witnessed, on 9 May 2005, the abject misuse of state machinery for Maharashtra Seamless against the agitating tribals. One woman protester was crushed to death and many were detained for 22 days at Kalinganagar Police Station. It was only after eight months, on 2 January 2006 hundreds of Adivasis from 25 villages heard that Tata was about to start a construction on their land near Champakoili village.[54] Just as the bulldozers were about to start levelling the ground, and a delegation of tribals had met with no response from the authorities, it seems that a stick of dynamite exploded in a group of advancing Adivasis, injuring four and blowing the foot off one man. The state government could realize how barbaric its attacks could be, but at the cost of 12 innocent tribal lives and the life of a policeman. The Kalinganagar incident has numbed everybody and left even the corporate confused.

For 23 days, the Adivasis had blocked the state highway at Kalinganagar, protesting against the takeover of their farmlands by a steel company. Then the Adivasis attacked a *havildar* and killed him. This death triggered the police firing, which lasted for about an hour. 13 Adivasis died and 38 Adivasis were seriously injured. Police took six bodies away immediately afterwards, and when these were returned, their hands and genitals were cut off. There was also an attempt to tag the movement as 'Maoist'. Kalinganagar Adivasis continue their opposition and face threats from the company mafias. Adivasis have teamed up in Kalinganagar through an association named Visthapan Virodhi Jana Manch (VVJM) to protest the proposed steel plant by Tata and the move to displace people.[55]

PARADIP MOVEMENT AGAINST POSCO (2006)

Pohang Steel Company of South Korea was also drawing up plans for a contentious steel plant at around this time on the coast near Paradip port, in Jagatsingpur district. The primary aim was to get a lease for mining iron in an area of un-spoilt forest on the beautiful Khandadhara mountain of Sundargarh district. Resistance to POSCO is led by betel-vine farmers, who refuse to leave their fertile fields on the proposed factory site. People of the Pahari Bhuniya tribe are preparing to resist this invasion. Since 2006, the Adivasis were under constant pressure. They erected barricades and in May 2007 kidnapped POSCO officials for a couple of days. The project received environmental clearance in August 2007 and serious violence erupted on 29 November when the company goons threw bombs at a crowd consisting largely of women. The POSCO Pratirodh Sangram Samiti has resisted all attempts to mine Khandadhara mountain.

In Gobindpur village of Dhinkia gram panchayat, a 20 platoon strong police force met with unprecedented resistance, with thousands of people forming a human barricade with women and children. They kept their struggle alive even during the imprisonment from October 2008 to August 2009 of their leader, PPSS President Abhaya Sahoo. The movement against POSCO is primarily a people's movement. As has been established time and again, the people dictate the leadership. One may at times find the leadership showing signs of fatigue, but not the people, especially the young.[56]

LALGARH MOVEMENT (2008)

Lalgarh comprises Binpur I, some parts of Binpur II and Jhargram blocks of the West Medinipur district, in West Bengal. The area is mainly inhabited by Santhal tribals. The area has had a history of neglect and discrimination, with little to offer in terms of development and basic necessities for the people. The Lalgarh movement began in a different context. It started as a response against the brutality perpetrated by the police on 5 November 2008. It was, at the same time, a fight against age-old deprivation and humiliation and for the assertion of dignity and the rights of the people. However, the landmines attack on the West Bengal chief minister on 2 November 2008 as a mark of protest against the Jindal Special Economic Zone (SEZ) at Shalboni.[57]

From 2 November onwards, the police arrested four schoolboys, a schoolteacher and other villagers for 'investigation'. Deepak

Pratihar of Kantapahari village was arrested on 3 November when he was coming back from the block office. The policemen reportedly kicked his pregnant wife on the abdomen when she tried to intervene. Eight people, including Gopal Sareng and Lakhiram Murmu, were arrested in this manner from different villages. On 5 November, the police beat up women in Chotapelia village when they were resisting the arrest of a labour contractor, injuring ten women seriously and permanently damaging the eye of Chintamuni Murmu. By the morning of 6 November, as police atrocities continued unabated, the anger of the people reached a peak. Thousands of Adivasi men and women gathered in front of the Lalgarh police station and blockaded it. Vigil committees formed in each village by the Pulish Shantrash Birodhi Janashadharaner Committee (PSBJC, People's Committee against Police Atrocities). Although the Lalgarh movement started with a spontaneous outburst of people's anger, it quickly assumed an organized form under the leadership of the PSBJC. The people of Lalgarh have launched a profound struggle for justice and the right to self-determination. Although the region faces widespread poverty and neglect, the primary demands of the movement are not economic in nature. Rather, the people are demanding the restoration of their dignity and apologies from state functionaries for their highhanded behaviour and atrocities.[58]

NARAYANPATNA MOVEMENT (2009)

Chasi Mulia Adivasi Sangha (CMAS) in Narayanpatna, a predominantly tribal populated block in Koraput district, has fought for Adivasi land rights in poverty-ridden south Orissa for over two decades, CMAS became a grave threat to the local *sahukars* (traditional moneylenders and landlords), the liquor traders, the forest mafia and ultimately, the district administration, as it fought to eradicate the slave-like conditions of agricultural labourers, the widespread production and sale of country liquor, and for the redistribution of land among agricultural labourers. The people were protesting against the harassment and violence they were subject to during combing operations in their village when police firing of 20 November 2009 took place in which two Adivasis were killed, several injured and many in the area tortured and arrested. There was a split of CMAS between Narayanpatna and Bandhugaon blocks. The CMAS in Bandhugaon led by the CPI(ML) has expressly criticized the assault and hostility against poor Adivasis and poor non-Adivasis and appealed that the land seized from the Dalit families be returned and the destroyed houses reconstructed. The CMAS in Naryanpatna, instead, views the Bandhugaon section as being close to the *sahukars* and liquor traders.[59] Thus the people's movements have also exhausted myriad democratic means to draw attention to basic needs or in saying no to forms of development that will impoverish them further.

PATHALGADI MOVEMENT (2017)

Pathalgadi movement has challenged the current model of development and also asserted Adivasi identity by proposing an alternative of a powerful *gram sabha* as a village agency at the grassroot level. The Pathalgadi movement in this neo-liberal era is a lesson that revives the memory of the Adivasi movement during colonial era which claims their authority over their own territory. The movement has fostered the sub-national consciousness among the Adivasis in the country. The Pathalgadi movement in Jharkhand is strong among the Munda and the Ho Adivasis, who are of Kolarian origin.

Pathalgadi means erecting stones on a dead person's tomb or just to mark any memorable occasion is a well-known custom of the Adivasis. Adivasis inscribe messages on these large stones which are locally called as Pathalgadi, that are painted green and measure about 15 ft by 4 ft and the messages are written in white, apparently to demonstrate their close association with their green landscape. *Sasandiri* was the original term the Mundas used to describe this practice. These stone slabs are erected by the gram sabhas of the villages, which purport, on the one hand, to assume powers by drawing legitimacy from the constitutional provisions. On the other hand, they draw on the customary practice of *parha* panchayat (traditional panchayats of the Adivasis of Chota Nagpur) to assign more power to the *mankis* (head of *parha*) and the *mundas* (head of the village).[60] British exploitation of the past was the central theme of the movement, by which the Adivasis demanded a complete ban on the free passage of the *dikus* and making *gram sabhas* the chief authority.[61] This has led to the revival of the native system of village governance[62] and the notion of the golden past where there was no displacement, no poverty. The Adivasis of Jharkhand are awfully in crisis as the influx of outsiders is increasing at an alarming rate. Besides, the *gram sabhas* have never been consulted before any acquisition of land in spite of having clear provisions in Jharkhand Panchayati Raj Act (JPRA), 2001, amended in 2010 as well as PESA in this regard. Pathalgadi movement is aimed to strengthen the role of the *gram sabhas* through PESA.[63]

In February 2017, the government of Jharkhand organized a global investors' summit titled 'Momentum Jharkhand' in Ranchi. A lot of MoUs were signed to make the state one of the richest hubs of mining and industrial investments. Companies like Usha Martin Group, RSB Group, Tata Steel Growth Shop (TGS) and others showed interest.[64] The government declared that it would form a 'land bank' in which thousand acres of non-cultivable land will be included to materialize the development programmes.[65] This was the background of the Pathalgadi movement. After the declaration made by the chief minister Adivasis got really afraid of being displaced by the development projects. In a small village called Bhandra of Khunti district in Jharkhand, a stone slab was erected on the boundary of the village on 9 March 2017.[66] Initially, the Khunti district of Jharkhand was the stronghold of the movement which later spread to neighbouring districts of Latehar and Singhbhum, and the areas of Jashpur in Chhattisgarh.[67] The movement first came to the news when on 21 February 2018, 25 policemen were detained by the villagers of Kanki in Khunti district for entering their locality without prior permission of the *gram sabha* and arresting the *gram pradhan.* Since then, arrest of leaders of the movement and *gram pradhans* has resulted in *gherao* of police stations, stopping armed policemen for questioning for trespassing in their area and holding policemen hostage for releasing persons arrested on the charges of Pathalgadi which has become a regular feature. On 23 May 2018, villagers of Baruhatu of Khunti held an anti-landmine vehicle and eight policemen hostage in return for the release of Durga Munda who was associated with the Pathalgadi movement.[68]

Several villages of the district—Kanki, Kochang, Jilinga, Udburu and others—erected stone slab inscribed with the order given by the *gram sabha* for implementing constitutional provisions, such as Article 13(3)(a), Article 19(5)(6), Article 244(1) part (b) Para (5)(1) of the Fifth Schedule. Significantly, the slab recorded a similar order by the *gram sabha* imposing restrictions on the entry of outsiders which included police, government officials, medical staff and strangers. This way, the traditional cultural practice of 'Pathalgadi' was employed with political motives, first, drawing legitimacy from the Constitution and second, on its facade declaring their landscape as an autonomous zone.[69]

The Pathalgadi movement received a huge response from the Adivasis of Jharkhand. Adivasi organizations such as Desh Parganas Mahal and Adivasi Mahasabha[70] are currently working towards raising awareness of the Adivasis about their autonomy and complete control over their own landscape called *abua disum, abua raj* (our village, our governance). The movement has spread over Chhattisgarh and Orissa.[71]

KOEL-KARO MOVEMENT (2001)

The Koel-Karo movement in Jharkhand is a movement of Munda, Oraon, and other Adivasis against the construction of two big dams of a hydroelectric project planned on the South Koel and Karo Rivers going on for about 30 years. Undoubtedly, it is one of the successful examples of prevention of the construction of massive dams on Adivasi lands in a long and rich history of struggles in India by tribal people against displacement and dispossession. Koel-Karo movement has set an exemplary instance of stopping any significant land acquisition by the state for the hydroelectric project in the Koel and Karo River valleys. The project aimed at acquiring 55,000 ha of land from a minimum of 112 villages, threatening about 1,50,000 people, for the generation of 710 megawatts of electricity.[72] According to the Koel-Karo Jan Sangathan (KKJS), an organization consisting of only and all the local villagers of the submergence area, the number of affected villages is 256 and the number of threatened families is obviously very high. It has been estimated that a total of 1,50,000 to 2,00,000 people face displacement as a result of this dam. The project was planned in 1955 and needs to acquire 55,000 acres of land in order to produce 710 mw of electricity.

In 1998, the Supreme Court of India passed a judgement whereby all development projects that threaten to displace Adivasi populations must work with a land-for-land rehabilitation plan as opposed to rehabilitation through monetary compensation. Today, this has become standard for all projects displacing Adivasis; rehabilitation cannot be done in the form of monetary compensation but only through land-for-land exchanges. Yet this policy is not very practicable in a country as densely populated as India. Legally, at least, it is quite complicated to accomplish, and as a result there is increasing pressure from bureaucrats and industrialists to override this landmark judgement.[73]

When the new government took the charge it proclaimed that the construction of the Koel-Karo dam was its principal aim and it would invest more power and money in curbing Maoist guerillas militarily in the vast rural areas of Jharkhand. Over the next few months the rural police were rearmed and put on high alert. Bunker-like structures were built at police stations and outposts.[74] On 1 February 2001, the police opened fire on villagers demonstrating in the Tapkara market in Ranchi district of Jharkhand, again an instance of police brutality.[75] Police opened fire from rifles for a full hour on a 4,000-5,000 strong crowd of mostly Munda Adivasis. Nine local people died from the firing and at least 22 other Munda persons were seriously injured. Several injuries have not been officially reported while there are a few persons who seem to be missing. It was an entirely peaceful crowd which was fired upon savagely and relentlessly for almost an hour without any provocation. In Jharkhand, the Koel-Karo movement stands as the great symbol of the continued struggle and survival of Adivasi society in spite of the forces of capital and globalization arraigned against them.[76]

For the first time in the history of the Koel-Karo movement that the Adivasis resorted to violent means. After police firing, the movement was successfully carried on by the Adivasis in 2002. In January, NHPC (National Hydro Power Corporation) pulled out, citing the total lack of land acquisition for the project. The Department of Land Acquisition said that it wanted that NHPC officials were the ones in charge of this job, because 'to go into those tribal villages is to risk your life. You can be lynched any moment. Not a single of our employees are willing to go there any more.'[77] The Koel-Karo movement was chiefly non-violent in nature even after the recent unprecedented police firing on a group of peaceful protestors; followed by the state government and the police's nonchalance and the largely, one-sided press reports which have not deterred them in its resolve to continue its struggle, firmly espousing the path of peace and democracy.

The police had also surrounded several villages in Balitutha and Potko in Jharkhand and had fired on thousands of protesters resisting the takeover of their lands by the Tata and Jindals. As Arundhati Roy has rightly said that, political parties and individuals who have not, in the last 25 years, ever lent their support to say, the Narmada Bachao Andolan, or marched in solidarity with any one of the many peaceful people's movements in the country, have suddenly begun to extol the virtues of non-violence and Gandhian *satyagraha*. On the other hand, those who have been actively involved in these struggles may strongly disagree with the Maoists; they are wary, even exasperated, but they do see them as a part of the same resistance.[78]

NOTES

1. B.R. Ambedkar, 'Gandhism: The Doom of the Untouchables', in *What Congress and Gandhi have Done to the Untouchables*, ed. Vasant Moon, New Delhi: Dr. Ambedkar Foundation, Ministry of Social Justice & Empowerment, Government of India, 1991, p. 283.
2. M.K. Gandhi, *An Autobiography or My Experiments with Truth*, tr. Mahadev Desai, Ahmedabad, Gujarat: Navajivan Prakashan, 1969, p. 352. For more details, see R.P. Mitra, 'Mahatma Gandhi and Tribal Development', *Journal of the Anthropological Survey of India*, 68(2), 2019, pp. 234-44.

3. Ernesto 'Che' Guevara, *Guerrilla Warfare: Introduction by Marc Becker*, New York: Monthly Review Press, 1998, p. 7.
4. Nivedita Menon, 'Radical Resistance and Political Violence Today', *Economic and Political Weekly*, vol. 44, no. 50, 12-18 December 2009, pp. 16-20.
5. T. Karunakaran, et al., ed., *Appropriate Technology Lineage Gandhi, Kumarappa, Schumacher*, Gandhigram: Gandhigram Rural Institute, 1993, p. 61.
6. Ramachandra Guha, 'A Nation Consumed by the State', *Outlook*, 31 January 2011, pp. 30-44.
7. Giuliano Pontara, 'Reflections on Gandhi: Between Ethics and Politics', in *Between Ethics and Politics: Gandhi Today*, ed. Eva Pfostl, New Delhi: Routledge, 2014, p. 53.
8. Shiv Visvanathan, 'Reinventing Gandhi', in *Debating Gandhi: A Reader*, ed. A. Raghuramaraju, Oxford: Oxford University Press, 2010, p. 208.
9. Giuliano Pontara, 'Reflections on Gandhi: Between Ethics and Politics', op. cit., pp. 56-7.
10. *Harijan*, 1 September 1940.
11. *Harijan*, 17 March 1946, in M.K. Gandhi, *The Moral and Political Writings of Mahatma Gandhi*, ed. R. Iyer, Oxford: Claredon Press, vol. II, 1986, p. 83.
12. M.K. Gandhi, *The Moral and Political Writings of Mahatma Gandhi*, ed. R. Iyer, Oxford: Claredon Press, vol. III, 1986, p. 49.
13. Y. Chada, *Rediscovering Gandhi*, London: Century, 1997, pp. 9-10.
14. *The Englishman*, 28 January 1902, in M.K. Gandhi, *The Moral and Political Writings of Mahatma Gandhi*, ed. R. Iyer, Oxford: Claredon Press, vol. III, 1986, pp. 264-5.
15. *Harijan*, 13 October 1940.
16. *Harijan*, 7 December 1947, p. 174.
17. *Harijan*, 29 April 1939, p. 101.
18. M.V. Naidu, 'Gandhian Humanism and Contemporary Crises', *Peace Research*, vol. 21, no. 4, November 1989, pp. 53-5.
19. *Harijan*, 31 August 1947, pp. 25 and 302.
20. *Young India*, 29 October 1931, p. 325.
21. W.P. Kabadi, ed., *India's Case for Swaraj*, Bombay: Yeshanand & Co., 1932, p. 209.
22. *Harijan*, 11 February 1939, p. 8.
23. M.V. Naidu, 'The Gandhian Revolution: A Comparative Analysis', *Peace Research*, vol. 32, no. 4, November 2000, pp. 1-30.
24. *Harijan*, June 1940; *Young India*, April 1926.

25. Sumanta Banerjee, 'Gandhi's Flexible Non-Violence', *Economic and Political Weekly*, vol. 48, no. 31, 3 August 2013, p. 4
26. Giuliano Pontara, 'Reflections on Gandhi: Between Ethics and Politics', op. cit., p. 69.
27. W.H. Roberts, 'A Review of the Gandhi Movement in India', *Political Science Quarterly*, vol. 38, no. 2, June 1923, pp. 227-48.
28. Felix Padel and Samarendra Das, *Out of this Earth: East India Adivasis and the Aluminium Cartel*, New Delhi: Orient Blackswan, 2010, pp. 25-6.
29. Nehru to Gandhi, from 'Selected Letters', *The Selected Works of Mahatma Gandhi*, vol. V, 9 October 1945, pp. 122-5.
30. Felix Padel Samarendra Das, *Out of this Earth*, op. cit., 2010, p. 26.
31. David Hardiman, 'Towards a History of Non-violent Resistance', *Economic and Political Weekly*, vol. 48, no. 23, 8 June 2013, pp. 41-8.
32. M.K. Gandhi, 'The Fiery Ordeal', *Young India*, 4 October 1928, in *Collected Works of Mahatma Gandhi*, vol. 43, electronic book (CD-ROM), Publications Division, Ministry of Information and Broadcasting, Government of India, New Delhi, 1999, p. 59.
33. Ramachandra Guha, 'Mahatma Gandhi and the Environmental Movement', in *Debating Gandhi: A Reader*, ed. A. Raghuramaraju, Oxford: Oxford University Press, 2010, p. 223.
34. Felix Padel and Samarendra Das, *Out of this Earth*, op. cit., pp. 569 and 575.
35. Prathama Banerjee, 'Culture/Politics: The Curious Double-bind of the Indian Adivasi', in *Subaltern Citizens and their Histories*, ed. Gyanendra Pandey, New York: Routledge, 2010, p. 133.
36. Ramachandra Guha, 'Mahatma Gandhi and the Environmental Movement', in *Debating Gandhi*, op. cit., 2010, p. 235.
37. Gandhi in *Young India*, p. 421. From N.K. Bose (1957) *Selections From Gandhi*, 26 December 1924, pp. 38-9.
38. Gandhi in *Young India*, p. 381. From N.K. Bose (1957) *Selections From Gandhi*, 15 November 1928, pp. 38-9.
39. Felix Padel and Samarendra Das, *Out of this Earth*, op. cit., 2010, p. 393.
40. Prathama Banerjee, 'Culture/politics: The Curious Double-bind of the Indian Adivasi', op. cit., p. 139.
41. B.D. Sharma, *Unbroken History of the Broken Promises*, New Delhi: Freedom Press, 2010, pp. 28-9.
42. Alpa Shah and Judith Pettigrew, 'Windows into a Revolution: Ethnographies of Maoism in South Asia', *Dialectical Anthropology*, vol. 33, no. 3/4, December 2009, pp. 225-51.

43. Manoranjan Mohanty, 'Adivasi Swaraj is the Answer to Violence', *Economic and Political Weekly*, vol. LII, no. 21, 27 May 2017, pp. 66-70.
44. Manoranjan Mohanty, *Red and Green: Five Decades of the Indian Maoist Movement*, Kolkata: Setu Prakashani, 2015, p. 298.
45. Sumanta Banerjee, 'Revolutionary Movements in a Post-Marxian Era', *Economic and Political Weekly*, vol. 47, no. 18, 5 May 2012, pp. 55-61.
46. Nivedita Menon, 'Radical Resistance and Political Violence Today', *Economic and Political Weekly*, vol. 44, no. 50, 12-18 December 2009, pp. 16-20.
47. Arundhati Roy, 'The Trickledown Revolution', *Outlook*, 20 September 2010, pp. 26-51.
48. Felix Padel and Samarendra Das, *Out of this Earth*, op. cit., p. 25.
49. Arundhati Roy, 'The Trickledown Revolution', op. cit., pp. 26-51.
50. Deba Ranjan Sarangi, 'Surviving against Odds: Case of Kashipur', *Economic and Political Weekly*, vol. 37, no. 31, 3-9 August 2002, pp. 3239-41.
51. Felix Padel and Samarendra Das, *Out of this Earth*, op. cit., p. xx.
52. Vidhya Das, 'Kashipur: Politics of Underdevelopment', *Economic and Political Weekly*, vol. 38, no. 1, 4-10 January 2003, pp. 81-4.
53. Sarmistha Pattanaik, 'Does Environmental Degradation Escalate Naxalist Violence? Reflections from Orissa', in *Discourses on Naxalbari Movement 1967-2009*, ed. Pradip Basu, Kolkata: Setu Prakashani, 2010, pp. 172-87.
54. Banikanta Mishra, 'People's Movement at Kalinga Nagar: An Epitaph or an Epitome?', *Economic and Political Weekly*, vol. 41, no. 7, 18-24 February 2006, pp. 551-4.
55. Chandi Prasad Nanda, 'Dislocated by Development: Discourse on Development and People's Movement in Post-Colonial Odisha', *Proceedings of the Indian History Congress*, vol. 73, 2012, pp. 1357-65.
56. Banikanta Mishra and Birendra Kumar Nayak, 'Paan or POSCO?', *Economic and Political Weekly*, vol. 46, no. 26/27, 25 June-8 July 2011, pp. 12-13.
57. Amit Bhattacharyya, 'Is Lalgarh Showing the Way?' *Economic and Political Weekly*, vol. 45, no. 2, 9-15 January 2010, pp. 17-21.
58. Manika Bora and Budhaditya Das, 'The Movement in Lalgarh', *Economic and Political Weekly*, vol. 44, no. 26/27, 27 June-10 July 2009, pp. 15-17.
59. Ranjana Padhi, Pramodini Pradhan and D. Manjit, 'How Many More Arrests Will Orissa See?', *Economic and Political Weekly*, vol. 45, no. 10, 6-12 March 2010, pp. 24-6.
60. S.C. Roy, *The Mundas and their Country*, Calcutta: Kuntaline Press, 1912, pp. 117-21.

61. Asoka Kumar Sen, *Indigenity, Landscape and History: Adivasi Self Fashioning in India*, New York: Routledge, 2018, p. 81.
62. The traditional system of self-governance is called the *patti* system among the Mundas, the *parha* system among the Oraons, the *manjhi parganait* system among the Santhals, the *munda manki* system among the Hos and the *doklo sohor maha* samiti among the Kharias.
63. *Hindustan*, 'Jhakhand Main Poori Tarah Laagoo Nahi Hai "PESA" ', Supplement, Ranchi, 25 February 2018.
64. Sourav Mukherjee, 'Momentum Jharkhand: 21 Projects Launched', *Times of India*, 19 May 2017, viewed on 9 April 2018, https://timesofindia.indiatimes.com/india/momentum-jharkhand21-projects-launched/articleshow/58770157.cms; also see, *Daily Pioneer* (2017): 'Over 100 Investment Proposals for Momentum Jharkhand-3: CS,' 5 October, viewed on 13 April 2018, https://www.dailypioneer.com/2017/state-editions/over100-investment-proposals-for-momentumjharkhand-3-cs.html
65. Swati Parashar and Anju O.M. Toppo: 'Patthalgari Challenges the Republic in its own Backyard', *Indian Express*, 7 April 2018, https://indian express.com/article/opinion/patthalgarhi-jharkhand-challenges-the-republicin-its-own-backyard-5128458/
66. *Hindustan*, 'Adivasiyon Ko Train Aur Viman Sewa Muft Mile', Ranchi, 2018, 8 March, p. 1.
67. Rajiv Goswami, 'Sirf Khunti Ke 1,500 Acre Main Afeem Ki Kheti Darr ya Kamai . . . Police Vahan Kabhi Jaati Hii Nahi', *Dainik Bhaskar*, Ranchi, 6 March 2018.
68. *Dainik Bhaskar*, 'Khunti Main Gramino Nain Phir 8 Police Jawano Ko 4 Ghante Bandhak Banaya', Ranchi, 24 May 2018.
69. Anjana Singh, 'Many Faces of the Pathalgadi Movement in Jharkhand', *Economic and Political Weekly*, vol. LIV no. 11, 16 March 2019, pp. 28-33.
70. *Dainik Bhaskar*, 'Pathalgadi Ki Aar Main Hungama: Sarkar Aur Rajneeti Dal Bhi Bhramit', Ranchi, 25 February 2018.
71. For details please see Debasree De, 'Tribal Land Alienation and Resistance in Jharkhand: A Case Study of Pathalgadi Movement', *Journal of Kolkata Society for Asian Studies*, vol. 6, no. 1, 2020, pp. 200-214.
72. Madhukar, 'Koel-Karo Battles On', *Down to Earth*, 15 June 1992, pp. 18-19.
73. Kaushik Ghosh, 'Between Global Flows and Local Dams: Indigenousness, Locality, and the Transnational Sphere in Jharkhand, India', *Cultural Anthropology*, vol. 21, no. 4, November 2006, pp. 501-34.
74. Kaushik Ghosh, Sarada Balagopalan and Meghnath, 'Adivasis Massacred

in Koel-Karo, Jharkhand', *Economic and Political Weekly*, 3-10 March 2001, pp. 717-21.

75. Bela Bhatia, 'Resistance and Repression', *Frontline*, March 2001, pp. 3-16.
76. Kaushik Ghosh, Sarada Balagopalan and Meghnath, 'Massacres of Adivasis: A Preliminary Report' *Economic and Political Weekly*, vol. 36, no. 9, 3-9 March 2001, pp. 717-21.
77. Navika Kumar, 'NHPC Gets Ready to Pull Plug on Koel Karo', *Indian Express*, 31 March 2002.
78. Arundhati Roy, 'The Trickledown Revolution', op. cit., pp. 26-51.

CHAPTER 6

A Postscript: Gandhi in Adivasi Folk Traditions

1

The system of the zamindars broke down,
With it went away the begari performed by the Kisan
The big baboo is now handling the Kudal
We won't have either police or village chowkidar
Do not sleep brother Kisan
A Bihari wolf enters Chota Nagpur
Awake the Kisan!
Collect stones, to drive it away.
O children of Bharat, listen to the word of Gandhi
Let us confront the Sarkar
The forest bush was taken away,
The bush, the hills were also taken away
We were cheated.[1]

[The English translation of the speeches delivered by the Kherwar speakers at Chunga, Daltonganj Sadar on 8 February 1958. Deputy Commissioner's Confidential Section papers, Confidential Section of the Deputy Commissioner's Office, Palamau.]

2

Birsa and Gandhi (*Bhajan*)

O Mother, like the rising sun Gandhi was born,
Like the rising moon Birsa had come up.
O Mother, Gandhi was born for Swaraj,
Birsa had come up to put the Mundas on their feet.[2]

3

Rana-Nimantran

By Umesh

Hai chheda jang azadi ka, ye hukma hamare Gandhi ka,
Ab chhida Bagad men bhi vahi phisana
Le shastra ahinsa ka kara men viron! Data jao, ja-rana men.

[The Dungarpur Rajya Prajamandal published a journal in Hindi called *Dungarpur Rajya Prajamandal Patrika* to publicize its social and political programme among the Bhils and non-Bhils. The above-mentioned poem was composed on 9 May 1946 which advised men and women to join the non-violent struggle under the leadership of Mahatma Gandhi for the overthrow of the British imperialism.[3]]

4

Ganji dongar chadla bai,
Kachha sutane Salabai.

[This song was sung during the Devi movement in South Gujarat. It means, the woman Salabai was the Devi and she came from the hill of Gandhi. Ganji was a wrong pronunciation of Gandhi.[4]]

5

Gandhi Bapu—Gandhi Bapu
Salabai—Salabai
Saladevi—Saladevi
Daru nahi pivo—tadi nahi pivi
Machhi nahi khavo—mas nahi khavu
Darroj nahavu—sachu bolvu
Rentio kanto—rentio kanto
Gandhi Maharaj—Gandhi Maharaj

[This means, Gandhi Bapu—Gandhi Bapu
Salabai—Salabai
Saladevi—Saladevi
Do not drink daru—do not drink toddy
Do not eat fish—do not eat meat
Take a bath everyday—speak the truth

Spin on the spinning wheel—spin on the spinning wheel
Gandhi Maharaj—Gandhi Maharaj.[5]]

6

Charkha biur biur-te,
Swarajem agukeda,
Gandhim agukeda.
Sutam takui takute,
Swarajem agukeda,
Gandhim agukeda .
Ulgulan kete,
Chotanagpurem agukeda,
Birisam agukeda.

[A Mundari *bhajan* song meaning,
By working the spinning wheel,
You got *swaraj,*
O, Gandhi, you got it.
By spinning cotton,
You got *swaraj,*
O' Gandhi, you got it.
By causing a tumult,
You got Chota Nagpur,
O Birsa, you got it.][6]

7

Ame khadi no Pyjama Paheria
Gulam Pandu na kariaye
Ane Mandini Nankari kariye
Sansunina kariye Gulam Pandu Na Kariye.

[The above stanza of folklore is quoted in: P. G. Shah, *Tribal Life in Gujarat,* Chap. X, Folklore Art, Mumbai, Popular Prakashan, 1955, p. 224.]

8

This is your last chance, come to the feet of Gandhi,
Leave the drink-habit and take to the spinning-wheel,
Leave the use of flesh and fish, and take to producing yarn,

Leave the worship of spirits and ghosts, and believe in Holy Rama,
Leave foreign and British articles and take to khadi, for this is
your last chance.

[This is a *bhajan* sung by the *bhajan mandalis* organized by educated Adivasi reformers. This particular *bhajan* has a nationalist content.[7]]

9

Do you know what Gandhi tells you,
Give up liquor, eating meat, stealing, rioting,
Spin the *charkha*;
Let every house echo with the sound of the spinning wheel
Thakkar Bapa says, educate your children
Give up your false deities, and worship Ram, the true God.[8]

[A Bhil *bhajan* originally in Hindi and rendered by Thakkar Bapa in 1955.]

10

Bhajan

Nimin din Gandhi takliph janae,
Gandhi takliph janae,
Chotanagpur me swaraj lele Gandhi,
Swaraj lele Gandhi,
Bhakti bhai sange Gandhi swaraj lele,
Swaraj lele.

[Gandhi suffered so long!
Gandhi suffered.
O Gandhi, you got *swaraj* for Chota Nagpur.
Gandhi got *swaraj.*
With Bhagats (behind him) Gandhi got *swaraj,*
He got *swaraj.*[9]]

11

Bhajan

Singi turoleka numa Gandhi doe janamlen.
Chandu turoleka numa Birisa doe upaelen.

Swaraj natin numa Gandhi doe janamlen,
Mundako bird natin numa Birisa doe uparlen.

[O Mother, like the rising Sun Gandhi was born,
O Mother, like the rising Moon Birsa had come up.
O Mother, Gandhi was born for *swaraj.*
O Mother, Birsa had come up to put the Mahatma on their feet.[10]]

12

The Spinning Wheel and Swaraj

Bhajan (Sadani)

Dutu kati kati ke swaraj lele Baba,
Swaraj lele Baba.
Kori Korke swaraj lele Baba,
Swaraj lele Baba.
Baro joti jotike swaraj lele Baba,
Swaraj lele Baba.
Kapas boi boi ke swaraj lele Baba,
Swaraj lele.
Kapas oti oti ke swaraj lele Baba,
Birsa Bhagwan swaraj lele,
Rua dhuni dhuni Baba swaraj lele,
Charkha kati kati ke swaraj lele.

[O Father, by clearing the jungle, you won *swaraj.*
O Father, you got it.
O Father, by digging (the earth) you won *swaraj,*
O Father, you got it.
O Father, by ploughing (the field) you won *swaraj,*
O Father, you got it.
O Father, by sowing cotton seeds you won *swaraj,*
O Father, you got it.
O Father, by sowing cotton seeds you won *swaraj,*
You got it.
O Father, by ginning cotton from seeds you won *swaraj,*
O Father, by combing cotton wool you won *swaraj,*

You got it.
O Father, by spinning the working wheel, you won *swaraj*.]

13

Wearing of *Khadi*

Dress we in *khadi pyjama*
Tolerate we no servitude
Serve we never as Halis bonded servant
Tolerate we no srvitude
Serve we our mothers
Serve we never our mother-in-law
Tolerate we no servitude.[11]

14

On Prohibition

This was the last occasion to seek, the protection of Gandhi,
Sing the merits of Gandhi
Leave wine and leave toddy
Drink milk and butter milk
Leave to eat meat and fish
Eat but Jaggery and Bajra leaf,
Leave Buva (priest) and belief in ghost
Utter Ram, the last word
Leave foreign cloth and
take resort to *khadi*.[12]

15

On Spinning

Unbroken is the thread from the spinning wheel,
Broken could be the iron shakles and golden ornaments,
Thousands of gun could be defeated but not this Kachha Safar thread.[13]

16

Adibasi 1952

By Verrier Elwin

How tired they are, and what a somber grace
  Time has drawn on the wise old faces, grey
With the death of children, and no release
  From want that rules day after anxious day.
There was life there once, and joy in recreation,
  Dancing and laughter, love among the trees,
But little now save sullen speculation
  Of what the future has and where it leads.
Old rules are broken, boys go to the town;
  Children are married in a loveless tie;
The ancient forest is no more their own;
  The women lose their treasured liberty.
New customs which are little understood
  Drive out the old, leave nothing in their place.
The old men suck their wooden pipes and brood,
  And tremble for the future of their race.[14]

NOTES

1. K.S. Singh, 'A Forest Satyagraha', in *Tribal Movements in India*, vol. II, ed. K.S. Singh, New Delhi: Manohar, 2015, p. 190.
2. K.S. Singh, *Birsa Munda and his Movement (1874-1901)*, Delhi: Oxford University Publication, 1983, p. 285.
3. Vijay Kumar Vashishtha, *Role of Gandhi's Ideas in Mobilization of Adivasis of Southern Rajputana Princely States (1921-48)*, Shimla: Indian Institute of Advanced Studies, 2014, p. 150.
4. David Hardiman, *The Coming of the Devi Adivasi Assertion in Western India*, Delhi: Oxford University Press, 1987, p. 34.
5. Ibid., p. 172.
6. K.S. Singh, 'The Mahatma and the Adivasis', *Gandhi and the Social Sciences*, 1970, pp. 125-6.
7. David Hardiman, *The Coming of the Devi*, op. cit., 1987, p. 197.

8. K.S. Singh, 'Mahatma Gandhi and the Adivasis', *Man in India*, vol. 50, no. 1, January-March 1970, pp. 1-25.
9. Ibid.
10. Ibid.
11. Shirin Mehta, *The Peasantry and Nationalism: A Study of the Bardoli Satyagraha*, New Delhi: Manohar, 1984, p. 87.
12. Shirin Mehta, 'Social Consciousness of "Historyless": A Study of Folk Literature of Tribals of South Gujarat during the Colonial Period', *Proceedings of the Indian History Congress*, vol. 48, 1987, pp. 467-77.
13. Ibid.
14. Ramchandra Guha, *Savaging the Civilized*, op. cit., 2014, p. 206.

Conclusion

> I cannot believe this army. As far as consumption goes, it's more Gandhian than any Gandhian, and has a lighter carbon footprint than any climate change evangelist. But for now, it even has a Gandhian approach to sabotage; before a police vehicle is burnt, for example, it is stripped down and every part cannibalised. The steering wheel is straightened out and made into a *bharmaar*, the rexine upholstery stripped and used for ammunition pouches, the battery for solar charging. (The new instructions from the high command are that captured vehicles should be buried and not cremated. So they can be resurrected when needed.) Should I write a play, I wonder—Gandhi Get Your Gun? Or will I be lynched?[1]
>
> ARUNDHATI ROY

Under the British colonial rule, most of the tribal populations have a history of resistance of the outsiders for their nefarious acts of encroachment and exploitation.[2] Even after Independence, many, with a strong sense of sons of the soil, have continued to assert for their rights. A live indigenous tribal identity is an integral part of any tribal awakening for rights, whether a revolt or a movement, though its expression might be latent in some cases.[3] In Chota Nagpur the first revolt took place in 1789, closely following the actual occupation of the region in 1772. In 1831-2 when Western forces had hardly reached Chota Nagpur, the tribals, being harassed by their adversaries, spontaneously felt to rise against the enemies.[4] Most of the Adivasi movements of the post-colonial era have powerfully engaged with the repressive mechanism represented by state-corporate combine in the latter's attempt at land grab mostly legitimized invoking the 'myth of public/national interest'. Analysing these movements in the wake of neo-liberalization of economy and the brief traumatic history of development dislocation since Independence, it is crucial to conclude with the final words about the influence of Gandhian methods on the tribal resistance of today.

The most crucial aspect of these resistance movements has been the development-induced-displacement. The development paradigm followed by the government so far has ended up destroying the social organization of Adivasi people, their cultural identity and resource base. It has also generated multiple conflicts, undermining the communal solidarity of the Adivasi people, which has cumulatively made them increasingly vulnerable to exploitation. The problem is that the state has always treated Adivasis as 'sacrificial lambs' who can be dispensed with in the pursuit of development activities. Non-recognition of indigenous rights has compounded the problem. Adivasi people, who bear the brunt of industrial development, have been fighting tooth and nail against the acquisition of forest land and mineral bearing land and hills. Be it in the case of the Niyamgiri hills at Lanjigarh in Kalahandi, which Vedanta Alumina Limited was trying to mine, or the Khandadhar hills in Sundargarh district, which the government was hell-bent on handing over to POSCO for iron ore extraction, they have come out in large numbers to oppose mining, which would adversely affect their livelihoods and water availability. Worse, people's movements are branded as pro-Maoist, and innocent people and activists questioning the land acquisition moves are jailed and charged with having links with the extremists. Various reports have substantiated that over 75 per cent displaced due to land acquisition remain without proper rehabilitation. Those who owned and tilled their own land, or eke out a living from forests and other natural resources, have been reduced to being landless workers, doing jobs in unorganized sectors for a living and leading lives of penury.[5]

Another very important aspect of today's tribal movements is a combination of both violent and non-violent quotient. The dose non-violence is being supplied by the civil society whereas the Maoists are supporting them with the ideology of armed struggle. But the Adivasis themselves are unequivocally and undeniably non-violent which is unprecedented in nature. Both these features were absent during the colonial era. The so-called *bhadralok samaj* or civil society had practically no role in the Adivasi movements during colonial times. Sometimes they even condemned the movements. Since the Adivasis themselves were violent at times during this period, there was no question of Naxalism which is quite evident in the movement of today. Widespread displacement, land alienation, forest loot, onslaught on the Common Property Resources (CPR), humiliation, and increasing insecurity of Adivasi livelihood—all have contributed to the emergence of Maoist activities in the Adivasi region and in spite of violent means taken by them to overthrow the state they are getting support from the tribal masses. Sometimes they even carry out socio-economic reforms in the tribal region. Felix Padel had rightly said that,

> Unlike Gandhi's ideal, however, Adivasis are not vegetarian. They hunt and kill animals to eat. They drink and swing their axes in anger. Many have been drawn to the Naxalite path. Yet the movements . . . are remarkably non-violent, partly from the sense that this is more effective—since violence is invariably met by much greater violence from the security forces—and partly from the example of Gandhi and countless other activists in the tradition of *ahimsa*.[6]

Gandhian non-violence method still has relevance and has been adopted by more or less all anti-globalized protesters. According to David Hardiman, Gandhi deployed several strands of non-violent protest in India and elsewhere in the world to develop a highly effective form of civil protest that deployed an emphasis on non-violence to wrong-foot opponents and gain the moral advantage. Waging non-violent civil resistance does not necessarily require that we should be rigidly 'Gandhian' in every particular way. One does not even have to believe in non-violence as a moral imperative, rather should understand that its deployment has advantages that have time and again proved highly fructified in a wide range of conflicts in many different countries. What is more, its use in the long term is more likely to enable the creation of a more open and democratic society, in which disagreements are resolved through dialogue and negotiation rather than through violence.[7]

NOTES

1. Arundhati Roy, 'Walking with the Comrades', *Outlook*, 29 March 2010, pp. 1-26, downloaded from https://www.outlookindia.com/magazine/story/walking-with-the-comrades/264738 on 2 June 2019.
2. K.S. Singh, *Tribal Movements in India*, New Delhi: Manohar, 1982, cited by Joseph Bara, 'Alien Construct and Tribal Contestation in Colonial Chhotanagpur: The Medium of Christianity', *Economic and Political Weekly*, vol. 44, no. 52, 2010, pp. 90-6.
3. Joseph Bara, 'Alien Construct and Tribal Contestation in Colonial Chota Nagpur: The Medium of Christianity', *Economic and Political Weekly*, vol. 44, no. 52, 26 December 2009-1 January 2010, pp. 90-6.
4. J. Reid, *Final Report on the Survey and Settlement Operations in the Ranchi District, 1902-10*, Patna: Superintendent, Govt. Print, Bihar and Orissa, p. 22.
5. *Frontline*, 17 June 2011, read online at https://frontline.thehindu.com/cover-story/article30175728.ece, accessed on 26 September 2018.
6. Felix Padel and Samarendra Das, *Out of this Earth: East India Adivasis and the Aluminium Cartel*, New Delhi: Orient Blackswan, 2010, p. 592.
7. David Hardiman, 'Gandhi's Adaptable Non-Violence', *Economic and Political Weekly*, vol. 48, no. 33, 17 August 2013, pp. 4-5.

Abbreviations

AICC	All India Congress Committee
BDO	Block Development Officer
CLA	Christian Life Assembly
CMAS	Chasi Mulia Adivasi Sangha
CPI (Maoist)	Communist Party of India (Maoist)
CPI (ML)	Communist Party of India (Marxist-Leninist)
CPR	Common Property Resources
CSS	Christa Seva Sangh
CWMG	Collected Works of Mahatma Gandhi
FSO	Feudatory States of Orissa
IDCO	Industrial Development Corporation
INC	Indian National Congress
JPRA	Jharkhand Panchayati Raj Act
KKJS	Koel-Karo Jan Sangathan
MKSS	Mazdoor Kisan Sangram Samiti
MoU	Memorandum of Understanding
NAI	National Archives of India
NEFA	North Eastern Frontier Agency
NHPC	National Hydro Power Corporation
NMML	Nehru Memorial Museum & Library
NNC	Naga National Council
PESA	Panchayat Raj Extension to the Scheduled Areas Act
POSCO	Pohang Steel Company
PSBJC	Pulish Shantrash Birodhi Janashadharaner Committee
PSSP	Prakrutika Sampad Surakshya Parishad
SEZ	Special Economic Zone
SOLR	Selections from Official Letters and Records
SPG	Society for the Propagation of the Gospel in Foreign Parts

ST	Scheduled Tribes
TGS	Tata Steel Growth Shop
TISCO	Tata Iron and Steel Company
UAIL	Utkal Alumina International Limited
VAL	Vedanta Alumina Ltd.
VVJM	Visthapan Virodhi Jana Manch

Glossary

Achhoot	Untouchable
Adivasi	Tribes
Ahimsa	Non-violence
Asal vatani	Original inhabitants
Ashram/ashramshalas	Hermitage
Atmashuddhi	Self-purification
Banias	Trader
Beth begari	Forced labour
Bewar	Shifting cultivation
Bhadralok	Middle class educated urban elite
Bhagwan	God
Bhajans	Hymns
Bhakti	Devotion
Bharmaar	Glut
Bhathi	Liquor distillery
Bhuinyas	A title used to refer to a landlord or chieftain
Bongas	Malevolent spirits
Charkha	Spinning wheel
Chela	Pupil
Chowkidari	Watchman
Cutcheries	A public office for administrative or judicial business
Daks	The postal service
Dapa	Bride price
Daridra narayan	God in the shape of the poor
Darshana	Sight
Dasas and *Dasyus*	Savages
Des log	Sons of the soil
Desh	Country
Dewan	The chief treasury official

Dewar	Magico-medicine men
Dharam raj	Kingdom of righteousness
Dikus	Outsiders
Disum	Country
Fituri	Rebellion
Ghatwalls	A feudal tenure for quasi-military service in Santhal Parganas.
Gherao	Protestors encircling the targets of the protest
Ghotul	Dormitory
Gram pradhan	Village headman
Gram sabha	Village assembly
Gurus	Spiritual teacher
Haats/hatu	Village market
Harijan	God's people or the Dalits
Haripani	Holy water
Havans	Ritual offerings in the fire
Havildar	Constable
Himsa	Violence
Hul	Rebellion
Jagirdars	Feudal lord
Janeu	Sacred thread
Jhanda	Flag
Khadi/khaddar	An Indian homespun cotton cloth
Khetwaris	Market-garden owner
Khuntkatti	Communal ownership
Kirtans	A devotional song
Kurukh Dharam	True religion
Mahajans	Moneylenders
Mahua	Honey-tree from where alcoholic drink is produced
Mankis	Circle headman
Meriah	Human sacrifice
Moujas	A village consists of a group of houses, together with other buildings such as a church and school
Pirs	A Muslim saint

Podu	Shifting cultivation
Purdah	Seclusion
Raj	Rule
Raja	King
Ramnama	Recite the name 'Rama'
Ram-rajya	Kingdom of Rama
Sahukars	Moneylenders
Sannyasi baba	Religious mendicant
Sapha hors	Pure men
Sardars	Leaders
Sarna	Sacred grove
Sarpanch	Head of the Panchayat
Sarvodaya	The economic and social development of a community
Sasandiri	Place where the Mundas bury the bones of their ancestors
Satyagraha	Passive resistance
Shuddhi	Purification
Sogan	Oath
Swaraj/purna swaraj	Independence/complete independence
Tana	Pull
Tapasya	Penance
Thikadars	Contractors
Tulsi	Holy basil
Ulghulan	Uprising
Umrao	Nobility
Zamindars	Landlords

Bibliography

PRIMARY SOURCE

Annual Progress Report tin Forest Administration of the Province of Bihar and Orissa, 1921-2, Ch. 2, para. 13, Go&O Rev. (Forest) Progs., no. 1-7, November 1922, OIOC, p. 11152.

Bihar and Orissa Government, Police Department, Abstract of Intelligence, vol. V, Palamau, 11 April 1916; Bihar and Orissa Government, Police Department, Abstract of Intelligence, vol. V, Palamau, 15 May 1916.

Bihar and Orissa Political Special File no. 50/21, 'Note by the Chaukidari Magistrate of Ranchi showing the attitude of the Tana Bhagats, Commissioner, Ranchi, to Chief Secretary, 1 April 1921'.

Bihar and Orissa Political Special File Nos. 50/1921, 51/1921 and 219/1921.

Bihar and Orissa Political Special File no. 5011921, 'From Deputy Commissioner, Ranchi, to Commissioner, 3 February 1921'.

Bihar and Orissa Political Special File no. 153/1921.

Bihar and Orissa Annual Administration Report 1921, Patna.

Bihar and Orissa Political Special File no. 478/1921, 'From District Magistrate, Singhbhum, to Lyall, Commissioner of the Chota Nagpur Division, 2 September 1921'.

Chanda, R.P., *Selections from Official Letters and Records (SOLR), Roughsedge to Swaiton*, Secy. to Govt. of Bengal, 7 May 1821.

Circular letter from A.V. Thakkar of 12 September 1940, in Box VIII, File D, Hyde Papers, Centre for South Asian Studies, Cambridge.

Cobden-Ramsay, *Feudatory States of Orissa (FSO)*, (Bengal Gazetiers), Howra.

Confidential File, Political (Special) Department, No. 75 of 1921; *Social Scientist*, vol. 16, no. 11.

Deputy Commissioner of Singhbhum Report, R.P. Ward to Tuckey, Confidential D.O. No 132/C, 30 July 1931, para 8, GoB&O, Pol. (Special) Dept., File no. 57, 1931, BSA.

Elwin Papers, Nehru Memorial Museum and Library (NMML).

File no. 86 of 1919, Political Department, *Special Section*, Government of Bihar and Orissa; File no. 313 of 1920, Political Department, Government of Bihar and Orissa; File no. 75 of 1921, Political Department, *Special Section*, Government of Bihar and Orissa.

Fortnightly Report of Bihar and Orissa for the second half of January 1921, Govt. of India, Home Department (Political), File no. 42/1921, NAI.

Fortnightly Reports of Bihar and Orissa for the first half of May 1921, Govt. of India, Home Department (Political), File nos. 63/June/1921, NAI.

Interim Report of the Excluded and Partially Excluded Areas (other than Assam) Sub-Committee, New Delhi, 1949, Appendix D, Minute of Dissent, 19 August 1947.

'Judgement in the Oraon Case', June 1916, Proceedings No. 280-1.

Letter from L Van Hoeck, Rector, Manresa House, Ranchi to C. Van den Driessche dated Ranchi 17 August 1916, *Correspondence on the Tana Bhagat Movement*; 'Hari-Baba', *The Chota Nagpur Mission Letter*, November 1931, pp 236-7.

Lewis, K. to Sir Alfred Lyall, Commissioner of Chota Nagpur, demi official letter no. 149- TC, 17 August 1921, para 2, Government of Bihar & Orissa, Pol. (Special) Progs, File no. 465, 1921, BSA.

Memorandum dated 18 April 1946. Submitted by Adivasi Congressmen of Chota Nagpur to Mahatma Gandhi; Memorandum dated 1 May 1947, in Subject File 37, C. Rajagopalachari Papers, Fifth Instalment, (NMML).

Police Department, Special Section, Confidential, No. 104C, Ranchi, 4 May 1934.

R.P. Ward to A.D. Tuckey, Confidential D.O. No 132/C, 30 July 1931, para. 4, GoB & O, Pol. (Special) Dept., File no. 57, 1931, BSA.

Reported by Collector of Surat, J.R. Martin, 7 December 1921, BA, H.D. (Sp.) 584 of 1921-2. B.P. Vaidya (1977), *Rentima Vahan*, Ahmedabad.

SECONDARY SOURCE

Ambedkar, B.R., *What Congress and Gandhi have Done to the Untouchables*, Bombay: Thacker & Co., 1946.

Areeparampil, Mathew, *Struggle for Swaraj: A History of Adivasi Movements in Jharkhand: From the Earliest Times to the Present Day*, Chaibasa: Tribal Research and Training Centre, 2002.

Bajpai, K.D., R. Jamindar and P.K. Trivedi, ed., *Gleaning of Indian Archaeology, History and Culture*, New Delhi/Jaipur: Publication Scheme, 2000.

Banerjee, Prathama, *Politics of Time: 'Primitive' and History-writing in a Colonial Society*, New Delhi: Oxford University Press, 2006.

Baske, Dhiren, *Gana Andolane Santhal Samaj*, Calcutta: Maitreyi Prakasani, 1996.

Basu, Pradip, ed., *Discourses on Naxalbari Movement 1967-2009*, Kolkata: Setu Prakashani, 2010.

Bose, Nirmal Kumar, *The Structure of Hindu Society*, New Delhi: Orient Longman, 1996.

Brown, Judith, *Gandhi's Rise to Power: Indian Politics 1915-1922*, London: Cambridge University Press, 1972.

Cederlof, Gunnel and K. Sivaramakrishnan, ed., *Ecological Nationalisms: Nature, Livelihoods, and Identities in South Asia*, Delhi: Permanent Black, 2005.

Chada, Y., *Rediscovering Gandhi*, London: Century, 1997.

Chakravarti, Adhir, ed., *Aspects of Socio-Economic Changes and Political Awakening in Bengal: From the Eighteenth Century to Independence*, Calcutta: State Archives of West Bengal, Education Department, Govt. of West Bengal, 1989.

Chattopadhyay, D.P., ed., *History of Science, Philosophy and Culture in Indian Civilization*, vol. XIV, part II, *Social Sciences: Communication, Anthropology and Sociology*, ed. Yogendra Singh, Pearson Longman, Delhi: Centre for Studies in Civilization, 2010.

Chaudhuri, A.B., *State Formation among Tribals: A Quest for Santhal Identity*, New Delhi: Gyan Publishing House, 2013.

Chaudhuri, Buddhadeb, ed., *Tribal Transformation in India*, vol. III [Ethnopolitics and Identity Crisis], *Tribal Studies of India Series*, New Delhi: Inter India Publications, 1992.

Choudhary, Valmiki (ed.), *Dr. Rajendra Prasad: Correspondence and Select Documents*, New Delhi: Allied Publishers, 1984.

Chowdhury, Arun, *Adibasi Jibon: Samaj O Sangram*, Kolkata: Gangchil, 2013.

Constituent Assembly Debates: Official Report, New Delhi: Lok Sabha Secretariat, vol. 4, 1988 (rpt.).

Das Gupta, Sanjukta, *Adivasis and the Raj: Socio-Economic Transition of the Hos, 1820-1932*, Delhi: Orient Blackswan, 2011.

Das Gupta, Sanjukta and Raj Sekhar Basu, eds., *Narratives from the Margins, Aspects of Adivasi History in India*, Delhi: Primus Books, 2012.

Datta, K.K., *History of the Freedom Movement in Bihar*, vol. I, Patna: Govt. of Bihar, 1957.

——, *Writings and Speeches of Gandhiji Relating to Bihar from 1927 to 1947*, Patna: Government of Bihar, 1967.

Desai, Mahadev H., *Day to Day with Gandhi: Secretary's Diary*, vol. V, Varanasi: Sarva Seva Sangh Prakashan, 1970.

Devalle, S., *Discourses of Ethnicity: Culture and Protest in Jharkhand*, Delhi: Sage, 1992.

Datta-Mazumdar, N., *The Santals: A Study in Cultural Changes*, Calcutta: Government of India Press, 1956.

Dinesh, V.N., *National Movement in Jharkhand*, Rampurhat, West Bengal: Santhal Parganas Forum Publication, 2006.

Dutta, K.K., *Anti British Plots and Movements*, Meerut: Meenakshi Prakashan, 1970.

Elwin, Verrier, *Leaves from the Jungle: A Diary of Life in a Gond Village,* New Delhi: Oxford India Paperbacks, 1936 (rpt. 1990).

——, *The Loss of Nerve: A Comparative Study of the Contact of Peoples in the Aboriginal Areas of the Bastar State and the Central Provinces of India*, Bombay: Wagle Press, 1941.

——, *The Foreign Missionary Danger*, published by H.C. Vidyarthi, Ranchi: All India Divine Light Mission, 1944.

——, *Gandhiji: Bapu of his People*, Shillong: North East Frontier Agency, 1956.

——, *A Philosophy of Love*, Delhi: Publications Division, Ministry of Information and Broadcasting, 1962.

——, *The Tribal World of Verrier Elwin: An Autobiography*, Oxford: Oxford University Press, 1964.

Firth, C.B., *An Introduction to Indian Church History*, Madras: Christian Literature Society, 1976.

Fisher, Louis, *The Life of Mahatma*, London: Granada Publishing, 1982.

Fuchs, Stephen, *Rebellious Prophets: A Study of Messianic Movements in India*, Bombay: Asia Publishing House, 1965.

Galbraith, J.K., *The Anatomy of Power*, London: Hamilton, 1984.

Gandhi, M.K. *Collected Works of Mahatma Gandhi* (*CWMG*), all volumes (1 to 98) Delhi: Publications Division.

——, *Christian Missions and their Place in India*, Ahmedabad: Navajivan Press, 1941.

——, *Constructive Programme: Its Meaning and Place*, The Navajivan Trust, 1945.

——, *Hind Swaraj*, Ahmedabad: Navajivan Publsihing House, 1951.

——, *Gandhi, Drink, Drugs and Gambling*, Ahmedabad: Navajivan Publishing House, 1952.

——, *Self-restraint vs. Self-indulgence*, Ahmedabad: Navajivan Publishing House, 1927 (rpt. 1958).

——, *Prohibition at Any Cost* (compiled by R.K. Prabhu), Ahmedabad: Navajivan Publishing House, 1960.

——, *An Autobiography or the Story of My Experiments with Truth*, tr. Mahadev Desai, London: Penguin Classics, 2001.

——, *The Message of Jesus Christ* , ed., A.T. Hingorani, Bombay: Bharatiya Vidya Bhavan (n.d.).

Ghosh, Subodh, *Bharater Adivasi*, Calcutta: Indian Associated Publsihing Co. Ltd., 1948.

Guevara, Ernesto 'Che', *Guerrilla Warfare: Introduction by Marc Becker*, New York: Monthly Review Press, 1998.

Guha, Ramachandra, *India After Gandhi: The History of the World's Largest Democracy*, London: Picador, 2008.

——, *Savaging the Civilized: Verrier Elwin, His Tribals, and India*, Haryana: Penguin Books, 2014.

Guha, Ranajit, ed., *Subaltern Studies I*, New Delhi: Oxford University Press, 1982.

Harald Fischer-Tine and Jana Tschurenev, eds., A *History of Alcohol and Drugs in Modern South Asia*, New York: Routledge, 2014.

Hardiman, David, *The Coming of the Devi Adivasi Assertion in Western India*, Delhi: Oxford University Press, 1987.

——, *Gandhi in his Time and Ours*, New Delhi: Permanent Black, 2016.

Hari, Viyogi, *Thakkar Bapa*, New Delhi: Publication Division, Govt. of India, 1977.

Iyer, R., ed., *The Moral and Political Writings of Mahatma Gandhi*, vol. II, Oxford: Claredon Press, 1986.

Jagadisan T.N. and Shyamlal, eds., *Thakkar Bapa: Eightieth Birthday Commemoration Volume*, Madras: Diocesan Press, 1949.

Jha, Hetukar, ed., *Perspectives on Indian Society and History: A Critique*, New Delhi: Manohar, 2002.

Kabadi, W.P., ed., *India's Case for Swaraj*, Bombay: Yeshanand & Co., 1932.

Karunakaran, T., et al., eds., *Appropriate Technology Lineage Gandhi, Kumarappa, Schumacher*, Gandhigram: Gandhlgram Rural Institute, 1993.

Kela, Shashank, *A Rogue and Peasant Slave: Adivasi Resistance 1800-2000*, New Delhi: Navayana Publishing, 2012.

Khoshoo, T. N. and John S. Moolakkattu, *Mahatma Gandhi and the Environment: Analysing Gandhian Environmental Thought*, New Delhi: Teri, 2017.

Kujur, Ignes, *Jharkhand Dumuhane Par*, Ranchi: Sudarshan Press, 1955.

Kumar, N., 'District Gazetteer', Ranchi, 1970.

Mahtab and De, ed., *History of the Freedom Movement in Orissa*, vol. 1, Cuttack: Secretary State Committee for Compilation of History of the Freedom Movement Orissa Publishing, 1957.

Malik, S.C., ed., *Dissent, Protest and Reform in Indian Civilisation*, Shimla: Indian Institute of Advanced Study, 1977.

——, ed., *Indian Movements: Some Aspects of Dissent, Protest and Reform*, Shimla: Indian Institute of Advanced Study, 1978.

Mashruwala, Kishorelal, *Gandhi-vichar Dohan*, New Delhi: Sasta Sahitya Mandal, 1991.

Miri, Mrinal, ed., *Continuity and Change in Tribal Society*, Simla: Indian Institute of Advanced Studies, 1993.

Mishra, Asha and Chittaranjan Kumar Pati, eds., *Tribal Movements in Jharkhand: 1857-2007*, New Delhi: Concept Publishing, 2010.

Mohanty, Manoranjan, *Red and Green: Five Decades of the Indian Maoist Movement*, Kolkata: Setu Prakashani, 2015.

Munda, Ram Dayal and S. Bosu Mullick, eds., *The Jharkhand Movement: Indigenous Peoples' Struggle for Autonomy in India*, Copenhagen: IWGIA, 2003.

Naik, Dahyabbai, *Bhil Sewa Mandal: Dahod—Progress Report*, Ahmedabad: Navajivan Press, 1967.

Nanda, B.R., ed., *Essays in Modern Indian History*, New Delhi: Oxford University Press, 1980.

Nehru, Jawaharlal, *Nehru Abhinandan Granth: A Birthday Book*, New Delhi: Nehru Abhinandan Granth Committee, 1949.

O'Connell, J.T., ed., *Organizational and Institutional Aspects of Indian Religious Movements*, Shimla: Indian Institute of Advanced Study, 1999.

Ojha, P.N., ed., *Bihar: Past and Present*, Patna: Kashi Prasad Jayaswal Research Institute, 1987.

Padel, Felix and Samarendra Das, *Out of this Earth: East India Adivasis and the Aluminium Cartel*, New Delhi: Orient Blackswan, 2010.

Padel, Felix, *Sacrificing People: Invasions of a Tribal Landscape*, New Delhi: Orient Blackswan, 2011.

Pandikattu, Kuruvilla, ed., *The Meaning of Mahatma for the Millennium*, Washington: The Council for Research in Values and Philosophy, 2001.

Pandey, Gyanendra, *The Ascendancy of the Congress in Uttar Pradesh: A Study in Imperfect Mobilization*, Oxford: Oxford University Press, 1978.

——, ed., *Subaltern Citizens and their Histories*, New York: Routledge, 2010.

——, *A History of Prejudice: Race, Caste and Difference in India and the United States*, Cambridge: Cambridge University Press, 2013.

Pandya, Jayant and Amrut Modi, ed., *Sarvodaya: Gandhi Sevaso Smithi Granth*, Bhavnagar: Bhartiya Sarvodaya Sammelan, November, 1994.

Parel, Anthony, ed., *Gandhi: Hind Swaraj and Other Writings*, Cambridge: Cambridge University Press, 2009.

Pati, Biswamoy, ed., *Adivasis in Colonial India: Survival, Resistance and Negotiation*, New Delhi: Orient Blackswan, 2011.

Pfostl, Eva, ed., *Between Ethics and Politics: Gandhi Today*, New Delhi: Routledge, 2014.

Phizo, A.Z., *The Fate of the Naga People: An Appeal to the World*, London: Privately published in July, 1960.

Pradhan, M.C. and Verrier Elwin et al., eds., *Anthropology and Archaeology: Essays in Commemoration of Verrier Elwin, 1902-64*, London: Oxford University Press, 1969.

Praharaj, D.M., *Tribal Movements and Political History in India*, New Delhi: South Asia Books, 1988.

Prasad, Archana, *Against Ecological Romanticism: Verrier Elwin and Making of an Anti-Modern Tribal Identity*, New Delhi: Three Essays Collective, 2011 (2nd edn.)

Prasad, R., *Mahatma Gandhi in Bihar*, Bombay: Prabhat Prakashan, 1949.

Raghavaiah, V., ed., *Tribal Revolts*, Nellore: Andhra Rashtra Adimajati Sevak Sangh, 1971.

Raghuramaraju, A., ed., *Debating Gandhi: A Reader*, Oxford: Oxford University Press, 2010.

Rana, L.N., 'Party Politics in Chota Nagpur 1937 to 1987', PhD Thesis, Ranchi University, 1991.

Rajgarhis, Shushil, *The Tribal Soldiers of Mahatma Gandhi 1920-47*, New Delhi: Satyam Publishing House, 2010.

Rath, G.C., ed., *Tribal Development in India: The Contemporary Debate*, Delhi: Sage, 2006.

Reid, J., *Final Report on the Survey and Settlement Operations in the District of Ranchi, 1902-10*, Patna: Superintendent, Govt. Print, Bihar and Orissa, 1926.

Riley, Leanne and Mac Marshall, eds., *Alcohol and Public Health in 8 Developing Countries*, Geneva: Substance Abuse Department, Social Change and Mental Health, World Health Organization, 1999.

Risley, H., *The Tribes and Castes of Bengal*, vol. I, Kolkata: Harvard Library: Bengal Secretariat Press, 1891.

Roy, Sarat Chandra, *Oraon Religion and Customs*, Delhi: Gyan Publishing House, 2012.

Roy Chowdhary, P.C., 'District Gazetteer', Santhal Parganas, 1965.

Rycroft, Daniel J. and Sangeeta Dasgupta, eds., *The Politics of Belonging in India: Becoming Adivasi*, New York: Routledge, 2011.

Sahu, M., *The Kolhan under the British Rule*, Jamshedpur: Utkal Book Agency, 1985.

Sarkar, Sumit, *Swadeshi Movement in Bengal*, New Delhi: Peoples Publishing House, 1973.

——, *Modern India (1885-1947)*, Macmillan: New Delhi, 1983.

Sen, Padmaja, ed., *Changing Tribal Life: A Socio-Philosophical Perspective*, New Delhi: Concept Publishing, 2003.

Sewak, Ram, *History of Bihar between Two World Wars 1919-39*, New Delhi: Inter India Publications, 1985.

Sinha, S.P., *Conflict and Tension in Tribal Society*, New Delhi: Concept Publishing, 1993.

Sinha, M.P., ed., *Contemporary Relevance of Gandhi*, Bombay: Nachiketa Publications Limited, 1970.

Sinha, N. and L. Singh, *Jharkhand, Land and People*, Delhi: Rajesh Publication, 2009.

Singh, K.S., ed., *Tribal Situation in India*, Shimla: Indian Institute of Advanced Studies, 1972.

——, *Birsa Munda and his Movements 1874-1901*, Delhi: Oxford University Press, 1983.

——, *Tribal Society in India*, New Delhi: Manohar, 1985.

——, *Jawaharlal Nehru, Tribes and Tribal Policy*, Calcutta: Anthropological Survey of India, 1989.

——, *Tribal Movements in India*, vol. II, New Delhi: Manohar, 2015.

Singh, Lata, *Popular Translations of Nationalism: Bihar, 1920-1922*, New Delhi: Primus, 2012.

Sharma, B.D., *Unbroken History of the Broken Promises*, New Delhi: Freedom Press, 2010.

Sundar, Nandini, *Subalterns and Sovereigns: An Anthropological History of Bastar 1854-1996*, New Delhi: Oxford University Press, 1997.

Tarlo, Emma, *Clothing Matters, Dress and Identity in India*, New Delhi: Penguin, 1996.

Tendulkar, D.G., *Mahatma: Life of Mohandas Karamchand Gandhi*, New Delhi: Publication Division, Government of India, New Edition, vols. 7-8, 1962 (revised).

Thakkar, A.V., *The Problem of Aborigines in India*, R.R. Kale Memorial Lecture, Poona, 1941.

Tiwary, R.K., *Jharkhand Ki Roop Rekha*, Ranchi: Shivangan Publications, 2012.

Troisi, J., *Social Movement and Change*, New Delhi: Indian Social Institute, 1979.

Vashishtha, Vijay Kumar, *Role of Gandhi's Ideas in Mobilization of Adivasis of Southern Rajputana Princely States (1921-48)*, Shimla: Indian Institute of Advanced Studies, 2014.

Venkatarangaiya, M., *The Freedom Struggle in Andhra Pradesh (Andhra)*, Hyderabad: Andhra Pradesh State Committee appointed for the compilation of a history of the Freedom Struggle in Andhra Pradesh, 1965.

Vidyarthi, L.P., ed., *Aspects of Religion in Indian Society*, Meerut: Kedar Nath Ram Nath, 1961.

Vidyarthi, L.P., B.N. Sahay and B.K. Srivastava, eds., *Gandhi and the Social Sciences*, New Delhi: Bookhive [Seminar on Gandhi's Contribution to Social Sciences, 1969, Ranchi University], 1970.

Weiner, Myron, *Sons of the Soil: Migration and Ethnic Conflict in India,* Princeton, NJ: Princeton University Press, 1978.

Xaxa, Virginius, *State, Society and Tribes: Issues in Post-Colonial India*, New Delhi: Pearson Education India, 2008.

Yagnik, Indulal, *Atmakatha*, vols. II-III, Ahmedabad: Gujarat Grantharatan Karyalay, 1970.

JOURNALS

- *American Anthropologist*
- *Archaeology and Anthropology*
- *Asian Folklore Studies*
- *Bulletin of the Department of Anthropology*, Government of India
- *Bulletin of Bihar Tribal Welfare Research Institute*, Ranchi
- *Bulletin of the School of Oriental and African Studies*
- *Critical Inquiry*
- *Cultural Anthropology*
- *Dialectical Anthropology*
- *Down to Earth*
- *Economic and Political Weekly*
- *Environment and History*
- *Frontline*
- *Harijan*
- *Indian Anthropologist*
- *Indian Historical Review*
- *International Bulletin of Missionary Research*
- *Journal of Bihar Research Society*
- *Journal of the Indian Anthropological Society*
- *Journal of Southern African Studies*
- *Madras Legislative Council Proceedings*
- *Man in India*
- *Modern Asian Studies*
- *Navajivan*
- *Outlook*
- *Peace Research*

- *Political Science Quarterly*
- *Proceedings of Indian History Congress*
- *Social Scientist*
- *Social Science Quarterly*
- *Studies in History*
- *The Calcutta Review*
- *The Eastern Anthropologist*
- *The Historian*
- *The Illustrated Weekly of India*
- *The Indian Economic and Social History Review*
- *The Indian Historical Review*
- *The Journal of the Royal Anthropological Institute*
- *The Modern Review*
- *Young India*

NEWSPAPERS

- *Andhra Patrika*
- *Hindustan Times*
- *Indian Express*
- *Indian Nation*
- *New Age*
- *Sentinel*
- *The Englishman*
- *The Times of India*

Index